The Breast Stays Put

No Chemo — No Radiation — No Lumpectomy —
No Thank You

(Put your scalpel back in your pocket and nobody gets hurt!)

*How One Woman Overcame Breast Cancer with
Alternative Medicine Alone*

By

Pamela Hoeppner

PRESS

Disclaimer

The information in this book is the true-life story of the author and is intended for informational purposes only. The author does not recommend, advise or imply that the information in this book be used as a substitute for medical advice and/or treatment by a competent oncologist or health care professional. Should you choose to use any of the information, products or treatments discussed in this book, without the approval of your doctor, you should know you are prescribing for yourself, and although that is your constitutional right, the author in no way recommends it and assumes no responsibility. Every case is unique, and it is up to each person to make their own treatment choices and decisions.

The author also is not responsible for any treatment, therapy, supplement or product referred to in this book that changes in quality, content of ingredient, process of manufacturing and/or effectiveness.

Dedication

This book is dedicated to my mother, Marjune Mary Kushion (1923-1987), without whose nurturing belief in the human body's innate ability to heal itself with natural elements, and the courage and fierceness with which she alternatively fought a diagnosis of breast cancer herself, my life would have been void of the empowerment I received in the example she lived. Because of you, Mom, no further proof was needed to convince myself why my decision to refuse conventional cancer treatment was nonnegotiable. Your beauty, love and devotion live on in our hearts today, and the legacy you lived will affect our family profoundly for generations to come.

Acknowledgments

To Willie, the love of my life, who still can't understand *why* Rome *wasn't* built in a day, and yet had so much patience when "I received a diagnosis; I beat it; this is how I did it" took me longer to write than a week. To the man I walk beside and dream big dreams with of a bright, exciting, adventure-filled future that I can't wait for us to get on with, now that I've finished this book!

To my children and grandchildren—my reason for living and my passion for life, including all the little "noses and tiny toeses" that are still yet to come! Every time you look into my eyes and hug my neck you embrace my heart and fill it like nothing else can!

To Kerri, who showed so little fear and stood steadfast in faith with me, as she held a constant vigil throughout my recovery, either by phone or at my side. My source of strength on a daily basis, ever there for me when I needed her most! And for her and Shawn giving me so much to live for by creating a future for me to "live in" . . . at a time when I so desperately needed one I could move into!

To Josh, whose strong faith, daring and resilience in life has been a source of inspiration and encouragement to me from a small child on up. And whose devastation turned to hope when he thought about where a recovery like this would take me, putting it all in perspective for me with, "How could I ever doubt you could write a book, Mom? Even your emails are epic!" And to Randi who was there for me in ways no one else was or could have been, as I labored to turn this manuscript into a book!

To Glenn and Kathy who are about to give us our third grand-child, just days after my book is scheduled to go to print! Their genuine support and votes of confidence in what I had chosen to do meant more than they can know. We look forward to this new little bundle with such anticipation and seeing what the years ahead hold for the *three* of them!

To my dear friends who didn't hear from me for so long and gave me the space I needed at a time in life when I needed it. And for all their prayers that were so instrumental in keeping me here in the meantime.

To Daystar and TBN for providing the programming and airtime for the pastors and Bible teachers who made it possible for me to sit and glean the saving knowledge of Scripture I'd need—to stand in that day.

To Twinkie Toes, my "Twinkie Twin"—who entered my life with all the flare of "Loretta Young," without whose mentoring and constant source of encouragement through the years I'd never have been able to birth this dream of authoring a book into a reality. Forever "We be Berries!" I could only hope she'll stay for a lifetime!

And to everyone who has ever faced the pain and devastation of being diagnosed with and having to battle cancer, in any form, for whom I have the utmost respect!

Contents

THERE WILL BE NO WHITE FLAG

THEN CAME THE MORNING

Introduction

"Can you meet us in Mexico?" Daddy called to ask, and the words just tore me apart. Mom thought she'd be going for more treatment. But I knew the real reason Daddy said they needed me. Mom didn't have much time.

So just days later I flew to connect with them in San Diego. And when I met them at the airport, Daddy was exhausted—and scared. So for three days I cared for Mom alone in a clinic in Tijuana. And somewhere amidst the pain of watching her be taken—I made a vow. I knew my mother was in heaven, but this thing was hell orchestrated, and *hell* could expect to hear from me! There would be a score to settle—in the form of "unfinished business!"

On July 7, 1987, my sister, Sally, had flown in, and with Daddy by our side, we lost our mother to metastatic breast cancer. And the constant reminder of it in the years that followed, from the first time I had to check the box marked "cancer" on a medical form, under "family history," only galvanized my resolve. Convinced Mom's diagnosis came from a source that couldn't possibly hand me *anything*—I resented the category "they" said it threw me into . . . that I knew would inevitably be perpetrated on to my children and grandchildren.

Then, completely blindsided when cancer found an opening and I actually *was* diagnosed with it in 2004, I seized the opportunity to win it all back—by waging three separate battles!

First, I had a diagnosis to beat. And, with the way I'd be going about it, I knew it meant going against the grain of the medical establishment.

Secondly, I had to prove that the only thing I "inherited" from my mother, with regard to cancer, was in the legacy she lived, as she so bravely fought something even she knew she'd never have had were it not for what she'd been handed by the same "machine" that more and more, with each passing year, *insisted* I was next in line.

And, thirdly, I had to empower my family with facts and evidence, so that no matter what they were told throughout the course of their lives, they could rest assured—this was more than genetic, and they need never buy into the "if your mother had it" lie.

So I had to overcome a death sentence while discovering the root cause of two diagnoses—in order to free my family from a curse! And with what I would soon uncover, which I realized countless others could also benefit from, I found myself facing a fourth monumental challenge. I had to author a book.

As I wrote, although being aware of the number of lives this information could touch, it was always the individual who would one day have a *desperate* need that I thought about the most, wishing so much we could somehow sit and talk—so they could tell me about their life, their family and what they were now dealing with, in the uncertainties they faced. I know the terror and the gripping hopelessness for which no descriptive exists that adequately captures the devastation associated with a diagnosis like breast cancer. And if you happen to be that individual today, my heart aches for you, and I feel your pain—because not long ago I *was* you. Which is why I not only chose to tell my story, but I also endeavored to provide life-saving information in the way of answers, solutions and keys to preventing a diagnosis like this from ever occurring to begin with.

It might surprise you to discover, as you enter my world, that the principles, truths and attitudes I clung to, as I maneuvered through the murky waters of my recovery, might actually be as meaningful and helpful to you as my telling you about the treatment I used to recover with itself—since so much of it applies, regardless of what treatment one chooses. And, therefore, I labored to give you everything I knew to give, with what I found to be the "diamond-cut" precision tools to my recovery—that inevitably made all the difference in the final outcome.

When I took on this project, you, along with my family, relatives, friends, everyone I'd ever met, and all who are and will one day be searching for answers, were in my heart and the health of your future was on my mind. And it's been my goal from the start to create for you "a window to look through." To provide you with a form of empowerment against cancer and, in many ways, whatever else might one day decide to threaten your life, or the lives of the ones you love. An empowerment you might otherwise never have, without first having read *The Breast Stays Put.*

Since no one seems to be telling them, and feeling compelled to answer the call, I could, of course, individually, one by one, pay them a visit—to sit a while. But then, perhaps a better plan would be to apply ink to collectively bound parchment, where all who chose to, could instead, at their convenience . . . simply come and visit me.

I'm so glad you're here.

THE LUMP

CHAPTER 1

Disbelief—Denial—Desperation

At the Mammogram Boutique

What could be taking so long? I asked myself, glancing up once again at the clock hanging directly across from me, as it ticked away on the cold, drab, antiseptic-yellow, cement-block hospital wall.

I don't recall it ever taking this long for a radiologist to read a mammogram on any of my prior appointments, I reasoned.

Decked out in what I presumed was the latest fashion design in hospital gowns, I was a little cold sitting there. I'm sure it was thought to be very "user friendly" by the staff though. It had *three* armholes. (I'll let you figure that one out.)

I'd been flipping through a book of mammogram jokes and cartoons I'd found sitting on the desk next to me, to pass the time.

Someone obviously went to a lot of trouble to put these together. (A little "boob-smashing" humor to lighten the mood, I supposed.)

They were actually pretty funny—I even laughed right out loud at a few of them. But I was starting to get bored and I wanted to go home.

My thoughts drifted toward my husband, who was out in the waiting room . . .

Willie normally didn't come with me on appointments like this, but this time there was a little cause for concern. If he was worried he didn't let on, and I was just glad he was there. Knowing he was out there waiting was the least of my concerns. He's such a sweetheart; so patient and easygoing. Waiting for me at anytime, for any reason, is never a problem—just one of so many things I love about him.

He was probably getting hungry by now though. This was taking much longer than either of us had anticipated. More than likely he'd been sitting there thinking about where we'd go for lunch as soon as we got out of this place today. (I, for one, wished we were already there.)

The technician had said she'd be right back. She just needed the radiologist to take a look at the films—to be sure she didn't need to "do any over."

"Do any over?" I mused. *That's just what I need—a few more "radiation vibes" shot into my system.* She'd already taken two extra images as it was when I told her about the lump, or swollen gland, I wanted checked. Well, I had news for them. They'd better have gotten what they needed the first time, because there would be no "do-overs." Not today. I didn't plan to be nuked again—especially considering how I didn't even want to be there in the first place!

It was probably only a few minutes that she'd been gone, but it seemed like an eternity. The longer I sat there, the more I realized just how edgy I was about this whole ordeal.

I had told the technician how I'd found a lump while showering. She showed no reaction, alarm or concern. But my guess is that technicians are instructed not to, which was fine with me—I just wanted to get dressed and get out of there. The place was giving me the creeps. I could read the report later. At least that's how I thought this would go down. Now, I wasn't so sure. *What could she be doing that was taking so long?*

I found myself thinking back to the day, about a month ago, that had brought me here today.

The Day It All Began

It was turning out to be such a great Christmas. Josh, twenty-three, and the youngest of our three children in our blended family, had flown in from New York City. Kerri, our oldest, and her husband of five years, Shawn, had driven up from Saginaw.

Glenn, who is our middle child, and his wife, Kathy, newlyweds of just one year, had been up from Novi the week before, so we had already enjoyed a great Christmas with them a little early. (Just so you know, before we became this blended family, Kerri and Josh were mine and Glenn was Willie's; Kerri and Glenn were teenagers; Josh was nine.) No grandchildren yet, but we loved the times when the kids all came home. We had planned it that way.

When Willie retired we moved to what Michiganders fondly refer to as "Up North," in Northern Michigan. It's where everyone in the state heads for the lake during the summer, and where they hit the slopes and snow mobile trails in the winter. So, regardless of the season, there's always something for everyone.

There's actually this phenomenon, unique only to Michigan, which occurs mostly on the weekends, and especially in the summer. It's like the entire state *tips,* as the bottom empties out, with bumper to bumper traffic filling all the lanes on I-75 heading north as far as the UP (Upper Peninsula). People from as far south as Ohio set out for their weekend getaways and vacation destinations and the little bit of heaven they know awaits them. It's a four-hour drive from Detroit, but, for Michiganders, the rewards of coming Up North far surpass the headaches of dealing with all that traffic.

To hear the locals tell it, though, it's the very same people who leisurely boat through Northern Michigan's Inland Waterway that connects Crooked, Burt and Mullett lakes in the two-way boat traffic, smiling and waving to each other as they pass in the rivers, who will be flipping each other off on I-75 as they make their way back home in the Sunday night exodus! But while they're here, it's all about the sun, the fun and the beckoning crystal clear waters of Michigan's pristine lakes—and we love being a part of it all.

It started out as a vacation spot for us, too. Just thirty miles south of the majestic Mackinaw Bridge and the romantic vacation draw, Mackinaw Island, Willie designed and built a gorgeous home for us on one of Michigan's largest and most beautiful lakes. It has bedrooms for all the kids. And, no matter the season, with all the exciting things one can venture out into up here, it makes it even more enticing for the kids to find their way back to us.

Today it was Christmas. Everyone was downstairs fixing breakfast, which meant Mom didn't have to cook. So I was upstairs—getting ready for what was promising to be yet another wonderful family holiday. I was taking a quick shower, and that's when I discovered it. I distinctly felt a *lump*—and a cold chill came over me.

Where in the world did this thing come from? I thought, standing there stunned. *Lord? What is this? I've never noticed anything there before. And if it had been there—for even a few days—I certainly would have detected it before this! Wouldn't I?*

Stepping out of the shower, I reached for a warm towel. (A towel I would soon find myself burying my face in, as the gripping reality of the significance of this *untimely* discovery began to take hold!) Over and over, I checked and *rechecked* for some kind of reassurance that this *had* to be all in my imagination. But it wasn't. The existence of something foreign was undeniable—and a sick feeling came over me because it had to be something, because *something* was definitely there!

Christmas morning. Of all days! To find something like this? Well, Merry Christmas to me! I wanted to cry!

It Had to Be the Chocolate

The smell of blueberry pancakes wafting up from the kitchen below quickly brought things back into focus, reminding me I had a family downstairs waiting—I had to get dressed!

I started reassuring myself, with every justifiable reason I could come up with, as to why this had to be nothing. I knew I had to regain my composure before I could even *think* about going back downstairs to join in on the fun-loving atmosphere of celebration.

I don't dare tarry, either, or Kerri will be up those stairs looking for me. I have to find a way to pull myself together. I have to snap out of this.

Forcing myself to just stop and take a deep breath, I looked up at heaven and told God (and myself), "If ever there was a time in my life when a good healthy dose of flat-out denial was in order (and justified!) *this* would be it!" *Just because I found out about this today doesn't mean anyone else has to. I'll simply file this little piece of information away somewhere in a remote compartment of my mind for the time being. I'll deal with it tomorrow, or even next week—but certainly not today! Like I'm going to go downstairs when we're all having such a great time and drop this bombshell? Perish the thought! Besides, it has to be just a swollen lymph node, or one of those annoying fibroid cysts I've had to deal with throughout the years. Probably from all the chocolate and sugar I got into between Thanksgiving and Christmas. Ugh! Why did I eat that stuff? (Funny though—I've never noticed one in that spot before—and certainly never while standing up . . .)*

Well, whatever it was, all I knew was that one day it wasn't there and the next day it *was*. And surely cancer doesn't act like that—does it?

Okay . . . hooked, fastened and buttoned; hair fluffed; one last look in the mirror at that "haphazard" attempt at makeup: Good to go, I thought. Grabbing my makeup case, I headed downstairs—and put it out of my mind!

Now, in late January, here I sat—in this "boutique" waiting for some kind of answer.

I had also expressed to the technician earlier that I was sure this was nothing. It wasn't very big; it was quite soft; it didn't feel fixed or attached, so to speak. (All the things I'd heard to look for.) She was probably in there right now, though, telling on me. My answers on the questionnaire they require you to fill out in regard to past mammograms weren't exactly those of a model patient. Now, add this lump thing into the mix, and I figured I probably wouldn't get out of here today without *some* type of lecture. Oh, the joys of dealing with the medical industry's system and "rules." Well, I'd had confrontations with doctors in the past, so this wouldn't be the first time.

I hadn't had many mammograms over the years. I don't think they're very dependable or accurate. In fact, I've always thought with the radiation involved they can actually be harmful—and may even *cause* breast cancer. I know that's controversial, but it's my opinion. Even the news media often reports on the inaccuracy of mammograms. And what about all those women who were told their report came back negative, only to discover a suspicious mass or lump that turned out to be malignant, just weeks or months after having a mammogram? I find it appalling that women radiate their body like the medical industry insists we have to, and then "Whoops! A pea-size mass was missed!" (If it actually was even *there* at the time of the mammogram!)

They could at least offer a few more color choices, I thought, looking down once again at the proverbial fashion statement I was wearing. *Most women have an aversion to mammograms to begin with. Why add insult to injury by making them wear puke green on top of it? This place is a real trip. For two cents I'd bolt and get out of here.* But I decided I'd better behave myself, stay put and face the music, whatever it was. Because I was definitely beginning to sense—*something* was coming!

The Dreaded "C" Word

Finally, the technician appeared from behind the block-wall partition. The radiologist was with her, and the look on her face was sobering. I braced myself. Because it was evident—she was *not* happy!

Her eyes were fixed. Her jaw was set. Her body language spoke volumes. Even the sound of her footsteps got my attention. This chick was *upset,* and, quite honestly, I was all prepared to say, "Okay, okay, so I'll get them done more often!" But I started to sense that what she had on her mind was a little more serious than my breaking any "mammogram early detection laws." This woman was on a mission. And whatever she was delivering—it was *not* good news!

"I have to talk to you," she said. "What I'm seeing on your mammogram films looks extremely suspicious, and I couldn't let you leave this hospital today without you understanding how serious I think this is. I'm strongly recommending you see a surgeon about a biopsy. And, in my opinion—this can't wait!"

Whoa! Engulfed by the flood of thoughts and emotions coming at me at warp-speed with that little information-packed outburst, instantly my mind was sent swirling!

But that was it. She didn't say anything more. She just stood there looking at me. Then I realized. She was trying to tell me something . . . without saying it. But I couldn't even move, let alone speak, so I just sat there looking at her. And she just stood there—

looking back at me! *This can't be good*, I thought. (*That* was an understatement!)

Meanwhile, she still stood there staring at me. They both did. It probably only involved seconds, but it seemed like forever. It was like "the first one who speaks loses" kind of a thing.

Finally, I managed to come up with something I thought sounded *somewhat* intelligent, and I heard myself say, "So what you're saying is . . ."

"I'm not 100 percent certain it's *cancer*, but I am *90 percent!*" she said.

Okay—that's it! Now she did it! She just said the "C" word! The words *stung* as they echoed through my head. I know I didn't flinch though. I couldn't have—*I was too numb!* The words *certain, cancer*, and *90 percent?* All in the same sentence? And *all* pertaining to me? *This was insane!*

Reality as I knew it started to shift, and I felt powerless to stop it, or even slow it down! I tried to respond, but nothing was there to come out. All I could do was nod my head to acknowledge I'd heard what she had just said—even if I didn't comprehend it. *And I didn't!* I had taken so many precautions and preventative measures through the years to prevent the kind of diagnosis she was talking about. *How could this be happening?*

Damage Control—Damage Control!

Somewhere between the thoughts flooding my head and trying to make *some* kind of sense out of what had just been dropped on me, I began telling myself that I *had* to get on top of this situation. I wasn't about to lose it before I knew for certain what this radiologist was implying even had any validity to it!

Aware that I had become frozen, and must have had a blank look on my face, I started doing a mental assessment of what was going on with my reactions.

What is my face saying? Do I have the "deer in the headlights" thing going on? Are my eyes as glazed over as they feel? And, oh, dear Lord—please don't let my mouth have dropped open! It was surreal and like being suspended in time. Even my hearing had become muffled. The only thing I knew for certain I had going for me was a keen sense of awareness that I felt compelled to appear together, on the outside, all the while knowing, on the *inside*—it was *pure* mayhem!

It's amazing how the mind goes into overdrive in a situation like that, as mine had—leaving me sitting there in a numb state of silent internal chaos!

I immediately began telling myself, *It's okay! Whatever is happening here—it's going to be okay!*

But in the same instant, my heart wanted to break. I had experienced loss at times in my life, but never did I *ever* remember such a feeling of profound sadness. This was so much more than a personal letdown. This was *far* from being just about me! If this ended up being as serious as she was indicating it was, there was no question about it—this was going to throw all the people I loved right into a tailspin with me. That fact, and all it entailed, magnified the trauma of what I was facing—*tenfold! How would I tell my kids?*

I knew I somehow had to fight to keep my wits about me. Caving in to self-pity was a luxury I couldn't afford. If I started allowing myself to go to those kinds of places in my thoughts and emotions, I felt as though I might never get back. The room wasn't spinning, but it felt like my entire *life* was!

This was definitely not going down the way I had hoped it would. If this was really happening, if her suspicions were founded—then life as I knew it *was over!* This wasn't just some little bump in the road. This was a major *train wreck* going somewhere to happen! And the worst part was—*I was on the dang train!*

(Little did I know at the time, but those few words she just spoke over me were about to change the course of my life— *forever!*)

The Bad News Room

Again, I heard the radiologist say something. "Would you let us see if we can get you in to see a surgeon, and set up an appointment for you before you leave today?"

At first I couldn't even respond. "Yes, of course," I finally managed to say.

"Then, you go ahead and get dressed, and we'll get right on it."

Now, all I had to do was get up out of the chair, walk across the room to the little booth partitioned off by a curtain and hope when I got up all the blood hadn't drained from my head—so I didn't do something stupid—*like faint!*

It hadn't. I didn't. And now all I wanted was to find Willie!

As I left the mammogram room, the lady at the desk asked if we would prefer to sit in a separate little room off to the side, rather than the waiting room. I agreed, and she proceeded to take us to where Willie and I would, once again, sit—*and wait.*

The room was "little" all right. There was barely room to turn around. Then it occurred to me. This had to be their "Bad News Room." They put us in here because they just knew I was going to fall apart. (Probably most women do.) *Well, I wasn't about to!* I had too much riding on this to cave in and lose focus. I had to fight to keep my wits about me. I knew I had to maintain my composure and stay on top of the situation.

It's Not the Circumstance—It's the Thought

In the seconds that followed, I stayed in one continual state of assessing the situation and doing damage control. And I was starting to notice that, surprisingly, in spite of what the radiologist was indicating, I had remained relatively calm. *Numb!* But calm.

I also kept a strong sense of awareness of my surroundings. Because, although I had come to these people for this "test," I knew there wasn't much else in the way of treatment (at least not the type *they* were steeped in anyway) that I wanted any part of.

Willie, bless his heart, had remained calm, too. He picked up a magazine from the table next to him and showed no reaction. And I was glad he didn't. It gave me time to process what had just occurred, and more importantly—*what might still be coming!*

No, I didn't fall apart. Instead, a tangible feeling of peace began to wash over me. And I was quick to embrace it.

There's *power* in holding your peace. Waiting to speak, or pass judgment; getting quiet before God to listen and hear first what He has to say about a matter. I had already heard loud and clear what the radiologist had to say about the situation—now I wanted to hear what *God* had to say! Recognizing the real Authority hadn't yet weighed in on the subject. And I knew He was there. The room had become *thick* with His calming presence!

Maybe I had no control over what the radiologist just spoke over me, but you can bet, in the suspended state of *guarded confidence* I'd created, I was determined to have full control over the first words I chose to speak — over *myself!*

The second we stepped into that room and the door closed behind us, I made the deliberate conscious decision to keep my mouth *shut!* To refrain from making even *one* comment about what had just occurred until I knew I was in complete charge of my senses, thought processes and emotions. This was serious stuff! I knew full well — the *first* words I spoke *would* set forces in motion. I needed words that would count for something; words that could and would affect the outcome of this possible *pending* diagnosis, and ultimately — *my destiny!*

I spend a lot of time with the Lord, in His Word. Standing on His promises has long since become a way of life. And, in times of pressure or crisis, I know the importance of being able to remind God of those promises. I'm certain it's so much more for our sake than it is His. It not only reminds us of who He is, and *who's* in control, but that there's also creative power in the Word of God. After all, He used it to speak the entire *universe* into existence!

The Bible says, "Put Me in remembrance of My Word.[1] And, "My Word shall not return unto me void, but it shall accomplish that which I please, and it shall prosper in the *thing* whereunto I sent it."[2]

Well, I was that "thing" and I *needed* some of that "accomplished" stuff. Because my definition of "prosperity in life" certainly didn't include me being done in "early" by any vicious death sentence! And neither would my dying of cancer bring glory to God. I knew that these promises, and any others I could cling to, would be the exact evidence and lifeline I needed to prove this whole thing could somehow be *turned around!*

Drawing a Line

Through the years I have memorized scores of scriptures, even whole chapters, but in the heat of the moment my mind was a complete blank.

"By His stripes we were healed"[3] would have been good. "I am the Lord thy God that healeth thee"[4] would have been *perfect!* But none of them were coming up! Fear was trying to grip me—and it was beginning to *tick me off!* I had always made a point of living on *top* of my circumstances, not *under* them!

In fact, whenever anyone would say, "Well, *under* the circumstances . . . ," it wasn't unlike me to ask, "What in the world are you doing down there?"

The Bible says in Romans, "We are more than conquerors[5] and no weapon formed against us can prosper."[6]

I told myself I just needed to slow down, breathe deep and relax—and find a way to throw the care of this over on God (where it belonged!).[7] My mind may have wanted to "check out," but my *spirit* was ready to fight! And down in my spirit, I could feel it. The troops were beginning to mobilize—I had to establish order.

They say the first thing to do in a situation involving desperation *(especially of this magnitude)* is find out where God is in it—and get on the side *He's* on. I knew God didn't do this to me. He's all Life, Light and Love. He's not the author of death. He's not even the author of sickness! No, this was a blatant all-out attack from the pits of hell!

As I attempted to sift through all the self-talk going on in my head, I could also hear things from that *other* side attempting to penetrate my defense mechanisms; seemingly screaming at me, demanding to know, "So just *where* is your *God* in all this now?" But I wasn't buying into any of it. I knew better! I pray for protection daily, for Willie and myself, and our entire family—and I purpose in my life to walk in health. If I was facing a bad diagnosis, I knew it wasn't *my* God who put it on me. He's not in the business of making people sick. It's not His style. So where in hell (literally) did this come from? And how was it able to do it?

But I told myself that at the moment, *for the moment*, none of the above mattered—except that little part about "choosing sides." *I couldn't choose God fast enough!*

It wasn't about being brave. It wasn't about finding fault. It wasn't even about feeling guilty in thinking I hadn't lived a healthy enough lifestyle. And I sure don't believe in "the-luck-of-the draw"—or "luck" at all (good *or* bad) for that matter. It was about knowing: It's not so much about what happens to you in life as it is *how you react to it!*

Well! This was one diabolical plot the devil could consider foiled! He may have crossed one line, but I just drew another one! One he *couldn't* cross. One drawn in blood. *The blood of Jesus Christ!* The devil can't cross the bloodline!

Don't Quit Your Day Job

Sitting in that cold (and what could easily have become *depressing*) hospital environment, I knew without question that whatever it was that was going on, whatever was happening to me, when I overcame this thing—I was going to make the devil sorry *(sorrier than the sorry thing already was)* he ever decided to pick *me* to put this on!

"If they had only known, they would have never crucified the Lord of Glory."[8]

Well, by the same token, if the devil had only known what he was setting in motion when he tried to pull *this* stunt, he'd have found something better to do that day! If he thought he was going to succeed at making me one of his "pet projects," he could think again. *Because I intended to become his worst nightmare!*

It was right about then that I remembered: *The little book!* The one I'd picked up on my way out the door that morning. Suddenly, I realized . . . it was no coincidence that *this* particular book was left sitting there so easy for me to snag as we hurriedly left the house. In all this darkness, God was about to shine His light on my behalf! And I couldn't wait to reach in my purse and pull out the little book. Maybe when I left home that day I didn't have a clue as to what was coming, but—there was no question about it—this little book being with me was God's own "signature" way of letting me know *He* did! Nothing takes God by surprise! *Nothing!* And by now I knew Him well enough to know—*He was about to call in "the reinforcements!"*

30

CHAPTER 2

God Had My Back

One Word from God

There in my hand was the little book I knew so well, by Kenneth Copeland, entitled *One Word from God Can Change Your Health.*

Earlier that morning I had thought, *Great! This is perfect for today. Thank You, Lord!* (Now I realized just *how* perfect!)

No, this book being so handy for me to grab today was no coincidence. This was a *God-incidence!*

As I opened the little book it was as if I'd found a pool of water in the desert, thinking, *Oh God, if <u>ever</u> You were going to speak to me to console me or show up to reassure me everything was going to be all right, this would be an incredibly perfect time to do it, because it doesn't get much more desperate than this!* (I wasn't to be disappointed.)

As I fanned the pages, yellow highlighting caught my eye that I vaguely recalled having done years earlier. And, seeing it, I melted into a warm embrace of anticipation. There before me were words that couldn't have been any more alive and real if Jesus Himself had appeared in the room and spoke them to me . . . because to me He just had!

> **John 14:10** *"The Father that dwelleth in me, he doeth the works.*
> Remember that. It's the Word that does the work, not the
> one holding onto it. It will work for anyone who will put

31

it to work. It will work for you just like it did for Jesus. Just put it out there and get in behind it and hide. Let the Word fight its own fight."

Well, "get in behind it and hide" works for me! I thought. I was overwhelmed with relief! I was going to be okay—I had God's Word on it! Whatever it was I was facing, I knew I wouldn't be in it alone. Not only did I have the Word of God and know how (and *know-how*) to use it, I also had a secret weapon I had already heard about months earlier. An alternative cancer treatment called Protocel® (originally named Entelev®) that had remarkable testimonies to vouch for its outstanding track record of effectiveness—for all types of cancer. I had heard about it just three months earlier through close friends who had a teenager in their family who had been battling leukemia for several years.

Out of the blue one day they were informed by their doctors that there was nothing more medical science could do. They sent the child home with just weeks to live. Desperate for answers, they searched the Internet and came across a product called Protocel®, which they ordered and started the child on the next day.

Within the first month, the doctors were so taken aback by the child's drastic improvement that they wanted the parents to "stop the treatment." They didn't know "what it was doing" to the child, in that they had never seen anything like this dramatic reversal and radical improvement in numbers. The parents, of course, continued to administer the Protocel®, and after just a few months the child was in remission!

How comforting was that? Talk about "A word fitly spoken"— "For such a time as this!" To already know three months ahead of time there was something out there (and without horrible side effects) that could be used effectively to take down a diagnosis of cancer was for me—*off the charts!* Another "co-inky-dink?" I think not. I could see God's handwriting all over this!

My Weapon of Choice

I should tell you right now: Witnessing firsthand over and over again, throughout the thirty-year span of my career in nutritional consulting, the body's innate ability to heal itself when given the "tools" it needs—coupled with what I knew to be true about the "Big Three": radiation, chemotherapy, and surgery (which to me is nothing more than burning, poisoning and mutilation)—I was intrigued by Protocel®'s curative properties from the minute I heard about it. I had just begun to look into and research this "non-toxic dietary supplement" (which is exactly what this little powerhouse formula is!), and from all I'd read, unlike conventional treatments, the only things people were reported to have experienced with it "on the side" were *benefits*. It looked remarkable.

I had only scratched the surface, but what I was hearing was impressive with regard to its effectiveness, including with several other degenerative and autoimmune diseases. And this dark liquid formula, containing properties that are said to literally cause cancer cells to fall apart, was surprisingly economical—and could even be purchased without a prescription!

I had lost my mother to breast cancer several years ago, so naturally prevention has always been something I've actively pursued. I had already pretty much determined, after hearing some of the reports of what Protocel® had done for others, if ever I were to receive a diagnosis of cancer, it would be Protocel® I'd reach for. In fact, I had already decided weeks earlier to start taking Protocel® as a preventative—right after the holidays! (Best laid plans, huh?)

So—if what I was now facing ended in a bad diagnosis, I wouldn't take it lying down. I'd beat it—and when I did I'd tell the *world* about Protocel®! And you could take *that* to the bank! I had no intentions of having anything conventional done. I would see a surgeon, and I'd think about a biopsy, but that's as far as it would go. I'd keep my system strong and healthy, coming at this from a completely different angle. (Completely different from what *they* had planned for me, anyway.)

Suddenly, I realized—here we were, once again, stuck in that room for a whole lot longer than they had indicated. For all I knew the clock was running and I could already be out doing something!

The radiologist had said they needed to get me in their system as soon as possible. *Wrong.* The last thing I wanted was to be involved in their "system"—or anything it had to offer! Sitting there wasting

33

precious time, waiting on whatever it was they *thought* they were setting up for me—was ridiculous. Okay, so:

Note to Self #1—No one is setting anything up for me! *I'm outta here!*

I looked over at Willie, and I knew I had to say *something!* And it had to be words that put both heaven and hell on notice—leaving little doubt as to where I stood on all this.

That's when I heard myself say, *"I REFUSE to fear!"*

Pivotal Moments

I had heard Kenneth Copeland, one of my favorite Bible teachers *ever* and the author of the little book I was holding in my hand, speak many times of a situation where his granddaughter had been diagnosed with spinal meningitis. The doctors were telling his daughter, Kelly, that her little girl might die because, at the time, so many other children in the same situation already had.

He tells how Kelly—steeped in Scripture, armed with determination and decisiveness—walked across the room to where her sister stood, gritted her teeth, stared her square in the face and spoke those same exact words over her daughter's situation. And *those* were the words I chose to speak over mine!

Earth-shattering?—maybe not to anyone else, but to me, and more importantly, my circumstances—the good, the bad and the ugly—those four little words spoke volumes! And, as I spoke them, I could literally feel all of hell tremble.

In the end her little girl lived! And I intended to live, too!

I told Willie I wanted out of that room! I had things to do, the first of which would be for me to call Kerri to get things rolling with Protocel®. She'd get me the phone numbers and websites I'd need to set out on this journey. The last thing I needed to be doing right now was sittin' in this place—burnin' daylight! I opened the door to that "Bad News Room," started looking for a phone—and I felt better already!

On the way home, we stopped for lunch at a place we like—but I don't remember eating. I didn't even remember eating thirty minutes after we left the restaurant. I was in a fog. I kept telling myself the verdict wasn't in yet, but it was the "90 percent" comment I couldn't get away from. It's just way too close for comfort to that all-defining 100 percent mark. And the look on the radiologist's face was something else I couldn't shake. She was filled with terror for me. It may not have even been legal for her to tell me what she did. It's probably why she stood there staring at me: She was waiting for me to ask the right question so she felt entitled to give me her opinion.

The whole thing was surreal. I could feel myself vacillating back and forth somewhere between denial and the stark reality of it all.

This was "The Big C" we were talking about. I mean, if you think about it . . . when someone says the word *cancer* the word you really hear is *death!* And it shouldn't have to be like that. There's just way too much fear and terror given to this vile disease: a disease that should have been brought to its knees decades ago. And, in my opinion, were it not for the greed associated with the astronomically profitable multibillion-dollar "business" they've built out of it (and *around* it)—it would have! This has gone on for decades now—with no progress that I'm aware of. (And I do think, more and more, people are beginning to question why!)

The Real Pain Begins

Before we left the hospital, I did find a phone to call Kerri. But as soon as I dialed I quickly hung up. Engulfed by another surge of heartbreaking disbelief that this could even be happening, I cringed at the thought of having to make this call. I was so not prepared for this. What a sobering moment! One I painfully recognized as being the first in a series of continual "firsts" I'd be facing with all the unknowns that were waiting, as I entered into uncharted territory. I had to keep it together. This was definitely not the time to let myself fall apart. I knew I had to decide ahead of time what I was going to say to her—and more importantly—*what I wasn't*. I sat up straight, took a deep breath, put a *smile* on my voice and dialed again. And, thank God—she answered!

"Kerri," I said quietly, "it's Mom." And in the most reassuring tone I could find, I said, "I'm at the hospital, and I've finished with the mammogram. But the radiologist just spoke with me—she's telling me she sees something 'suspicious.' They want me to make an appointment to see whether or not I should have a biopsy."

I didn't tell her the appointment would be with a surgeon. I thought this would go down easier if I just left that word out for the time being. (Along with all the others that were way too hard at this point to swallow!)

I didn't cry, and I didn't choke, but there was silence on the other end of the line. My sweet, precious daughter's voice began to crack as she tried to talk through the tears. She was trying to be brave—but I knew she was in shock. And it was tearing my heart out. I knew (all too well, in fact) the sickening terror she must be feeling. After losing my own mom to breast cancer, I was *never* going to do this to my family!

This wasn't new to Kerri either. She knew what the pain and sorrow of losing someone you love dearly was all about. I may have lost my mom, but she lost her adoring grandma—and all the years of her grandma's cuddles and kisses; and being showered with gifts and surprises; and all her tender words of wisdom she took with her when she left us. And here I was. Possibly in the middle of what? *The same unthinkable nightmare?* This was already bordering on unbearable! *And the worst part?* The looming, threatening shadow of realization that for a while—it was more than likely going to get even *worse!*

Still, I managed to keep my composure. I told Kerri I thought the sooner I got on this, the better. I needed to get some Protocel® ordered, regardless of the outcome of the diagnosis, because I had been planning all along to use it as a preventative.

She assured me that by the time I got home all the information I'd need would be waiting.

We didn't talk anymore. We didn't need to. More was being said in what *wasn't* being said anyway. She had to be reeling!

I'll probably never know what she went through that day. But she was there for me—as she always is. And all I could do at the time was tell myself that the day would come when this would all be nothing more than a bad memory. But for now we had no choice. We were going to have to walk this thing out and deal as best we could, with all the pain that was associated with the possibility of facing something as catastrophic as breast cancer. Oh, how I wanted for this whole thing to just *go away!*

Sometimes It's Okay to Color Outside the Lines

It was a warm winter day. The sun was shining. But as we drove, I was in my own personal private vacuum. I began assessing the day, going over things in my mind, and I started feeling *duped!*

You've had that mammogram script for six months. If this ends up being a malignancy—you've got major problems! All you've ever read about to look for is this "small pea-sized mass." Well—since yours is the size of a small grape—that means this thing is big! And if you had just gone ahead and made the appointment at the time you got the script, it might have been detected long before this. Now you can't go back!

The devil, of course, was right there telling me what a fool I was. "You and your not wanting to have mammograms! Well, just look at you and the mess you're in. How smart is this now?"

And I, who am rarely at a loss for words—had nothing. I could only sit there in the same *shell-shocked* stupor I had continued to fade in and out of ever since the radiologist dropped her bomb.

Then another thought occurred to me: *I'd probably let God down in all this, too! Had I really been so irresponsible that I had set myself up for this . . . out of sheer stupidity?*

I could feel myself on the brink of slipping into a very *deep* hole. And right about the time my mind was poised to click on "save"—buying into that *hell-generated* spam of propaganda—my cell phone rang. It was Kerri. She was calling to tell me the email with all the websites, names and phone numbers had already been sent. And then she proceeded to say, "Ya' know, Mom, I was sitting here thinking, *Why couldn't Mom have just had that mammogram months ago when she first got the prescription?*"

My heart sank. "I know. I've been going over all of it, too. And I have to admit . . . I've been sitting here thinking the very same thing."

"Well," she said, "the longer I thought about it, Mom, I real-ized if you had—you were given the script for it back in July—we didn't even find out about Protocel® until *October! What if you had been given a diagnosis like they are talking about months ago?* You would have been in such a mess. How would you have known what to do? Mom! That would have been *horrible!" She was so right!* And I was so relieved! "Out of the *mouths* of babes . . ."

That little revelation from my daughter, who has been wise beyond her years her entire life, had just put this in a whole new perspective. Here, in a moment clouded with uncertainty, I had begun to entertain the thought of having really messed up with my personal stance on mammograms, when in reality—it may very well have *saved* my life!

Thank You, Lord! For Kerri—and her perception. And for all these answers You're sending (and so quickly) in the midst of all this craziness! Now I can go home, make a couple of phone calls, print information off the Internet, order my first bottle of Protocel® and go to bed.

(Little did I know at the time—but that's where I'd be spending *much* of the next several months!)

CHAPTER 3

Taking Care of Business

To Boldly Go Where People Should Have Been Going All Along

As we arrived home, I was so in hopes that none of the people in our friendly lakeside community would be out.

Our Pointe is a mile loop where everyone walks or rides bikes, golf carts, go-carts and ATVs. And, since all of us are such good friends, it makes it almost impossible to get around the loop without being hailed down by someone you just have to stop and talk with. Well—today I did *not* want that to happen. Because today I had an *agenda*. And, thank God, no one was out!

As soon as we walked in our front door, I already knew the first place I'd head would be upstairs—straight for my "chair." It's where I go to sort things out and the first place I go with my Bible every morning. It's where I go to meet with God. I needed to regroup and get centered—so that's exactly what I did, and already I could feel the pain that was still so fresh start to subside. Still numb—okay, still in *shock* is more like it, but I felt better, and I'd be back there often, but right now I knew I had to head back downstairs, which I did—straight for my office . . . and my computer, where waiting for me was Kerri's email. I sat down, pulled up my chair, rolled up my sleeves and got comfortable. I was going to be there a while.

"This is so overwhelming!" I said to myself, knowing what I was facing. But, once again, I quickly reminded myself of what the "flip side" to all this was. And *that* option (which was *no* option at all) still made it a "no-brainer," so I immediately told myself to *drop the idea of it being overwhelming—or it would be!* Kerri had done a great job of gathering all the pertinent information, but this was my recovery and now it was time for me to step up to the plate and take *ownership.* If this was going to be a full and complete recovery, it was going to be because of relentless diligence on my part: *in finding answers to questions, solutions to challenges and keys to unlocking doors that would move me swiftly to my goals!* (We can talk about where all that came from later.)

There in front of me on the monitor was the list. And on that list were phone numbers and websites for:

- Elonna McKibben's website: <u>ElonnaMcKibben.com</u> – one of the most well-known Protocel® cancer survivor success stories.
- The website: <u>OutsmartYourCancer.com</u>: where the Protocel® e-Booklet, by Tanya Harter Pierce, could be ordered or downloaded. (The book, *Outsmart Your Cancer,* was not yet in print.)
- The phone number for Renewal & Wellness: the main distributor for Protocel®: 888.581.4442
- A couple of other websites with more information on Protocel®.
- The phone number for a biochemist who volunteered his time speaking with people using Protocel®.

Enrolling at OYCU

"Overwhelmed" still best describes what I felt as I looked over what she had sent. Knowing I had to empower myself with knowledge as fast as I possibly could, in a subject I knew little or nothing about (and didn't *want* to!) when I was so exhausted from the stress of the day, made the task at hand seem *daunting!* Flashbacks to those terror-filled moments in the mammogram department, reminding me of the *unthinkable* pending diagnosis, were continually showing on the widescreen of my mind—in high definition! The weight of this was enormous!

But, as persistent as those thoughts were, I refused to entertain them. I had to stay focused. It would serve me no purpose whatsoever to think about the fact that tomorrow I might actually be diagnosed with cancer. Because, regardless of the outcome, I knew I had work to do. Information is power—and right now I needed all the power I could get!

"I've already browsed all the websites, Mom," Kerri had called to say, "and while it's all good information, it seemed lacking. But then I came across www.OutsmartYourCancer.com where a woman named Tanya Harter Pierce has authored a book called *Outsmart Your Cancer.* The book won't be in print for several months yet, and so we'll get it when it comes out, but in the meantime it said that an e-booklet that contains the four chapters on Protocel® from the book could be downloaded. So I already downloaded it! I already have the stuff, Mom—and wait until you read some of this! This covers it all: The history of Protocel®; the story of the man who developed the formula; how it works; how to take it; and several testimonials of those who have beaten cancer with it, even after being given no hope."

"Mom, a lot of the people in these stories only had weeks to months to live. Conventional medicine had done all it could for them, so their doctors sent them home to die. When you read some of these stories, if it turns out you need something like Protocel®, you are going to be so glad you know enough not to do any of that other stuff! I've just got to tell you some of this before I get there tomorrow night, if you've got time. Wait till you hear what Jim Sheridan's daughter wrote in here!"

I, of course, was all ears!

"Listen to this, Mom. Jim Sheridan was a biochemist working at Dow Chemical, in Midland, Michigan." (That certainly got my attention—as if in covered in neon yellow highlighting. The words not only jumped out at me, but they were hitting amazingly close to home!) Dow Chemical was literally right up the road—thirty miles due north from the rural Mid-Michigan farm I grew up on! And I, too, had worked at Dow in my late teens. So that meant, from where I grew up as a child, this man had been only thirty miles away—working on a *cure* for cancer? A cure—that might one day *save* my life? According to his daughter, Marge Sheridan Dubuque, who wrote the story, they all were—it was a family affair. She referred to it as "The Project."

Kerri went on to read that Mr. Sheridan wasn't as interested in organized religion as much as he was a *relationship* with God. And he wanted his life to count for something, so he prayed and asked God for the cure for cancer.

Now she *really* had my attention! Jim Sheridan was all about "relationship" with God, when it was a relationship with God that I had made such a point of developing. That meant this man not only believed in prayer, he believed when he prayed that he was actually talking to God! *And so did I.* And, since he knew he could pray and ask God for the cure for cancer, it also meant that in order for God to give him the answer, he believed God would talk back to him. And I knew God did that, too!

She read how a specific formula had come to him in a dream, a formula he would have to wait two years before coming across again, to be able to understand its significance. In the pursuit of his dream, he had later moved his family to Detroit. But had this man once literally been living and working in my backyard, devoting his whole *life* to perfecting something that I might one day use to save *mine?*

As we hung up, since Kerri already had the information on Protocel® in hand from www.OutsmartYourCancer.com and would be bringing it up, I began looking into the other items on her list. I decided to start with a phone call. The first call I made was to the biochemist who volunteered his time to talk to people like me.

The Voice of Experience

It was two-thirty in the afternoon, Thursday, January 29. Once again, as I dialed the phone, I was so in hopes the other end would pick up. And, once again—it did. It was the biochemist himself who answered. I remember not knowing where to start, but it wasn't long and he quickly put me at ease.

The first thing he wanted to know was what my diagnosis was. I explained that there wasn't one yet, but it was breast cancer they were suspecting and they wanted me to see a surgeon about a possible biopsy, tomorrow at eleven a.m., and that I had already decided I wanted to begin taking Protocel® immediately. I just needed to know which of the two formulas would be best for me to use—*Protocel® 23* or *Protocel® 50*.

He took the time to explain to me that his connection with Protocel® began when his brother was diagnosed with terminal cancer and wanted to use it as his treatment. He said he didn't think it would work for his brother, so he wanted to look into it for himself—and the more he probed, the more impressed he became. His brother survived the cancer, only to die of something entirely unrelated years later. And years later his own wife, who was diagnosed with breast cancer that had metastasized extensively, took Protocel® and she also survived. Wow—how impressive was that?

As he explained it, because of his background in biochemistry, he wanted to learn more about how a dietary supplement could have such a powerful effect against something like cancer. It was witnessing firsthand how it saved the lives of two of his loved ones that caused him to follow literally thousands of stories throughout the years, of people who chose to use Protocel® against a diagnosis of cancer—cancer of all types. He has since continued to stay involved counseling people as a volunteer.

It was his opinion, from what he had observed in the cases he followed through the years, that Protocel® 23 Formula was the one most used for dealing with a diagnosis of breast cancer—even though both formulas are almost identical. He also recommended a supplement called "bromelain"—a minimum of 1000 mg. with each meal.

I couldn't believe the time he took. He let me ask questions, and nothing I asked was too stupid. And there was a calm about his demeanor regarding my diagnosis. It was obvious—he didn't think this was the end of the world for me. (Or the end of the line, either!)

When I hung up the phone I immediately called to order my first bottle of Protocel® 23. I had decided, if they still could, I'd have it sent Next-Day Air. Tomorrow was Friday—and I wanted to start on it *yesterday!* Whatever tomorrow held in the way of a diagnosis, I knew I'd be taking my first dose of Protocel® 23 tomorrow night. Our UPS man always comes by six.

My "Get Out of Jail Free" Card

Thinking back, even in the hospital mammogram department when they were doing something as simple as setting up the appointment with the surgeon, they were tiptoeing around me. They didn't say anything comforting, or reassuring, or even encouraging. Encouraging would have been good. (*Anything* would have been good!) They didn't even ask me any questions, let alone smile at me. What they did do—was act like I was facing a death sentence! It was morbid. I could tell by the looks on their faces that they were in pain for me. And I couldn't help but think that *they* were the ones needing comforting more than I did. It was obvious they were all thinking the same thing—*in unison:* You could almost hear it!

The poor thing. Look at her. She's about to be handed a death sentence!

I remember sitting there thinking just how much I wanted to stop the whole mess and shut them *all* up by shouting, *"But you don't understand! I have a 'Get Out of Jail Free Card.' It's called Protocel®!"*

What a barn-burner that would have been! Couldn't you just see someone like *me* trying to explain to all those "skilled professionals" that I actually had this "dietary supplement" I could take—that would cause cancer cells to literally *fall apart?* Not only would they have thought I had breast cancer . . . and was probably going to die. But they'd also be thinking I was a *mental case* with breast cancer . . . *that was probably going to die!*

When I was a kid, if someone had cancer you didn't talk about it. And the people who had it were few and far between. Then as I got older we started to hear things like, "If you think about it, everyone knows someone with cancer." Then it escalated to where one in a hundred would get cancer, and then they were saying one in ten would have it by the year 2005. (And now they're saying it's *two* in ten?)

It infuriated me to hear those statistics. It still does. Especially the one about "It's almost getting to the point where it's not *if* a woman gets breast cancer, but *when.*" And now it had hit home! What happened that day dug up a lot of issues I've had "issues" with for years!

I'm tired of pink ribbon campaigns and women being made to feel the only power they have against this *horror-show* called breast cancer is "early detection." Why sit around and wait to *get* something that would even require detection? If there are preventatives, let's find out about them, and if they're promising—let's perfect them. Except I thought I'd been using some of the best. So how do you re-think the last thirty years when you *know* you were in the right ballpark all along?—(Which is why I still don't *get* this!)

I can't overstate how frustrating it was for me, wondering where this mess could have come from, knowing how proactive I'd been for years, even decades, about prevention. There had to be something drastic I'd missed. Some void in my life where supplementing my diet was concerned. Or my having a very messed-up metabolism, for me to be facing the possibility of becoming the devastated recipient of one of the most *dreaded* pieces of news a woman can possibly get. (See Chapter 20—*A Window to Look Through*.)

The more the reality of finding myself smack in the middle of this mess sank in, *the madder I got*. Regardless of what the diagnosis came back as, I knew I was already way too far in it to ever be able to turn and walk away from it now! Life had already somewhat prepared me for something like this, and as a result I knew too much. And now, in light of what had just been dropped on me—I was determined to find out even more!

I'm sure those technicians were thinking about the horrors of the inevitable suffering that lay ahead for me as I started to walk this thing out in their *system*—trying to survive. They see it every day. But when I left there that day, I distinctly remember saying to myself, *"Well, people—I hope you remember me. Because when I beat this thing (and if I need to, I <u>will</u> beat this thing!), I'll be back one day—to tell you just exactly how I did it!"*

And Trust Me—I Have Plans

I also remember thinking: *And I don't care how long it takes! Preferably sooner than later—but whatever the case—benign or malignant; stubborn or easy to deal with; in one spot, or all over the place: I'm fixin' to straighten this mess out!* I was ticked off enough already, just having been put through this gauntlet of terror. And it only took minutes of being thrown into the ring with it to know, in the long term, I'd be doing everything I knew to do about it for years to come—so somebody else didn't have to go through this.

I knew keeping a strong immune system when dealing with a diagnosis of cancer is *paramount*. A strong immune system will *buy time!* And I needed to have that going for me—because this was cancer we were talking about. It is one frightening, vile, insidious disease that exists solely to prey upon and kill. It was clear Protocel® had worked for countless others, but what was yet to be seen was, if I needed it to—*would it work for me?*

In the world of alternative treatments, I was well aware of the fact: not all treatments work for all people. And in a worst-case scenario, if the one alternative treatment I felt *certain* would work for me *didn't*—I knew a strong immune system would play a critical role in buying the time I'd need if I had to find another that *would*. I was always prepared to look elsewhere if need be. But, from what I had heard and read about Protocel®, and the path being seemingly orchestrated that led me to it, I prayed that I had found my treatment and would never need to. And when this worked for me— "Nellie, bar the door!" I'd be off and running *with this, in this* and *on this— promoting "alternative cancer treatments" for the rest of my life!*

The environment cancer finds the most difficult to flourish in is a body equipped with everything it needs to fight back—which is why I knew there would *never* be any poisoning, radiating or cutting going on—as long as I still had breath! I hadn't had anything conventional done, which everyone in Protocel® circles said tipped the scales even more in my favor.

And, unlike what went on in the hospital mammogram department, there was no alarm, fear or terror in their voices or demeanor as I discussed my situation with them. I wanted to be on the "team" that wasn't scared of a diagnosis like this.

Pure gratitude best describes my feelings about having known of Protocel® before I ever knew I'd need it. And for Jim Sheridan, who was so willing to be used of God that he spent his entire life in pursuit of perfecting this powerfully *restorative* formula, along with his family and the current owners of the Protocel® Formulas, who've kept his dream alive.

But one man's dream, however valiant or valuable, can become another man's obsession to destroy if it somehow begins to threaten their pursuit of power—or amassing the almighty dollar. Because in the end "the powers that be" not only didn't appreciate Jim Sheridan's brilliance, and the "God-given" answer to cancer he had developed, but history records that they systematically did everything humanly possible to undermine and suppress his work. Which I personally found infuriating, since now it was *my* life they were messing with— as they played their greedy, self-interest-serving games!

Just one more fire-fanning reason why—if I actually did have to take on cancer—when I beat this mess I would spend the rest of my life in the *unrelenting, focused, endeavoring effort* of seeing to it Protocel® became a household word, along with any other alternative treatment I find out about that's as effective as Protocel® is against cancer! I'm even starting to sense this was the reason I was born, 'cause, like I said, "I didn't start this fight!" But—*seein's how* I've been sucked into it—for me—exposing it for what it is, is not something that's likely to *ever* go away!

ElonnaMcKibben.com

While I was waiting for Renewal & Wellness to return my call I decided to check out the www.ElonnaMcKibben.com website. And what a touching, impressive, miraculous story!

In October of 1989, Elonna was diagnosed with Stage IV Glioblastoma Multiforme, just five weeks after she had given birth to quintuplets—four of which survived. GBM usually involves the brain and is rare—and always fatal. The survival time for people diagnosed with GBM is: GBM in the brain; people can live twelve to twenty-four months. Most don't make it past twelve. GBM of the spine; three to six months. Elonna's diagnosis involved her spinal cord, which is the rarest form, and it meant she may not have had even *that* long. She wouldn't live to see her children's first birthday.

After being introduced to Cancell® (which was the name for Protocel® at the time) and a considerable amount of prayer, Elonna cancelled the radiation treatments and began taking Cancell® (now Protocel® 23) in November of 1989.

In February of 1990, just three months later, she showed so much improvement that a CT scan was ordered. The report came back saying there was no evidence of any cancer. Elonna had literally survived a form of cancer that no one else had—*ever!* And she did this at a time when there was no one to talk to about their recovery—and no Internet to surf. What an incredibly brave lady with an incredibly encouraging story! (For Elonna's complete story, visit www.ElonnaMcKibben.com.)

The Attack and the Plan

So many things were lining up, reassuring me that I was making the right choice. I was still hoping for a good report of a benign tumor, or possibly a lymph node that was, shall we say, *"having a moment"*—but at this point I knew—whatever was coming, I'd face it and I'd conquer it! Because I had God in my corner—and Protocel® for the *straightaway!*

Throughout the years I've known of many people who survived cancer using alternative methods, but, probably because the whole thing is so scary and unpleasant, like many others, I'd never given much thought to what I'd use if I found I ever had a need. (Why do any research on the subject, in any kind of depth, when, to begin with, you are convinced you're never going to be in a position to have to make this kind of choice?)

However, when I heard about Protocel® in October, I felt it could be an answer for those who were searching, and I had already begun telling people. And, now, since something may have slipped through the preventative measures I'd taken, it looked as if it was time to go into "Plan B." God always has a "Plan B." And God had literally given me an answer before I ever knew I had a problem. *How humbling is that?*

My confession to God for years has been, "You order my steps;[9] You direct my paths;[10] and You establish my thoughts."[11] Because in the Bible He said He would, if I just trusted Him for it. And I *do*. So He *does*. And that's how it goes for us. *We're buds!*

I immediately started strategizing and *living in the future*. I had too many sunrises to paint (I'm partial to them—just ask my kids), too many grandchildren who hadn't even been born yet to love and help raise—and there was still that "book" I always knew I'd write. I simply didn't have time to die with all my gifts still inside me— especially of something as *pathetic* as cancer!

It was time to set my face like a flint. No wimping out on this one! This could be the battle of my life. And if it was—I intended to win! Take no prisoners—*this was all-out war!*

First of all, there are specific do's and don'ts with regard to taking Protocel®. With the way Protocel® works, taking products along with it that cause an increase in "voltage" or "ATP" (adenosine triphosphate) activity at the cellular level will negate Protocel®'s effectiveness. I'll go into this in greater detail later, but suffice it to say that if someone is not prepared to diligently follow the few simple rules that apply to the use of Protocel®, they're better off not using it at all!

Many supplements cannot be taken with Protocel®. Lists of supplements and treatments that are considered "compatible" and "incompatible" have been compiled by Tanya Harter Pierce and are presented in her book, *Outsmart Your Cancer*, and a list also comes with every bottle of Protocel® ordered. However, below is a list of the supplements known to interfere with Protocel® the most adversely.

- **Vitamin C**
- **Vitamin E**
- **CoQ10**
- **Selenium**
- **Essiac Tea**
- **Ozone Treatments**
- **Burdock Root**
- **Alpha Lipoic Acid**
- **Cat's Claw**
- **IP-6**
- **Cesium**

I myself have taken a number of health-enhancing, wellness-promoting products for years, but when I decided to use Protocel® I knew, for the time being, I had to give the majority of them up. Anything that directly promotes the production of ATP at the cellular level and everything that is on the "incompatible list" I immediately dropped! And if I wasn't certain it was compatible with Protocel®, *it was out!* Because the non-negotiable rule to follow *when using Protocel®* is, **"When in doubt—***don't!"*

Take alfalfa, for instance. A vegetable plant rich in nutrients with no vitamin C or E, but its roots grow deep in search of trace minerals, including selenium—and a handful of alfalfa tablets could contain too much. The supplements I took for years would be waiting for me one day when I was off Protocel®, after being deemed cancer-free for a period of at least a year. But in the meantime, I went through what I was *taking* and everything I was doing with a "fine-toothed comb" to be certain I was doing everything right!

(Visit www.TheBreastStaysPut.com for more detailed information on optimum Protocel® usage.)

Other Protocel® Uses

Protocel® 23 has also been known to be effective against autoimmune and other diseases including: Lupus, Rheumatoid Arthritis, Multiple Sclerosis, Psoriasis, Mononucleosis, Crohn's Disease, IBS or UC, Endometriosis, Parkinson's, Viral Infections and for pets in general for any condition.

CHAPTER 4

Doctor Is Not Spelled G-O-D

Swimming Against the Current of Mainstream Medicine

I don't remember much about the drive back to the hospital the next morning to see the surgeon—except for the fact that I still could barely comprehend or accept this was happening. Willie and I didn't do a lot of talking. We were both in deep thought. I do remember him holding my hand as we drove, softly moving his thumb back and forth across the back of it for a *long* time. I still had the feeling of being in a vacuum. I thought about this "surgeon" we were about to see and all the stress this would no doubt involve. How I did *not* want to have to do this.

I was going to have to tell him I wasn't doing anything conventional—that I'd be using an alternative treatment. That's always fun!—Telling a doctor you know more than they do, about *what* they do. And, although the confrontations are never something I've looked forward to, I've done it so many times in life it seems like it's become a fine art to me anymore.

Before I go any further, there's something else I should tell you (which only adds to disbelief and frustration about finding myself in this situation). Just three months prior to Christmas, Willie suffered a heart attack. (Believe that?) So, within months, we'd been hit with two *unbelievable* shocks! And I just have to tell you a little about this one, too.

It was a little past noon on a beautiful Indian summer day. I was upstairs just finishing my makeup when I heard Willie's truck drive in. The next thing I knew, I heard the front door burst open and he was calling out to me. And he didn't sound like himself. *At all!*

I came running down the stairs to find the healthiest, most muscular, structurally sound man I've ever known—reduced to *nothing*. Collapsing in *massive* pain! (Even when he's in *real* pain, Willie never complains. I knew this was bad!)

Immediately, I grabbed the cordless and dialed 911 for an ambulance—and then canceled it almost as quickly as I had called for it. There was only one hospital I wanted him in; the 911 lady couldn't tell me which hospital they would be taking him to—so I cancelled it. And as I did, I turned and called out to Willie, telling him to "Get in the car!" *He was nowhere to be found!*

(I should note the 911 operator was thrown for a real loop when I told her to "cancel it." She kept asking me was I sure I wanted to. I kept telling her, if she couldn't tell me where they were taking him—*I had to!* I assured her we would be okay—thanked her, hung up and started looking for Willie.)

I went running through the house to discover he had *climbed the stairway* to our master suite. He had gone to bed! (Ugh! Is that a *man* thing?)

Insisting he was going to the ER, I made him go down and get in the car. My plan being as soon as we got to a certain point in the county (where I knew we'd be assured of getting to the hospital I wanted him in) I'd dial 911 again, requesting assistance. And that's *exactly* what I did! It worked like a charm! Willie giving me orders all the way! (Another "man thing," right?)

First he didn't want me calling 911 again—(but after it was all over, he was one grateful guy that I did!). And he didn't want me "driving fast" either. And I wasn't. But it wasn't like "Maria" Andretti here didn't try to floor it after every curve and stop sign. (All the while thinking, *He's just lucky I'm not running them!*)

I know he was sitting there going, *If this isn't "the big one," she's going to see to it that it is before we get there!* Because the next thing I heard him say was: "You aren't supposed to stress people out when they're having a heart attack!" Which was pretty funny, and we both knew it! (Ya' had to be there.)

The paramedics met us on the road, and from the time we left home, within ten minutes they were treating him; ten minutes later he was in the hospital ER; and ten minutes later he was up in the CCU, where a stent was implanted. It was *that* fast!

Good call on my part, canceling that ambulance! God was right there, once again, like He always is—giving me the presence of mind to think about what was happening, what was coming and how I wanted it to turn out! *(Don't you just love that about God?)*

That other hospital? They aren't equipped. They'd have had to transport him to the one I took him to anyway, costing precious *hou*rs—with Willie incurring more heart damage. I wanted him to have the best possible care, and as it turned out, he got it. The heart damage was minimal. I did the right thing!

The paramedics in the ambulance winked at me as they left, pointing at me, saying, "You did *so* good!" And the doctors in the ER were practically high-fiving me, telling me I couldn't have done any better! From the time of the onset of the heart attack, we figured as little as forty-five minutes had elapsed before they had the stent implanted. They told me, "You can't do any better than that unless you're right here *at* the hospital when it happens!"

Later, after it was all over, the cardiac doctor on call told both of us he wanted us to be certain to understand: "Willie did not have a heart attack like other people have 'heart attacks.' He had no blockages. His arteries were clean. Something in the form of 'soft tissue' had broken loose, traveling to where it lodged, plugging the artery and causing the attack," which the doctor added was actually a rare occurrence. ("A *rare* occurrence?"—now, just how did we happen to draw *that* card?)

The doctors in the hospital were incredible. It was the ones we were scheduled to see later, for follow-ups, who started throwing a wrench in the works.

Battling "the system" with the cardiac doctor they assigned Willie to, in regard to medication they wanted him on, became challenging, to say the least. And, in addition to that, even his general practitioner who he had follow-up visits with told him, "If you ever get off Zocor—you're a dead man!"

Now, that's an exciting thing to hear, especially for someone like Willie, who has a history of *low* cholesterol. Willie's never been back to him. (Like you want somebody dim-witted enough to make a statement like that as your doctor, or someone who speaks death over you for *any* reason—let alone in conjunction with some drug that the next doctor could decide to pull you *off!* Incidentally, every doctor we saw after that told him to stay off that drug and find a way to get off the others, and to stay on CoQ10, Omega-3's, enzymes and several other supplements that he was already on that would do the same thing, without the undesirable long-term side effects of a statin.)

So here we were, quite the pair. Two people who had spent years going to great lengths taking all sorts of preventative measures to ensure we would live out our years in health and vitality—and just look at us, "Gertrude and Heathcliffe," *wondering what hit us!* Willie suffering a heart attack, and now me—facing God only knows what!

What an example we were setting for our thirty-year established health and wellness business! And now, especially, with *my* situation—life for us looked as though it might be spiraling right out of control! Where was this stuff coming from? None of this was supposed to be happening. At least neither one of us remembered penciling it in on our list of "scheduled events."

So here we go again, I thought, *stepping into the world of them telling us what I* have to *do*—and me telling them (politely) what I was *going* to do—and, more than likely, what I was *not* going to do—and then waiting to see if sparks flew. (This could get ugly, people.)

Gazing out the window at the frozen snow-covered scenery, I was well aware of what I was facing as I contemplated my pending predicament. But suddenly something came to mind that caused a sense of *strength* to well up inside me.

Kerri was four years old, and it was my first confrontation with a doctor. And, although on a totally different level, I now realized it was one uncomfortable and scary situation that had prepared me for what I knew I had to do today! I didn't want to deal with it either at the time, but I knew I had to for Kerri's sake. And now, after being reminded of how I was able to do it, I was certain I could pull this off, too! (A great example of when reaching back into what otherwise may have looked like a downer of a situation in your past can serve as a good thing—providing direction and strength for today when facing something similar—which they say is about the only time we're supposed to look back on something like this.)

Did I Say Spot?

When Kerri was four years old, on a routine doctor visit, I mentioned to the doctor that she had a spot on her toe that wouldn't clear up. I asked if he thought it looked like eczema.

He said it was, and as he was finishing up he added, "And we'll get a shot for that toe of hers. It should clear it up in no time." And out the door he went.

A shot, I thought? *What kind of shot?* An antibiotic wouldn't do anything for what was wrong with her toe; there was no infection in it. So, if not an antibiotic—*then what?* What other kind of shot would they give a child? I wasn't going to let him give her an antibiotic just to make it look like he was doing something because I voiced a concern, which we all know doctors can be inclined to do from time to time. (Okay—a lot!) *Somehow I have to do something to stop this. I have to "say" something. He is <u>not</u> going to give her "a shot!"*

I remember agonizing over how I'd do it and what I'd say. I mean, this was a "doctor," and at the time I was only twenty-seven! (Back then people didn't tend to stand up to doctors. Back then they wanted us to think we weren't supposed to know anything.) No matter how you cut it, when I questioned him about it, I'd essentially be telling him he didn't know what he was doing—wouldn't I? *How* do you do that? *To a doctor?* (Couldn't we just forget I brought this up?)

Finally, he came back, and I found the courage, sucked it up and said, "What kind of shot were you thinking of giving her?"

"Cortisone," he said.

I couldn't believe my ears! *Cortisone? What was he thinking?* He wanted to give a steroid injection—for a tiny spot of eczema—*to a little four-year-old girl?* It can take seven years to get something like cortisone out of the system! And they say sometimes people never get rid of the problems it can cause. *And she was just a child!* Everything inside me was saying, *You're going to have to go through me to get to her!*

A Shot for a Spot—I Think Not!

Well, I'd already launched right out there even questioning him about it, so I figured I might as well finish it off. I had no choice but to call him on it. I was *so* not prepared for something like this at the time, and I can still remember how hard it was to do, but it was *my baby* he was getting ready to inject with that *poison.*

"No, I don't think we need to do that," I heard myself say.

He shot me (no pun intended) a puzzled look.

So I went on to say, "It's a little spot, and she's only four—and I don't want cortisone in her system."

Okay, there! I did it!

To which he replied (and this just floored me), "Well, don't get me wrong; I don't suggest giving cortisone for just *anything.*"

(No? You just did . . .)

"But you said you couldn't get it to go away, and I know this would do it, so that's why I suggested it."

Okay, so now it was *my* fault. (See what I mean? Voice a concern—get a drug.) Well—*whatever.* I did what I needed to do, and I could tell he was a bit embarrassed. But the important thing was—he backed off. And Kerri was safe!

They can't possibly just freely give children cortisone shots for something that simple—can they? I asked myself as I walked Kerri out to the car. (I knew the answer to the question before I even asked it. They do it all the time.)

I'm sure in the world of medicine he operated in he meant well. He really was, in my opinion, a good, caring doctor. But I knew even he had to be going, *What was I thinking?*

What a scary moment! But I made it through it—and I knew if I could handle the situation with finesse the way I had back then, I could do what I needed to do today and all the tomorrows to come, if need be, in the same manner. Because, just like little Kerri that day—no one was injecting Mom with anything either!

Show 'em Your Papers

Okay then, so how hard can it be to tell a surgeon that anything he has to offer wouldn't be anything I'd be interested in pursuing? Piece of cake, don't you think? *Ugh!*

So here I went again. And, can I just say, it would be a whole lot easier if they didn't have all those diplomas, licenses and certificates hanging all over their walls! I mean, they've had eight years of med-school, and I've had what? *A couple courses in nutrition?* I wondered if the surgeon would be interested in seeing *my* papers. (Probably not, huh?)

This brought to mind a joke that a friend of mine told at a sales seminar years ago. I've always loved this joke!

It was about a farmer who was sitting on his front porch minding his own business when the government tax assessor drove in and wanted to look into the farmer's land holdings—to take measurements. The farmer told him he didn't want him around.

But the man put his briefcase on the hood of his car, opened it and pulled out papers issued by the state, verifying he had legal authorization and every right to be there. The farmer had no choice but to let the man on his land.

As the afternoon wore on, the assessor kept demanding to see more and more of the acreage. And every time the farmer resisted, he would flash those papers of his under the farmer's nose. So he had no choice but to let him go wherever he wanted to go, doing whatever he wanted to do.

Finally, the assessor ventured out into the pasture, and right about the time he got in the middle of it, the farmer's bull that had been grazing over in a corner caught sight of him, got a bead on him and came barreling!

The assessor took off running for his life trying to make it to the fence, screaming at the top of his lungs for help, to which the farmer quickly responded by yelling out to him, *"Show 'im your papers! Show 'im your papers!"* (Somehow I didn't think this surgeon would be interested in seeing mine.)

I'm All Out of Cute!

And I couldn't wait till the "family history" part where I would have to tell him I lost my mom to breast cancer; that she'd been going to Mexico for an alternative treatment—because I was *sure* he'd ask. The frustration was that I knew he wouldn't have time to hear the real story about how Mom actually had the cancer beat, but in the end lost her battle because of one bad decision she made. (More on this later also). But he never asked.

And he probably wouldn't have time for me to fully explain Protocel®. Nor would he care. In most states, unless a treatment is FDA approved, by law doctors can't prescribe it even if they wanted to. They can, however, monitor your progress and advise you. And if they are a good caring doctor, they will.

Anyway, you see my point. I just asked God to please not let this guy be old, out of touch, narrow-minded or mean. Old I could handle, and even out of touch. But narrow-minded or mean would probably send me right over the edge. Because, in this "pressure cooker moment" in my life, I didn't have it in me to be diplomatic with a know-it-all, closed-minded *anybody*. And I didn't even *care* that I didn't! All I cared about was getting beyond whatever was coming—and home to my bottle of Protocel®.

As we walked into the hospital, turning into the wing where we'd been directed, I realized even more just how little I knew about what was coming, and how much I wished this day was over.

I was told that having the biopsy wasn't something I needed to be concerned about. (Although I couldn't understand how disturbing a tumor with an invasive procedure, even with something as tiny as a needle, wouldn't cause problems—especially if it *did* turn out to be a bad diagnosis). But even those involved in the world of alternative treatments told me the procedure was relatively safe.

Note to Self #2 – Find out exactly what age that is: You know—the one where, when we finally get to it, we actually stop believing everything we hear.

(More on this later, too.) (We have a lot to talk about, don't we?)

"Just don't let them take any 'nodes'," I'd been told by my Protocel® friends. "If they say they want to 'see if it has metastasized,' tell them to just assume that it already has—because, if it has, Protocel® also takes care of metastases."

Well, God answered yet another prayer. This guy was great! He was kind and personable, with such an easygoing manner. Still, I knew I had to tell him I wouldn't be doing anything conventional, hoping he'd be okay about it. (I wasn't looking so much for him to understand as I was for him to be *understanding*.)

His demeanor was so non-threatening. I mean, this was a really great guy. I'm sure he was an excellent surgeon, to be so young and in his position. And he didn't seem to have a pretentious bone in his body. Even the mammogram technician, when she handed me the appointment slip as we left to go home yesterday, had whispered, *"He's a good one!"*

And, you know, I knew she meant that to be reassuring. But at the time, the best I could get out of it was a minor element of dry humor—for two reasons: As opposed to what—all the others that *aren't?* And, good at what? Doctors are only good at what they *do*. This guy is a "surgeon." If he finds something he doesn't like, the first thing he's going to want to do is cut it out—or worse yet—*cut it off!* Because that's what a surgeon *does!* So this guy being "a good one" wasn't a fact I took much reassurance in. At all! All I wanted was *the diagnosis, please.* So I could know for sure what it was I was dealing with. So I could get on with my life! *(Whatever the definition of that would now consist of!)*

CHAPTER 5

The Verdict

This Biopsy's for You!

You know, somewhere in all this I did briefly consider the fact that I didn't even have to have a biopsy if I didn't want to. I'd heard that Protocel® takes care of not only malignant, but also benign tumors, so was there anything saying I couldn't just go on a program of Protocel® without one?—leaving the lump in question undisturbed? (I should also add that, from what I'd heard, Protocel® does not take care of cysts—but I felt certain that what I was dealing with wasn't a cyst.)

With a needle biopsy very tiny sections of tissue are extracted from a mass to determine if it's malignant. (Which, to me, just sounds like trouble!) I knew for Protocel® to take care of it, I didn't need to know if it was or wasn't cancer. But someday when this thing was gone, how would I have proof (for others *and* myself) it actually *was* cancer Protocel® took care of?

No, I wanted there to be no doubt, after I slayed this beast, if it was in fact cancer. Because if Protocel® worked against cancer there was a whole world out there that needed to know. Pure frustration for me (if this actually *did* end up being a bad diagnosis) would be if Protocel® kicked butt against cancer—*but I had no way to prove it!*

Looking back, the question never again crossed my mind. It was settled early on—I'd be having a biopsy!

From the minute I met the surgeon and we exchanged pleasantries, I felt so at ease. *At least he doesn't come across as being terrified for me,* I thought. *Or, if he is, he's good—because I certainly can't detect it.*

Of course not! I chided myself (as my brain went flying off on yet another tangent)—the guy's a surgeon. He's the guy with the knife! He's the guy who knows if it's malignant, he's going to get out his scalpel. So what's for him to be scared for me about? (Well, think again, Zorro. It ain't happenin'!) But he was a really great guy, and I could feel myself calming down.

He asked what was going on and how he could help me, and I explained that the radiologist felt the mammogram looked "suspicious." And at that he said, "Well, then—*let's check it out!*"

As he examined me, he couldn't find it. I told him I couldn't find it either unless I was sitting or standing. He immediately had me sit up, and he agreed—it was quite soft. And then, with a look of hope in his eye, in a lighthearted mannerism, he said, "You know what? What do you say we step into a little room across the hall and do a needle biopsy right now? I have the time, and maybe we'll find out that this is all much ado about *nothing!*"

"Fine with me," I said, thinking to myself, *Okay, this is good. At least I'll know something soon. And there can't be much to it if he's going to go ahead with it right now. Right?*

Note to Self #3 – For future reference: *Nothing* **involving a surgeon doing a procedure in a "little room across the hall"** *ever* **falls under the category of "not much to it."** (Which *I* was about to discover!)

I Am a Surgeon—and I Have a Gun

There in the room was a large, wide, flat, cushioned table for me to lie down on, in addition to *four* nurses and/or technicians. (Which, for me, had red flags going up all over the place!) *Why did he need four? I should have investigated this a little further maybe . . . before agreeing to it? (Gee—'ya think?) (Would it be too late to apply for one of those "do-overs" here?)*

62

As the surgeon began introducing me, he also reassured me that he would explain what was happening as he went along.

To my right, one of the technicians was setting up the ultrasound machine, which he explained he would be using "as a guide" . . . so he'd know exactly where to "go in." *(Gulp!)* And then I could hear what sounded like one of the other nurses fumbling through a drawer . . . as if she were looking for something.

And that's when I heard the doctor ask, "Has anyone seen my needle gun?" *(Okay, what's that about? What is a "needle" doing in a gun—and what's a "gun" doing in here?)*

Right about then the nurse who had been looking through the drawers proceeded to nonchalantly ask, "What size needles do you want today, Doctor—six inch or eight?"

(Nice. A gazillion biopsy teams in the world and I have to get "The Hole in the Wall Gang.") (I thought about making a break for it, but there were too many of them.)

With *that,* my already *off-the-chart* anxiety level smoked it right to the "I changed my mind—let me out of here" stage, and I began massaging my forehead with the fingertips of my free hand—much the same as someone who was totally stressed out! *(Because I was!)*

The doctor had to have picked up on my body language, because I heard him chime in, saying something to the effect of: "I'm not sure all the talk about needles and their sizes is giving much confidence to our patient."

To which the ultrasound tech immediately responded to by saying, "Actually, Doctor . . . I was thinking maybe it would be the little *gun* remark that would be more apt to give her cause to start *freaking* out on us!"

And, before she even got it out of her mouth, I broke my silence and said, *"No—kidding!"* which broke everyone up—*including* the surgeon!

Apologetically, he tried to reassure me that they just call it "a gun," but it really doesn't "shoot" anything, quickly adding, "and . . . although the needles *are* long, you don't need to be concerned. It's mostly just the *tips* of them that I use."

"Well, now I know *I* feel better!" I said, with a touch of sarcastic enthusiasm, once again prompting a roomful of spontaneous laughter. *(A regular fun-fest!)*

Note to Self #4. When a surgeon armed with a gun, with a barrel that holds *an eight-inch needle* — tells you "there's nothing to be concerned about" — *be concerned!*

(And I can be totally up front about this, because they now have a less painful procedure. And may I be the first to suggest if you ever find yourself in a situation where you have need of a biopsy — *find a facility that has it*. That thing hurt like crazy!)

Not Your Typical Good News Week

Tears were just rolling. And at one point the surgeon stopped. He wanted to know if the tears were from pain or anxiety.

(I think he'd noticed I'd quit breathing.)

"Pain," I told him. "It seems to get worse each time you do it. But maybe it *is* mostly anxiety. From not knowing what's coming." (Story of my life right now.) (I thought about asking him if he had any Novocain . . . but the thought of laughing with an "eight-inch needle" involved made me think again.)

"I should only have to go in one more time. I hope with this last attempt I'll have gotten all the tissue I need. And, so you know, it won't hurt any more than it already has."

(And me? I was hoping all those "attempts" he was referring to were all in *one* spot. Having it in there was bad enough. . . I sure didn't need the thing *shot* full of holes!)

And with that, the doctor was off to the lab.

(Ugh! Would someone please tell me I just survived that!)

The nurses were so comforting to me. They were great in there. And as he left, the only nurse who stayed with me began talking with me. I shared with her my plans to use Protocel®, regardless of how this turned out. She was genuinely excited for me, very intrigued, and wanted to know more about it. So I told her how to find it online.

About that time the doctor came back. He was looking through the drawers again, this time asking if there were any Band-aids in the room.

"If you're looking for Band-aids," I asked leadingly, "it must mean you got all the tissue you needed . . . *right?*"

Still moving around the room, he rather wistfully said, "Yes—but it's not good news, darn it. The pathologist said it's positive."

"Positive?"

"Yes—*I'm afraid it's cancer.*"

And that was that. It was what it was. And ya' can't shoot the messenger (especially this guy!). He felt so bad for me. But—surprisingly, I seemed to be okay. Either the shock had worn off, since I'd had time to process what might be coming. Or maybe I was just too tired to get all bent out of shape over some, albeit, "life-threatening diagnosis" that I knew I already had an answer for.

But, just to be sure, I had to check with myself again . . . because a *surgeon* just said, "*You* have cancer"—to *me*—and I didn't seem to feel much of anything. And even I found that hard to believe!

But I really did seem to be fine. So—like we used to say back in the day . . . *"Might as well go with it; can't dance; too wet to plow, and the car's out of gas"*—I guess I'll be doing the "Protocel® Shuffle" long term after all!

At Newsstands Everywhere

Interestingly enough, this wasn't as scary as the previous day. I had just gotten the dreaded diagnosis, and nothing inside or outside of me was freaking out, falling apart or even distraught. They just said I had cancer: I felt sad. Maybe a little numb. But all in all, compared to yesterday—I thought I was coping amazingly well.

And I (the eternal optimist) knew the final report could still come back saying it wasn't cancer after all. It wouldn't be the first time something they *said* was positive turned out not to be.

But, all in all, I had resigned myself to the fact that this was the way it was going to be: So . . . *"Next?"*

(Maybe I should have fought harder on that one.)

The relative composure I was feeling had to be because I knew God had my back and Protocel® would be waiting for me when I got home.

Still, it seemed strange to know their worst suspicions, all centered around the *last* diagnosis I would ever want associated with my life, were just confirmed, and I didn't feel much of anything. It wasn't as if I was okay about it *(by any stretch of the imagination),* but there was an obvious absence of fear or terror on my part. And *that* was a good thing! And…after all, "Tomorrow is (as they say) *another* day!"

Come morning I knew my feet would hit the floor running—and I'd be about the business of building the full-out strategy I'd be using over the next several months—*to win the battle of my life!*

After they got me all fixed up, the ultrasound technician gave me a hug and said, "I know I'll be *reading* about you one day and how you survived this!" (See! Even she knew there'd be a book about it!)

The room where Willie was waiting was in view. This was going to break his heart. I knew he could see it in my face the second he looked up. And, as I told him, for the first time since this whole ordeal started—Willie reacted. He was so sad for me. He had so been in hopes the pathologist report would come back saying it was benign.

Me, too! I was in hopes it would come back saying it was *nothing!*

As we sat there waiting for the surgeon, Willie told me he had overheard doctors in another room speaking with an elderly couple. "The wife has breast cancer, and the doctors were explaining to them what was going to happen and what decisions they'd have to make. And they weren't comprehending any of it. How sad. They've probably spent their whole lives together, and now they're facing something like this."

And, in addition to wishing I could tell them about Protocel®, I was also wondering if anyone in another room near us had "overheard" *our* conversation. I don't think that's supposed to happen. In fact, I know it's not. Just another reason to get out of there (and *stay* out of there!)—I didn't want everybody and their brother knowing what was going on in our lives! We were both just so relieved that Protocel® would be waiting for me when we got home: My *"Get Out of Jail Free Card!"* But as we sat waiting for the surgeon to return, I couldn't help but think: *It's too bad that little lady doesn't have a bottle of Protocel® waiting for her—to go home and hug—like I do.*

I Wonder Where That Road Goes

Well, the verdict's in, and not to minimize what's going on here, but it looks as though I'll be heading down "Recovery Lane" for the next *however long,* after all, in what looks to be what you'd have to call your basic "unscheduled detour." (Suddenly finding yourself being sent in an entirely different direction than you were previously headed—without having *any* say in the matter.) Yesterday, when I woke up, I had a whole agenda planned for weeks and months to come. Today I couldn't even tell you what it was. Funny how all that "stuff" you absolutely have to "get at" and "get to" can suddenly, in one fell swoop, shift to the other side of the pad under the heading of "The Insignificant and Irrelevant."

Welp!—All I can say to that is, "It's a good thing the sport of taking *side roads* is one of our favorite things to do in life. A favorite pastime, if you will." (Okay, maybe for Willie a little more than me.) So it's not like, for the two of us, this "detour" stuff is anything to get all crazy about. To this day when I hear Willie say, "I wonder where that road goes," I have to shake my head and laugh. If he's said it once, he's said it a hundred times, because he truly *does* want to know—where *that* road *goes!*

And, since it's apparent that I have no choice, if it's a detour I've been given, then it's an "adventure" I'll be taking. If I'm going to get through this I have to view it in that light. Taking myself, and what I've been handed, too seriously would only add to the weight of contemplating all the "unknowns"—making it far too heavy to deal with if I choose to look at this any other way.

It's probably not the best time to mention this (all things considered), but I'm seriously thinking of having *"I wonder where that road goes"* put on a grave marker for us one day. You know—like it's "our motto" or something. Because, decades from now, knowing us, we'll probably spend eternity doing the same thing. Talk about road trips!

But for now—as we're takin' the curves—"driven' crooked down the highway," we'll soon find out where "Recovery Lane" takes us on this *detour* of detours. Because the truth about detours is: Once you're on one, you're usually there for the duration. They take you a little, or a lot, out of your way. They're a tad inconvenient. They usually take you in an entirely different direction than you were headed. They cost you time you could have been using for what you originally had planned. And they can, at times, be *extremely* frustrating! But, if you really look, you usually see things along the way you never otherwise would have. And sooner or later you do eventually arrive at your intended destination.

And—let's face it: when it comes to detours, it's not like we're the only ones in life who've ever had to take one.

Note to Self #5 – The term "deal with it" does come to mind!

I'll Get Back to You on That

Early on in my appointment with the surgeon, before he performed the biopsy, I had told him that I had no intentions of doing anything conventional. There was only a slight pause or hesitation on his part. I could tell he wished he hadn't heard me say what I'd said. Even in his non-reaction, I could sense he was disappointed. And why wouldn't he be? Most doctors in mainstream medicine think if you choose to use an alternative treatment you're practically signing your own death warrant.

I wonder why that is? Does the world really not realize, even in this day and age, there are discoveries out there—viable effective natural treatments against disease that work? Even though the FDA, for whatever reason, refuses to certify them? And beyond that, do we really believe everything the FDA tells us anyway? It's hard to believe doctors are that naïve. They must think all the clinics in Mexico, like the Contreras Clinic, and places like The Oasis of Hope, have existed for years solely because gullible people have continued to patronize them. But how do they explain places, like The Oasis of Hope, saving the lives of so many who come to them *after* the doctors have sent them home to die, if alternative treatments don't work?

In *Dismantling Cancer,* by Francisco Contreras, M.D., Jorge Barroso-Aranda, M.D., Ph.D. and Daniel E. Kennedy, Dr. Contreras writes:

"In 1981 my father conducted a retrospective study to document the five-year survival rates of our cancer patients. It is important to note that 95 percent of these patients came to us with Stage IV cancers after conventional therapy failed to help them. Stage IV cancer is the most advanced stage of cancer. The disease reaches Stage IV when the cancer has spread to other parts of the body from the primary site. Once patients reach Stage IV, conventional doctors generally tell them there is no hope for survival. This is when they come to Oasis. They are desperate for hope.

These patients were treated by our total care approach and the Oasis over-all five-year survival rate for all types of cancer was 30 percent. We also noted that 86 percent of our patients outlived their prognosis and reported an improvement in their quality of life."

I asked the surgeon if he had ever heard of Protocel®. He said he hadn't. So I attempted to briefly explain what it was, but I knew nothing I said was registering. And I could sense he was sad for me. I expressed to him how much I appreciated him listening and not being upset with me about the choice I'd made. He assured me it was fine, adding, "This isn't the first time I've heard it," and then conceding "and I'm sure it won't be the last." Perhaps he was thinking about others he remembers who had refused conventional treatment, too, and had died. Causing me to wonder if any of his patients ever get back to him—*to tell him that they lived!*

Well, I had no intentions of becoming another "dangling participle" in this surgeon's life, leaving him hanging where my recovery was concerned. This was one chick who'd be getting back to him!

Maybe he'll forget us as soon as we walk out that door today, I thought—*but I'll bet he remembers us the day we walk back through it!*

Lose the Scalpel and Nobody Gets Hurt!

As we waited, neither Willie nor I had any idea what to expect next. He'd probably want to talk to us a little (or talk me *into* a lot!).

I just wanted to thank him and leave, but I knew that wasn't going to happen.

About that time the surgeon walked in, explaining things as he closed the door behind him. "Even though the pathologist said the biopsy showed cancer, the actual diagnosis won't be in for a day or two. And, although you've already told me you don't intend to do anything we recommend, by law, there are some things I have to advise you of, and what we believe your options are."

I didn't mind hearing what he had to say, and I agreed to listen.

"Normally I would spend about thirty minutes covering this, but since I know you won't be doing any of it, I'll only take about ten." (Which was fine with me—ten minutes was about all I had left. I felt weak from the biopsy, and I wanted this to be over.)

He got out a set of booklets, which included diagrams of the four stages of breast cancer, including the one of the pre-cancerous stage, normally referred to as DCIS—Ductal Carcinoma in Situ. Many in the medical world believe DCIS is a precursor to breast cancer. However, I'll say right here—many others *do not*.

He pointed out that the pre-cancerous stage, Stage Zero, was where all the focus on "early detection" by regularly having mammograms came into play. "This is the stage that we believe, if detected early enough, has the highest percentage rate for survival," he stated. Which I instinctively surmised was being a little over-emphasized by him for my benefit—given my mammogram history. (Or shall we say—"my *lack* of one?")

Well, we all knew Stage Zero didn't apply to me anymore. That boat had long since sailed! So it was on to Stage One and Two.

"Of what I saw of it on the mammogram," he said, "in addition to the lump, it's begun to infiltrate surrounding breast tissue, and it covers an area the size of a small tangerine, *but only in circumference*—which is why all that can be felt is a small grape-size lump." (He didn't show me the mammograms in his office, but I later signed them out. And what he spoke of was clearly visible. The images on the mammogram had something of a "roadmap" appearance. I found out later—it was a tumor that had already begun sending out blood vessels to create a food supply.) (Which I found as disgusting as I did alarming.)

He then went on to explain all four stages, stating that, in his opinion, I would fall into either the Stage One or Stage Two category. And then next he began talking about what was involved in having a lumpectomy.

"A lumpectomy would involve removing several lymph nodes for examination, to determine whether or not it had already spread to the lymph system."

(First of all—wrong! Nobody's touchin' the "nodes," Doc.)

"A lumpectomy would also require radiation."

(Nope—sorry. Anech! Wrong again.)

"With *both* the lumpectomy and mastectomy procedures, there's a 10 percent risk of developing lymphedema, where the entire arm swells and fills with fluid. And it's permanent. It never goes away." (It's also very painful, as toxins are trapped and can't get out.)

I just sat listening, only hearing about half of it. My mind was preoccupied, thinking about a friend of mine, Jo, who was diagnosed with breast cancer in the early 1980s. She underwent a double mastectomy, and what lingered with her afterward was the pain of having to deal with the discomfort, and *disfigurement*, of lymphedema, before she eventually died—of lung cancer. (He didn't have to tell *me* about lymphedema.)

"A mastectomy, on the other hand, is a different story. Two of the main features of a mastectomy are that you wouldn't have to have radiation, and nowadays they even have plastic surgeons on stand-by to do reconstructive surgery at the same time—which, incidentally, is now covered by most insurance companies!"

(How special! *A bonus boob-job.* And if I have insurance—it's on the house! *And he's telling me this "by law?")*

Everything was becoming *one big blur!*

He wanted to know if he could answer any questions, cautioning me that if I changed my mind, it was not something to delay! (Which brought on an overwhelming urge to look over my shoulder for another "little room" across the hall somewhere.)

I didn't want to ask him any questions; I was already on information overload. I could only think of one anyway—and I already knew the answer. He made it clear that because of the "tangerine size area" my best chance for survival would be mastectomy.

I was also still back at square one in my own thinking, wondering why they'd want to cut on *(or cut off)* my breast in the first place, *when cancer is* <u>*systemic!*</u> *If it's in my breast—duh! Aren't the chances pretty good that it's in other places, too? All it takes is* <u>*one*</u> *cell! And if he can't even tell me for certain what stage I'm in, how can he be so sure that it hasn't already spread?*

Well, Girl Wonder, first of all—I don't think you want to go there with him on this. Hello? If he <u>*isn't*</u> *"sure," he knows he doesn't have to be! He knows he's got chemotherapy!*

So on that note I just let it go. (He already knows he's not invited to this party anyway.)

So That's How the Other Side Operates

I was very disturbed by by how women are expected to make such life-altering decisions while being given virtually no time to think about it. And—the only good I could find in any of this was in knowing I had already made all the decisions I was ever going to have to make about it, before I ever set foot in his office. The whole thing was giving me the *heebie-jeebies*. All I wanted now was to just leave—so I could go home and continue to count my blessings that I knew I had options—*ahead of time!*

Before we left his office, the surgeon told me the booklets were mine to take, and he would see about setting me up with an oncologist, because, as a surgeon, he wouldn't be in a position to monitor me; but the oncologist he was referring me to "may agree to it." *(May?)* Adding, "You'll have to speak with him about it."

His demeanor seemed guarded. Almost as though he was carefully picking and choosing his words. And I remember thinking, *That's odd. Isn't it just "a given" that doctors are expected to help people? Something about a "Hippocratic Oath?" Or are they being selective about their patients these days, based on whether or not they plan to do anything conventional?*

My intuition was talking—but I missed it. It was at the end of the appointment, and I was probably just too tired to go there.

Before we left, he also told me he wanted me to have a chest X-ray to be sure the cancer hadn't metastasized, and blood testing done, too. I was certain the oncologist the surgeon was to set me up with would take care of ordering whatever I'd need.

Note to Self #6 – Never "assume" *anything* when it comes to "assuming" what you'd think the medical world should know with regard to what it's *supposed to be doing* for you!

I was so taken aback from the surgeon's attempt to convince us that what he spoke of was something I should be prepared to begin immediately. And, if I did decide to go ahead with a mastectomy, I wouldn't need radiation, and probably not much chemotherapy; unless, of course, they *found* something later. (Yeah? Well—from what I've heard . . . if they "find something" later, its curtains! Because, from all I've read about chemotherapy, the only thing that stuff seems to effectively kill—is eventually *the patient!* Nope: don't think I'll be setting myself up for that scenario anytime soon.)

I had no idea going into this how hard-pressed someone in my situation would be to make an on-the-spot decision. I don't know what I thought—I just know I sure didn't expect the day would go like this. What a reality check!

But the real kicker was when he told me, in case I was wondering about one breast maybe being a little "shapelier" than the other from the reconstructive surgery; "not to worry—the plastic surgeons actually do a little 'nip and tuck' here and there on the other one, too, making the necessary adjustments. So they would actually both end up looking quite the same."

Everything I'd taken in as I sat listening was pulsing through me. I felt weak and lightheaded . . . from the biopsy, but also from the images going off in my head.

Let me get this straight, I thought, as I struggled to make some sense of it all. *I was diagnosed with breast cancer just minutes ago, and we're already talking "boob-jobs" and "boob-makeovers"—to sweeten the pot? And the reason I just got that little "sales" number done on me is because he's "required to"—"by law?" It's like an assembly line! A cut* (no pun and no disrespect) *and dried, bloomin' assembly line!*

He was a great doctor, and I'm sure he believed with all his heart that what he was offering me was my best chance at life. But I still wanted no part of anything the conventional world of medicine he operated in (I know—puns, puns, puns!) was selling when it came to fighting for my life against this disease.

Walking out to our car in the parking lot, all I could think about was how absolutely over-the-top all that was. And just to be certain that what I *thought* had just occurred had really taken place, I asked my husband, "Was it my imagination? Or did he just . . ."

"No, it wasn't. And yes, he did." Willie couldn't believe what he'd heard any more than I could.

Behind Closed Doors

On the way home, I thought about all the women who find themselves in the same situation I just walked out of. Not at all unlike the elderly couple Willie overheard the doctors talking to. We had Protocel® to come home to that day—they didn't.

Oh well, I thought, *I've spent the last thirty years focused primarily on helping people find answers to health issues. It's who I am and what I do. Why should it be any different now just because this "cancer dance" was going on in my life?*

There I was again, with that desire to find a way to tell people, so they'd know they have options. Someone had to do it. It wasn't like anyone in the *pink ribbon crowd* was ever going to. (Okay—rude remark alert! I know. I'll explain later.)

Women are made to believe they can only have what's behind Door #1—*The Lumpectomy Door*, or Door #2—*The Mastectomy Door*, both of which lead to corridors where chemotherapy and radiation lie in wait. And all because somewhere, decades ago, something (or someone) set the stage for using the same line of treatment, and the same train (wreck) of thought, that "this is the only way it's ever going to be." If we've come so far with conventional medicine perfecting procedures for the heart, when it comes to curing breast cancer (or any cancer)—why are we still in the dark ages?

Well, thank God, I had another option—a Door #3. And what was behind it (that had already shipped yesterday) would be sitting in front of Door #4—*My Recovery Door*—by the time we got home today.

Thank God, months ago, without my even knowing it, someone had already *thrown me a rope!*

WELCOME TO MY WORLD

CHAPTER 6

Blessed Are the Adaptable

Reality Bytes!

Forced to deal with all these unfamiliar feelings, being totally clueless at times as to where they were coming from, and knowing my life hung in the balance with every life-altering decision I'd have to make caused even my skin to feel at times like it was on fire!

A catastrophic diagnosis like cancer, when it enters your life, throws you into a world of eerie "unknowns." There's a line that you cross, where no one else—as much as they love you—can go with you. As much as they are there with you and there *for* you, and they feel your pain—you still find yourself in a place of inescapable sorrow and sadness, saturated with such unfamiliarity that you know others can't possibly begin to understand . . . because you can barely grasp it yourself! And as strongly as I could sense God's presence, there was still no denying the existence of the hard-core moments when I felt so *totally* alone! My whole being was trying to mourn. Mourn the life that up until yesterday had been void of this whole cancer issue. Now it never would be. Cancer, and how it pertained to me, even when I was one day deemed cancer-free, would always and forever be a part of my life. Because beating it automatically meant I'd be telling someone how I did it. Every chance I got! 'Cause that's just how I am. *And I fully intended to beat it!*

But for now it was all about finding a way to adjust. And it was something I had to do on my own, because this was now—*my new normal.*

This Isn't Kansas—and You're Not Toto

Waking up the next morning brought with it the stark reality of all that had transpired in the two days prior, and the same raw disbelief that, from out of nowhere, all this trauma—like it or not—now applied to *my* life.

So where do you run to in a situation like this? Certainly not into some sidewalk phone-booth to change in, hoping to emerge "able to leap tall buildings at a single bound." Or into the arms of someone wearing ruby-red slippers, attempting to click and chant her way back to "Auntie Emm." (Even if there *is* "no place like home.") *People die from this stuff!* A situation like this calls for *big* answers, and you can only get those from a *big God!* And I personally know—*the biggest!* And, fortunately for me, we just happen to be on a *first-name* basis. And it's going to be some kind of somethin' else to see how He works this one out—because this one's *a doozy!*

I can honestly say, the more times I've faced seemingly insurmountable odds in life where the light at the end of the tunnel ended up being God, and not another screaming *oncoming locomotive,* it's made it that much easier through the years to find the courage to trust Him in the BIG stuff. Knowing He's going to be there for me no matter what giant I end up facing! The longer you walk by faith, and the more times you see God at the end of a situation, the easier it becomes to trust Him. In fact, it gets to where the bigger the obstacle, the bigger the opportunity for Him to show up, show off and show out on your behalf! *What a way to live!*

Options Ahead of Time—*Priceless!*

From time to time through the years, I had thought about what I'd do if I were ever faced with this type of diagnosis. Now that I have been, punt does come to mind. If only it were that easy.

And—if you'll allow me to step out of my element as an author for a moment I'd like to say right now, as a friend, from the voice of experience: "The time to make an informed decision is while you're still in a position to believe you'll never be forced to have to make one. Because, they don't give you time to think!" And then, when you do finally get time to sort it all out, it's like you can't, because your mind is so saturated with all you've just heard, things you're still trying to process when all you'd really like to do is get away from it. But you can't do that either! And it's so difficult to think and make rational choices when you're being dogged by the highs and lows of emotions and feelings so foreign you aren't even sure what they are or if they are even real, let alone know how to deal with them.

I realize not all people would choose something like Protocel®, and that's okay, because you have to do what you have faith in! But shouldn't people be able to at least have the opportunity and the right to choose—even if it's to say "no" to something alternative? Even at this early stage in my battle, I'm already envisioning how, after I beat this thing, I could play a significant role in creating awareness. People have a right to know that they have options!

I've spent more than thirty years helping people in the area of prevention and wellness, and also in regaining their health once they lost it (which, I might add, is what made this diagnosis come as even more of a shock!), and I heard years ago, "The body wants to begin righting itself within fifteen minutes, if given the proper tools."

Well, every time I take a dose, I'll be giving mine one great big "Have at it!" Since being able to cause the body to "right itself" is exactly what this product is designed to do, starting with the first dose! To me Protocel® looked like it was virtually the best kept secret on the planet!

The Definition of Risk

One thing I was certain of—I had answers and I had hope! And hope is what you wrap your soul (your mind, will and emotions) around until faith shows up!

Because of God and Protocel®, there was this huge chance that I could overcome this diagnosis of cancer without poisoning, burning and/or mutilation, and without compromising, weakening or damaging my immune system, or my body. There was an element of risk involved, but it was a "risk" I was willing to take!

79

I had the opportunity to hear astronaut Alan Shepard speak at a convention I was attending back in '79 in Vienna, Austria. He spoke of his life as an astronaut, and, having been in outer space, he said he felt he knew, better than most, the true meaning of the word "risk," and he wanted to share it with everyone.

"The *real* definition of risk," he said, "is sitting on a launch pad in a space shuttle, waiting for liftoff—knowing *every* part you're sitting on went to the *lowest* bidder!"

Note to Self #7 – Life is full of risks . . . some are just more worth taking than others.

Cancer—Unplugged

As I read about Protocel® and Jim Sheridan, the chemist who developed it, and just how scientific this formula is, I became so secure in the thought of being able to recover in the comfort of my own home, without flying off to Mexico, or having to search out other clinics around the country, and/or world, which made the opportunity use to Protocel® even more appealing—not to mention that it's so economical.

(What about all those women out there, single moms and others, who don't even have insurance for expensive medical procedures, let alone the resources to pay for them out-of-pocket. Flying to Mexico, or any of the alternative cancer treatment clinics in the world, doesn't come cheap. What will *all* those people turn to, the ones the National Cancer Institute claims will one day be diagnosed with cancer?)

For me, Protocel® was such a perfect fit for my life and my belief system. And, if this ends up being all they say it is, I just found my life's crusade. I thought I had one before, but this takes precedent. If Protocel® is not only an effective treatment, but also an economical preventative—the world needs to know it!

The way Protocel® works, it lowers the energy in the body by 10 to 15 percent, at the cellular level. Healthy cells don't miss this small amount of energy because they operate on such a high level to begin with. Anaerobic cells (cancer and other bad cells), even though we think of them as reproducing rapidly, are very sluggish and only operate on a minimal amount of energy. When that small amount of energy is taken away, simply put, they can't survive. They begin to lose their *cement* (what holds them together), causing them to "fall apart" and deteriorate—which is what "lysing" is. And they're *done for!* The body then processes them out through the lymph and other systems as a "simple waste."

Doesn't it just *floor* you that it could be that simple? Rather than attempting to pulverize every cell in your body with chemo and radiation, which ends up poisoning *everything,* isn't a better plan to just sneak up on it, *through the back door,* and "pull the plug?" Doesn't this make so much more sense?

All I have to do is *unplug the source of energy* to the cancer cells by taking 1/4 teaspoonful of this dietary supplement, five times a day; keeping a level of saturation in the bloodstream; depriving the bad cells of their power-supply.

The more I read, the more I could see this product's amazing potential. I'm not a drinking person, but this was one bottle I'd be tipping pretty regularly and hitting pretty hard—starting tonight!

Sure enough, when we arrived home, there it was, sitting on our front porch. As I carried it into the house, I couldn't help but think that there in my hands, I was holding what I prayed, for me, literally amounted to "liquid life."

And the liquid I chose to drink that "liquid life" in was water. Filtered, RO, distilled, spring – whatever I had access to. When I premixed doses for the day, I used RO water. Distilled is what they recommend. I chose to take my doses of Protocel® in water as opposed to risking ingesting vitamic C in juice, since vitamin C will shut Protocel® down. Many prefer to drink Protocel® diluted in water for this reason.

Let the Games Begin

So—I just took my first dose of Protocel®. Probably should have taken it in something elegant, in celebration of the moment. You know—flung the crystal. Right? So fitting! This was the beginning of "The Beginning" for me. But, the beginning of *"the end"* for a bad diagnosis!

Well, I was on my way. One dose down, and now it would be my job to be faithful and diligent about seeing to it I never miss not so much as one dose! That's me from now on, "The Doser."

Protocel® starts working immediately in the body and can start making cancer cells lyse within the first twenty-four to thirty-six hours, though in some cases it can take a little while to get on top of all the cancer growth. But my calendar was clear—I wasn't going anywhere, anyway.

That night as I lay in bed, I contemplated the days to come, and all the doses that lay ahead. *Five doses a day, for thirty days; that's one hundred and fifty doses a month. To be taken on schedule— doses. To be taken on schedule—no matter where I am or what I'm doing—doses. To be taken on schedule—no matter where I am, or what I'm doing— "my life hangs in the balance on it"—doses. Doses. It's all about the doses. <u>Definitely</u> about the doses!*

And I was facing months of this, with all the *known's* as well as the *unknown's* that would factor into it.

Well, whatever time was involved, however long it took—I knew those cells would soon figure it out—the c*avalry* was coming! The heavy artillery! The big guns, if you will! And all I had to do to make it happen *was stay on top of all those doses!* I fell asleep that night . . . thinking about *"the doses."*

And Suddenly . . .

Willie always gets up early, every morning. He's very big on sunrises. We both are. But I've never been much of a "morning person," so he usually comes to wake me whenever he sees a spectacular one. And, living on the lake—we've seen plenty.

This morning, I was aware he was getting up, but it was like something was telling me not to. Coherent enough to know something significant was going on—that once I woke up and knew what it was, I'd wish I hadn't—I tried to stay asleep!

Ugh! It's starting to break through! No! I don't want to know! But it was too late. Semi-consciousness gave way to stark reality, and there it was again—larger-than-life, in full-blown living color! *I <u>knew</u> I didn't want to wake up!*

I turned over, buried my face in my pillow, pulled the blankets up over my head—and lay there . . . wondering what the chances were if I just stayed in bed today this whole thing might just go away.

Whoa! Maybe it already had!

I whipped back the covers, sat up and checked to see if it was gone . . . but it was still there . . .

Well, it was a thought, I reasoned, settling back in bed. *This thing's going to go away one way or another, Lord. I was just giving You the benefit of the doubt, in case You decided to reach down and zap it in the middle of the night, as a little extra added bonus for me "livin' right" or somethin'.*

(You'll notice the more we talk, I live with an *outstretched neck;* constantly looking for those "And suddenly . . ." moments in life where God shows up on my behalf expectedly!—His wonders to perform! He just specializes in never letting me know when He's going to do it.) (That way He stays God—*and I stay me.*)

Note to Self #8 – Be vigilant. Be on the lookout! Conditions are right! With all this trauma, there's bound to be one "and suddenly" after another coming—and they're probably just over the horizon. I'm sure of it!

Life's Little Comforters

I crawled back under the warm goose down comforter that we depend on during the cold Northern Michigan winters and tried to put it out of my mind. I needed more rest. Sleep hadn't come easy the night before. I lay awake thinking about so many things.

Mom didn't think she was going to die either, I painfully recalled. But that's as far as I let that train of thought go before I derailed it. I refused to let myself entertain the thought of dying for even one moment, even though it did constantly try to be the dominant topic of the self-talk chatter going on in my head. Yet denial over all this wouldn't work either. I couldn't help but wonder just how many more major battles like this I'd face in life.

Lord, You know we've weathered some pretty severe storms . . . but together, we've always come out victorious. ("Come out" and "victorious" being the operative words here.) And, with the obvious way You've already had so much to say in this, I know we'll come out victorious on this one, too. (And, by the way, Lord, just so You know . . . I'm totally depending on Your full participation here. Cause without it—I'm sunk!)

(I know He appreciates my sense of humor—He gave it to me. And that makes it a gift—*so I have to use it.* You're supposed to use your gifts!)

Kerri and I had talked on the phone at length the night before . . . even though much of the time was spent sitting in silence. We were all so blindsided by this. I found it so comforting to sit there together with her. Even in the silence she was there for me. Somewhere in the course of life, my daughter, my little girl, had become my best friend. I couldn't imagine what I'd be doing without her.

Sorting It Out—and Doing It Afraid

The night before, I had tried to call Josh. Remember—he's the baby. He may be twenty-three, but he's always going to be the baby. And I get accused all the time that he's the favorite.

He's a sweetheart, all right, and Kerri had a part in spoiling him just as much as I did. There was almost six years between them, but, let me tell you, those two were tight! She mothered Josh from the day we came home from the hospital. In fact, she carried him around until she could no longer pick him up. She was always "waiting" on Josh. And he *adored* his big sister!

Being that he's the youngest, it's been challenging to watch Josh find his place in life. With his deep love for music, he left for Florida to get a degree in the recording arts. Then our little guy (who is now six-foot-two) moved to New York City in search of work in the music industry and wound up touring the U.S., Europe and Japan. In fact, he's on tour as we speak. I decided to take a chance and call to see if I could reach him—wherever he was.

When Josh answered his cell phone, he was his usual chipper self, always glad to hear from me. "What's up, Mom? I'm in L.A."

I told him I decided to call because I just wanted to hear his voice. (Boy did I want to hear his voice!) And I also wanted to stick close to him by phone, so he'd realize when I finally did tell him—how much I'd wanted to all along.

My face was wet with tears. I knew if I held them back he'd sense I was crying, so I told myself—*Just let 'em roll.* We didn't talk long. We never do. He's always so busy. It was just so foreign to me to hold something back from him like this, but he'd be back in the city in a day or two—I could tell him then.

I thought about calling Glenn and Kathy, too, but I knew it had to wait. I could barely understand what was happening and what it all meant myself, let alone try to explain it to them. They'd probably want to know more than we could even tell them right now. Unlike Kerri and Josh, Willie and I were certain they had never heard of Protocel®. They live four and a half hours away—and the thought of trying to explain all of this to them over the phone, and why I'd be refusing all conventional methods, seemed way too complicated. It was going to be difficult enough to explain it to Josh, even with his prior knowledge of Protocel®.

I hadn't told my sister yet either and didn't know when I would. I was sure Sally would be okay about it, but she and Bob live three hours away, and I just didn't have the energy to talk about all this over the phone; nor did I want to. She knew how I felt about conventional treatments, so there'd be no surprise here. In fact, she'd probably be all for what I was doing. But just because of the fact that we lost Mom to breast cancer, I'd really rather wait until I had something more definite to tell her. And the real plus was that Sally also had knowledge of the grandchild of our family friends who had experienced such a dramatic turnaround using Protocel® against leukemia. So I knew she would understand. Telling all of them could wait. It would have to . . .

Did I ever say—*"This is just so not fair? I loathe the fact that I've been diagnosed with cancer! I don't know how it could have happened! Yes, I've been brave! Yes, I've not allowed myself to do anything but stand against this horror show that's weaseled its way into my life! Knowing something this vile could just invade my life at will is completely incomprehensible!"* I was still in a daze. There was still so much left to deal with and all these decisions that had to be made . . . and I wasn't even sure I was thinking straight! Being concerned about what others might think kept creeping in. But I kept telling myself it was a *non-issue.*

Note to Self #9 – This is one time in life when others don't count. For the time being, like it or not—life has to be all about "the Pamster"!

And, me, the brave one? Not really. You can do anything in life once you realize the easiest way to do it is just *do it afraid!*

Face it, you can either be like the twelve spies that went on ahead into the Promised Land who came back and said, *"Are you nuts? There are giants in there!"* Or you can take the attitude of Joshua and his buddy, Caleb, and, after sizing up the situation, go: "Those guys are *huge*—but I think I can take 'em!" And then watch them little *hummers* start to shrink!

Some Go to Mayo—Some Go to Mexico— I Just Went to Bed

All that fatigue in the beginning was a strong indicator that the lysing process was underway. Protocel® was hard at work dealing with this diagnosis, and to assist it, my body was calling on all its energy stores. I started having what is known in the world of Protocel® as "cold flashes." Also a sign that the body is dealing with the bad (cancer) cells and they are being lysed away.

(I should point out: *Protocel® itself does not directly cause all these symptoms*. The symptoms occur *as a result* of the breakdown and subsequent detoxing, as the dead cell debris is being eliminated. And lysed cells can also come out, in the form of other symptoms, through many additional avenues of the body than even what I experienced.)

I would get to be so tired and so cold, I would have to lie down. I quickly figured out that when that occurred I could count on a two-hour deep sleep. As soon as I would crawl under the covers and get still, it was like a little electrical current would begin pulsing up and down both sides of my spine. I'd curl up in a fetal position. I became so cold and would sleep so soundly that when I woke up two hours later I would not have even moved. This phenomenon went on for at least three months, intensely.

I also learned, in addition to "cold flashes," you can also get "hot flashes." I referred to them as "hot sweats," because when I woke up I'd be wringing wet, and almost always my chest would feel "slippery," or for an even more accurate (although a bit distasteful) term "slimy." As cancer cells are processed and become a simple protein waste product, the body tends to use any avenue it can to get the waste out of the system and the skin happens to be the largest organ of elimination. The "hot sweats," for me, seemed to occur mostly between 4:00 a.m. and 6:00 a.m. I also soon noticed "sand in my eyes" and learned later that this "crustiness" when I woke up in the morning and, oddly enough, all throughout the day, is also a prominent sign of lysing.

My stools became paste-like in consistency, uniform in color and had such bulk that I would find myself, many-a-time, saying, "*Where* is all this coming from?"

And, as early as two weeks into my Protocel® regimen, I experienced what are referred to as "traveling pains." Little (sometimes pulsating) pains that tend to move around randomly throughout the entire body, causing what seems like symptoms of the flu.

Since I was sleeping so much, I began thinking about putting together a plan to be certain I'd get my doses on schedule. I began thinking about an alarm watch—and I found one online. For months it put my mind at ease about getting my doses on schedule. After that, getting my doses became (if you'll pardon another one)—*like clockwork!*

(In the beginning the alarm watch was like a security blanket and I was glad I had it, but I probably could have set different alarms in our home for those first few weeks until I settled into the dosing schedule. I also found that purchasing extra small bottles from a pharmacy and mixing all my doses for the day in the morning was helpful. They were in a cool spot away from sunlight, and served as a reminder as I would see them on the kitchen countertop throughout the day.)

Lysing Cycles

Lysing is not what you *see*. Lysing is the process that *caused* what you see. What you see is lysed *material* as a result of the lysing *process*. Lysing can also happen in stages and it can also go in cycles. You may see foam and /or bubbles in your urine or stools one day(s) and then you may not see it again for awhile. You may sneeze for several days in the beginning, almost like you have allergies – and then not do it again for awhile. Or it may never happen again. It varies with each individual.

(Visit www.thebreaststaysput.com for an excellent word picture: "Wet Wicked Witches," by Tanya Harter Pierce, author of *Outsmart Your Cancer*.)

CHAPTER 7

Circling the Wagons

Defining Moments

There are moments in life that define all others, emotionally charged moments involving an event, situation or circumstance which you have no control over—and you instantly recognize it as being pivotal in your life. Moments so seared and fused into your memory, you know you'll carry them with you into eternity. You'll remember forever what you were doing: who you were with, what you were wearing—and with vivid detail. The stronger the emotion wrapped around the situation or the event, the more crystallized and imbedded it becomes in your inner psyche—your spirit-man.

Creating a mental or spiritual reason as to *why* there is *hope* to hang onto can help you find the good in it, as soon as the situation presents itself. Shifting your focus immediately begins altering the memory of what gets crystallized, and what ultimately *sticks*. And it's important to make that shift, 'cause it's going to be there in your memory for a long, *long* time! And taking control in your inner-man also sets laws in motion that can literally *change* how the story will one day be told. For me—the day of the mammogram was one of those moments.

I recall my conversation with the radiologist practically word for word. I remember the rooms with unbelievable detail: what I was wearing, what they were wearing, and I also distinctly remember how desperately I purposed in my heart to stay on top of the situation. It's probably the thing I remember most, purposing in my heart to do whatever it took to take control of a situation that was completely out of it!

Yet I don't remember much about that evening or the next day. Outside of wishing when I woke up that morning that it had all been a bad dream—and then finding it wasn't. And then there were the details of being with the surgeon and the biopsy procedure with all it entailed—I remember everything with unbelievable detail. But what I don't remember much about was the ride home. Even with the knowledge that I'd just been diagnosed with breast cancer. I just remember that I didn't want to call Kerri until we were home. And you'd think that would be the conversation I'd remember most— telling my daughter her mother had just been diagnosed with breast cancer. But I don't. (I'd venture to say *she* does though.)

And I also remember how great it felt to successfully apply what I'd learned over the years, in an effort to get my mental act together, by being determined to not allow *what I was seeing and hearing* to convince me of how things *really* were!

Being prepared for something like this was so rewarding! Not prepared for the diagnosis (not by any means), but prepared for the encounter. All that knowledge from seminars and the Bible—never dreaming that one day the acid test of whether I'd learned anything for all my efforts would show up in a life-and-death situation where I actually applied it! One step at a time—one situation at a time. And every time I did and it worked, it gave me even more confidence that I could also handle the next! I had learned to walk according to the way I *wanted* things to go, not the way people were *telling* me they were going to! And *that*—was empowering!

And, just so you know—there's no distance in time with God. He'll pick up right where you jump in. Nothing says you have to have all this knowledge and experience to have His unconditional love and attention right out of the gate. (It helps . . . but it's not a prerequisite!) And, "God, I need You! Show me how to do this!"—is a *great* place to start!

Hibernating in Northern Michigan

Very early on, I pondered the issues of what I faced. And, often, in the quiet of the night, as if on cue, there they'd come—"The Parade of All the Unknowns." One by one, the thoughts would come. And the most persistent? *How would I deal with friends, relatives and neighbors?*

I didn't want *anyone* to know. I was firm about that. I didn't want to have to explain *anything* to *anyone*. The possibility of running across narrow-minded doctors was enough to deal with. Why risk putting myself in that scenario with people I cared about? Especially when you have no way of knowing *who* it's going to be that's going to flip out on you (or come down on you) for what you're doing. I was too vulnerable and too emotionally charged to deal with "well-meaning" people who didn't understand. And it would take the outspoken one, the one high on control, who felt compelled to be confrontational—to perhaps "talk some sense into me"—without knowing anything about what I was doing, and *why* I had chosen to do it.

So, at the risk of finding myself in the unpleasant position of having to "set someone straight," when, to begin with, it really was no one else's business—I decided to spare myself the trauma and do myself (and whoever else) a favor—and just lay low. And, in addition, since I *wasn't* having this "removed," I also didn't want anyone looking at me thinking I was carrying something around with me that I knew they'd view as *death*. Thus—two very strong reasons for wanting to walk this out in silence and seclusion.

"Hibernating" shouldn't be difficult in the Northern Michigan resort area where we live. More than two-thirds of our neighbors are gone for the winter. The day after Labor Day everything folds up around here. You can practically roll a bowling ball down the main thoroughfare and never hit a car.

I was glad it was this time of year. I could have quiet and solitude and the time alone that I needed to recover. I've owned my own business in Wellness Alternatives for over thirty years. My business is established and I have lifetime buyers. It goes on with or without me. This wouldn't be the first time I had to pull back. Starting my own home-based business was one of the best decisions I ever made in life. I'm free to focus on my recovery and take all the time I need, a perk worth its weight in gold!

So, "Blanket me up, Mom!" I could hear Josh say, while Kerri would be asking for her "nightdown"; two of the leftover warm-fuzzies from their "toddler days" that came to mind—as I now found my life centered on doing much of the same. When things got too heavy all I wanted to do was go lie down and sleep—and since I knew no one would be knocking on our door it wasn't a problem. And, maybe—*just maybe*—when I woke up in the spring, I wouldn't have to be a bear anymore.

All the King's Horses—All the King's Men Aren't Pink

How simple would it be to be able to just throw myself at the mercy of the doctors and the hospital—turn it all over to them and their expertise, and just let them fix it! It was a thought that made its presence known *daily* in the beginning, as I, too, wished so much an easy way out existed and they had something to fix it with, but they didn't. Not anything I'd want to subject myself to anyway.

It occurs to me that between the cut and dried there's always *"Not so fast!"* Between black and white you run into gray. And the absolutes—well, they sometimes just disintegrate under the pressure of all those *"buts."* And it winds up being *our* assignment in life to find our way through the maze, where, in the end, we're still the ones who have to choose and decide, or even take a pass, if life calls for one. In fact, the only place it doesn't happen like that is in the *uncompromising* Word of God. (Which is why I like to spend so much time in there!)

In the "out-of-control bad cell" scene, it's been my experience, even before this diagnosis, to feel as though people tend to come at you with "You have to do *this;* it's your only hope," plastering ads no human eye can miss—right down to the "slap you in the face as soon as you walk through the door" display table I almost tripped over *in my own bank!* I don't know what the popular opinion is, but my personal take on it is: *They've taken over pink!* It used to be one of my favorite colors. Now when I see it, I just want to get away from it! And as much as I've tried to find the good in it, I just can't see where the medical community is creating awareness for anything other than "Breast cancer is out there—and you're going to get it." Or for the woman who's already been through it and is praying that it's over, "It's out there—and it's coming back. So let's *fry* those boobs, ladies! On a regular basis! Oh, and let's be sure to *give* to the cause! So we can all fund 'Big Pharma' and they can develop even more toxic drugs—as a means to kill everything in their path, and, who knows—maybe even the cancer!"

I've done searches on the Internet, trying to prove myself wrong where the "pink awareness campaign" is concerned, but I don't see options. I don't see where they are informing women of supplements that block estrogen receptors or deal with a bad cell before it ever divides and becomes two the first time. They put women on birth control pills, knowing that down the road one of the questions they are going to ask her is how many years she's been on them, because there is a greater risk of getting breast cancer if they've ever used them. And now schools are attempting to hand out these "metabolism-altering" *drugs* to little *eleven-year-old* girls? *Where* are the NCI and the "pink ribbon people" in *this* situation? Shouldn't they be screaming, *"No!—Don't do it!* One of the first questions we ask women today is how long they've been on birth control pills— because the more years they've been on them, *the greater their risk for developing breast cancer!"*

Where do they provide people with information they *know* could save lives? I don't see anything on their website about vitamin-D3, ellagic acid, turmeric, EGCG, I3C, DIM, sesame lignans and the many supplements out there, including something like Protocel®, that have been proven to be effective preventatives. (And I'll just throw this in, won't charge ya' nothin' for it. According to a report on www.cancerfightingstrategies.com, and also stated in a 10 page Breast Cancer Protocol at www.lef.org, an 800% increased risk for *recurrence* of breast cancer is associated with a *CoQ10* deficiency.) (Although CoQ10 is *not* compatible with Protocel®—when people who use Protocel® against cancer finish their last bottle they would do well to reach for CoQ10!)

And, incidentally, has any doctor ever talked to you about your iodine levels? Or some of your lifestyle habits? Like the chemicals you bathe, clean and wash clothes with—and what those scents consist of that they want you to think cause everything to smell so clean and wonderful?

Or has your doctor ever recommended stevia a safe herbal sweetener, as a substitute to the laundry list of artificial sweeteners such as Nutri-Sweet (aspartame), Equal, Spoonful, Splenda, etc. that has flooded the market in this country? Women, especially, tend to be so concerned about their weight that they are constantly ingesting diet drinks and other products. Aspartame has been proven to cause brain tumors and breast tumors in mice and a host of other horrible health issues. Splenda is said to be "safe" by the FDA, *but* in an article in *Diet, Nutrition and Weight Loss*, "Sugar Substitutes and the Potential Dangers of Splenda," it states "On the other side of the argument are responsible experts who say that Splenda is unsafe. The latest in a succession of artificial sweeteners that claimed at first to be healthy—only later to be proven to be full of side effects. These authorities say that Splenda has more in common with DDT than with food."

Are we being told strongly enough, or at all, about the dangers associated with consuming processed meats, such as bacon, sausage, lunchmeats, when the nitrates they contain are known carcinogens? Or how perfumes (even the expensive ones) and cosmetics contain cancer causing phthlates?

And, as if the plethora of cancer causing insecticides, pesticides, herbicides and fungicides being sprayed on our crops, weren't bad enough—*now they're being sprayed with MSG?* All the more reason to go organic!

(Visit www.TheBreastSaysPut.com for more on this and information on breast cancer prevention.)

So that's what I get out of seeing pink! *Where's the prevention?* They've taken pink over with a campaign that *insists* women get regular mammograms. When all this talk about "early detection", with their *pink mantra* seed planting they're doing, could actually be *programming* women to *get* breast cancer! As in "Whatever you think about on a regular basis will move in and live with you." Especially if it's fear based—because whatever you focus on gets bigger, and it's what you draw into your life!

And how have they been able to "pull off" insisting everyone has to do what they say, when everyone knows the chances of surviving on their "absolutes" are 10 percent or less (which should really be called "slim to none"!)?

They say their cure rates are up. But when you look at where they come up with their figures (just one example being: They count DCIS (Ductal Carcinoma In Situ) recoveries as a cure—when much of the alternative world believes DCIS isn't cancer to begin with and *may never be*), you have to see the huge chasm. Where have all the multiple millions—okay *billions*—gone? If they had just taken a tiny percentage of what they've spent and designated it to research of alternative treatments like Protocel®, I can't help but believe the mystery to this cancer horror would have been solved long ago.

Then there are those who've been persecuted and prosecuted for making people aware they *do* have options. They've never claimed to have *all* the answers, but then neither does the medical world. (Although many in the medical world would like everyone to believe they're the *only ones* who have any!) What about the women who believe there has to be a more humane way, who can't bear even the thought of going the route of "the big three?" Don't they have the right to know what's available to them, so they can make informed choices? Which includes me! I have to be the one to make the choices with regard to my treatment because I'm going to be the one to deal (and hopefully *live*) with the outcome, based on the decisions I make, as I attempt to mend the "cracks" in the porcelain of my life!

No, I was on my own on this one. If anyone was going to put Humpty-Dumpty back together again, it was going to be God and me. But for now I needed rest and quiet. And although it wasn't much past noon, I was tired. So I took my little "shell-cracked" self upstairs and crawled into bed.

Note to Self #10 – Ask God in the morning how good He is with *duct tape!*

A Room with an Original View

Rounding the top of the stairs to our bedroom, I turned toward the windows overlooking our bay and our *magnificent* view of the lake. I couldn't help but notice how particularly *breathtaking* the winter scene was that day.

The lake was frozen over and snow covered, yet the sun was shining as though it thought this was supposed to be summer. The closer I got to the windows, the more intense the bright rays became as they reflected off the almost *blinding* white winter snowscape, setting the stage for the appearance of millions of those tiny, faceted, brilliant little sparkling diamonds. The ones everyone knows only come out to play on the most *perfect* of bright winter days. Glittering and shimmering—they twinkled and danced that day, as if only for me, across the deep fluffy-white, hand-sculpted, cascading mountainous snow.

"Oh God, I want to live," I said in a whisper, as my nose touched the cold glass. "Life is so cool. I wish Jack Frost still painted windows . . . like he did when we were kids. Who changed the window glass to double pane so he couldn't? And how did life all of a sudden get this complicated?"

As if forced to linger there by the vastness of it all, I recognized this was a scene whereupon few are privileged to gaze. It was like having my own personal gigantic, sugar-crème-coated, frozen delicacy, sporting generous layers of thickly whipped sky-fallen icing, resulting in the *purest* of sweet winter eye-candy—and I could have all I wanted. I could savor as much as I could take in.

As I stood there marveling at the magnificence of it all from the second floor of our cozy log home, I wished so much I could capture the moment forever. For a lifetime. *Especially* for a lifetime! Looking up into the heavens, I told God I was sorry if I had any part in creating this mess, and I promised Him I'd do whatever it took to overcome it! And, as He walked me *through* it, I'd trust Him in the process—*no matter what!*

Still caught up in the moment, captivated by that glorious panoramic winter setting, I also couldn't get over what an absolutely gorgeous, even "heavenly," shade of dazzling *crystal blue* it was that made up the clear winter sky that day.

"This has to be the color the sky was the day they named it 'sky blue'!" I told myself. I was sure of it!

Often referred to as "the *dead* of winter," it couldn't have been any more *alive* out there that day; which, the more I thought about it, was kind of how it was with me.

Then—considering the timing of it all and what had just "come to me"—my eyes began to well up with tears.

"You did this for me, didn't You, Lord? I've never seen a winter day so breathtaking, or so 'alive.' You painted this *original* especially for me today." As sure as I was standing there I knew He did. I could *hear* it in what I was seeing. He was telling me *He* wanted me to live as much as I did!

I felt small and fragile. Oh, but not insignificant. *Far* from insignificant! I knew I mattered to God and I knew *exactly* how much I mattered to my family. And I felt warm all over.

"I'm going to make it," I said with conviction, as I turned to crawl into bed, "and I won't be straggling, either. *Chariot's of Fire* will be goin' on when I come *screamin'* across that line!"

Pitifully or Powerfully Done

As I awoke—I could tell it was dark outside. I'd been asleep for hours. *I'm just glad I made it back to the window to see that unforgettable scene again before the "changing of the guard," as day relinquished its watch to the night—before I finally fell asleep.*

I began to reflect on the events of the day, and about what had popped into my head on the drive home from the hospital. *You know, you could just go ahead and fall apart and let everyone pick up the pieces. With a diagnosis as catastrophic as cancer you're probably allowed.*

Where do those thoughts come from? It must be the flesh, always desperate to find a way out from under unpleasantness. It hates discomfort. Well, self-pity is not something I get into—if anything can put you in a hole, it's self-pity. Besides, with the way I live, and what I believe in, it wouldn't have worked anyway. I'd have had to fake it. And I'm not good at that stuff either.

(Clarification: Any woman who receives this type of diagnosis is bound to "fall apart" one way or another. And rightly so! It isn't that I didn't fall apart. On the contrary! I *knew* I was falling apart! But I also intuitively knew refusing to let it take hold was my fastest way out of it. Because, as we've heard Joyce Meyer say so many times, while you're being pitiful, you can't be powerful, and I knew, in *this* situation, what I needed more than anything was "empowerment"!)

No, there would be no wimping out on my part in this deal. Life had dealt me a lousy hand, and now I had to figure out how to play it and see to it in the end, the winner—and the one left standing—was me! I would think before I spoke words into existence that I didn't want to reap a harvest on, and I would choose to take action, rather than just 'react"; choosing rather to happen to the circumstances I was facing than to let them run me over . . . *and happen to me.* Why let myself be victimized by the magnitude of this and end up landing in the *"victim pile"* when it was the *"victory circle"* I had my sights set on. *(Not to mention my heart!)*

From day one I chose to conquer rather than be conquered. I didn't have all the answers, but I knew from what I read in the Bible, and what I learned from a course I took from a self-development seminar: If I zero in and focus on what I want to have happen in life—instead of what I *don't* want—I don't *need* all the answers as to how it's going to happen. The "how" of the situation will figure itself out!

Something I don't remember doing after those first terror-filled days was crying a lot. Not that there would have been anything wrong with crying: I don't believe it's healthy to suppress feelings to that degree. If you're sad, cry and get it out, but just don't dwell on it. Maybe I was just way too numb after a while. The times I did cry were the times I had to tell Kerri things as they were developing, and the days before I was able to tell Josh. And then, of course, *the day I did.* That was definitely the hardest part. It was just tearing me up to think what all this trauma must be putting them through. I told myself that even if it was a long uphill battle, at least I had a product that wouldn't create all kinds of side effects that would affect my health. I was glad I didn't have to lose my hair. I also knew the day would one day come when my family would see my progress and begin to breathe their own sighs of relief. But right now there was a valley to walk through, the one that Psalm 23 talks about. "Yea, though I walk *through* the valley of *the shadow* of death."

Jerry Saville (another stellar man of God) says, "The shadow of a dog never bit anybody." It's only a *"shadow,"* and it's in a valley that God intends for us to walk *through.* So let's get a move on here!

When you live the life of an overcomer, you just go into "overcomer mode." You just don't know how to do it any other way. You pull yourself up by your bootstraps yet one more time, and you say, "Who is this uncircumcised Philistine?" and you go looking for your five stones. (David and I would have gotten along GREAT!)

Everybody Needs a Marleen

So there I was. It was just God, Willie, Kerri and me. I had my family, half of which didn't know yet, and then there was Marleen. Everybody needs a Marleen.

We've been friends for close to thirty years; she's one of my best friends in life! She lives in New York, but we have "talked" almost daily online since '97. Life has taken us through the births of our children (our youngest are just months apart); their marriages; the birth of grandchildren; losing parents and loved ones—and through it all we've always been there for each other. This crisis was no different—Marleen was actually the first one I told.

We both knew I was too healthy for it to be anything serious. I'd even located a graphic online that described the same shape, size and location—the whole nine yards. A swollen fibroid cyst with the exact description of what I had discovered. Marleen, too, thought all along it was a fibroid. She told me she'd be praying for me. And I knew she would.

After talking to the Protocel® people and placing my order, I could see Marleen on my buddy list. I just sat there staring at her name on my monitor, wondering how I was going to tell her. She was going to flip out at the first suggestion of it being malignant. Oddly, I remember feeling like a failure. I don't even remember how I told her, but I remember what she told me. She couldn't have been any more supportive.

"I am so glad you are not letting them do anything conventional to you," she said, "and you're going with something like Protocel®. So many people go along with conventional methods, and then after doctors have exhausted all their resources and tell the people there is nothing more they can do for them, they turn to something alternative and expect it to work for them. And that's just not fair. If people only knew how much better off they'd be by doing what you are. I am so in awe of your courage to go another route and so happy that you've made this decision that I can't even begin to tell you!"

Marleen would be my friend, my confidante, my sounding board, my encourager and my place to run to when I needed someone to mirror my strengths back to me throughout my recovery. She was always there for me. The wisdom of God just flows out of this woman. And I get to witness it and benefit from it on a daily basis.

My advice when facing something like this is to pick a friend, not just any friend, but one who loves you unconditionally—your own personal cheering section. Everybody needs a Marleen.

Just Between Friends

Kerri arrived in the afternoon after we returned home from my having the biopsy. Seeing her walk through our front door meant everything to me. She had probably felt sick all over thinking about how she'd find me, wondering whether I'd be as "together" as I had sounded on the phone. I'm sure she found the drive to be a stressful one, but we didn't talk about it. It would be months later—in fact, over a year—before she alluded to the drive up north that day as being "one of the *longest* drives of my life."

About an hour after Kerri arrived, the phone rang. I didn't hesitate to answer it. I had no reason to. It was our next-door neighbor, Valerie. She said she called to ask how I was doing.

"Okay," I said.

"Really? You're *really* okay?"

"Yes, I'm fine—*why?*"

"Well," she blurted out with genuine concern, "Willie told Mike you found 'a lump' and I had to call!"

I nearly dropped the phone! *What the heck?* It caught me so off guard—I was dumbstruck!

Concentrate so you can respond—I told myself, all the while trying to figure out how to avoid the obvious. *Without* lying! (I knew

100

this was one cat, if ever let out of the bag—there would be no getting the thing back in!)

When would Willie have told Mike of all people? And forget when—why? And how many people had Mike told by now?

Pulling myself back into the conversation, I heard myself say, "*What?* What was Willie thinking? Oh, Valerie, you know how fibroid cysts can be. I had a mammogram because I found something, but I can't believe Willie told Mike! I don't want this all over the place. Does *everybody* know?"

"Oh, no, no! Nobody else knows!"

"I'll bet! Mike tells Butch *everything!* The minute he finds something out he's on his cell phone to him!"

"No, Pam, I'm sure this was one thing he *didn't* tell Butch. And don't be upset with Willie—I didn't mean to get him in trouble. He was just so scared and concerned about you. And then Mike came in and said, '*Valerie*—Pam found a lump, you need to get yourself checked, too!' Then today I saw Kerri's car there, and I thought, *Oh, no!* So I had to call."

(She had it all figured out, didn't she? I thought there was no way anyone would find me out, but here she was *reading my mail!*)

Not believing what she was hearing, Kerri came around the corner wide-eyed with raised eyebrows that asked the question, "What is *that* about, Mom?"

I gave her the "I don't know" look. *(Because I didn't!)* And as the conversation continued, another rip-roaring *one-sided* one was taking place inside my head—right along with it!

I assured her I was okay (because I knew if I wasn't—I would be!). I didn't lie to her, I just segued right into talking about fibroids and avoided the whole issue. And the actual lab results wouldn't be back for a few days, so I really didn't have an official diagnosis yet. (Is this case I'm building here working at all?)

"Well, I'm glad I called, because I feel better now."

Then she said something I couldn't believe.

"But what if it *had* actually been cancer, Pam!—wouldn't that have been just *awful?*"

This was crazy! If she only knew *how* she was nailing it!

"Yup, that would have been pretty bad," I said.

101

By then, the whole thing had turned into a regular Seinfeld episode. I could not *believe* this conversation! I was wishing so much that I could just *tell* her, but she'd never see the humor in it!

"Well, I'm fine, so just put it out of your mind. Okay?"

She assured me they wouldn't tell anyone. She was just glad I was okay. And I knew Valerie. This was as far as it would go.

And before I ever got the phone back on the hook, I vowed to myself, *When this is over and I start telling people—Valerie's gonna be the first friend I tell! That was awful! And that was close! (But "close" only counts in horseshoes and hand grenades. And, thank goodness, an inch is as good as a mile!—Whew!)*

Keeping People Out of My Head

As we hung up, around the corner came Kerri. "Ohhh, Lord. Mom?—Why would Willie tell Mike?" I didn't have a clue—and couldn't believe he did! It was so crazy—we were *both* laughing.

"I'm telling you right now, Kerri—when the day comes that I'm cancer-free, Valerie is going to be the first to know. And Annette, too!" (Butch and Annette live downstate, but their cabin is three doors down from us.) I knew I'd also be telling Berneda and Noel, too, our next-door neighbors to the north, and such dear friends— along with several of our other great neighbors on the Pointe. But I knew I couldn't tell any of them now. Butch and Annette, for one, have constant company on summer weekends. I couldn't ask them to keep a secret like this. And I didn't want Berneda and Noel or any of the others worrying about me. And what if none of them got this at all, and were scared for me—questioning Willie constantly as to how I was doing! They'd be pressuring him to get me to "do *something*"—and Willie's not good at that sort of thing. It would have stressed him right out, and that would have driven *me* crazy.

This whole meltdown was such an eye opener! All of a sudden I had a glimpse of what it could be like for me if someone actually *did* know, and it was terrible. My head was getting all messed up. It felt like people were already in it, and I wanted them *out!* They weren't the issue here anyway. I knew the real problem lay within me. Because, for the sake of my own, very much needed peace of mind—I *knew* I couldn't chance even *one* person (that I wasn't

102

certain would support me in my decisions) knowing anything about any of this. I know it would have put me in a deep dark hole to know others were talking about me, good or bad. And besides, I hadn't even told Josh or Glenn and Kathy yet—*or my own sister!* I knew others would one day understand.

About that time—in walked Willie.

"What did you tell Mike, Willie?"

"Nothing."

"Willie, Valerie just called. You told Mike I found a lump."

"I did? I guess I did . . ."

I had thought Willie was handling things so well. But he had obviously been going through his own personal hell, too.

"I didn't know you weren't going to tell people," he said, in defense of himself. "When I wound up in the hospital a few months ago you called everybody."

Kerri very gently said, "Yes, Willie, but when you ended up in the ER your deal was a completely different situation. Mom's going to be living with this for a long time. She needs privacy."

"I know. You're right," I heard him say.

I told him that Valerie said she was sure Mike had told no one, so trusted that this was as far as it would go. We had to keep this in the family! I was more certain of it than ever now. What Willie said later was that he had actually told Mike when I first mentioned I had scheduled a mammogram. And what contributed even more to the comedy was that he'd also told Kenny (our neighbor next door to Mike and Valerie on the other side). They'd been out ice fishing (the perfect setting with plenty of time to talk). Willie said that Kenny wanted information on Protocel® to give to a friend who was facing serious issues. Well—we'd be having a talk with Kenny when we gave him that information! And we did. Later that day we saw him out on his snow mobile.

"Not to worry," he assured us. "I completely understand. Weezy and I just really hope this works for you, Pam!"

Thinking back, I remembered how Willie didn't question me when I first told him I'd set up a mammogram. In fact, he never brought it up again. But I was fine with it that he didn't—I didn't want to talk about it either. I mean, I believed it was *nothing*, so what was there to talk about? Willie doesn't jump to conclusions easily, but evidently I'd read him wrong on this one. He'd been distraught over this, too.

That night we ordered pizza. Comfort food. And again I tried to call Josh. He was flying back into New York City from L.A. that night. Finally—I could tell him.

CHAPTER 8

My Family—My Fortress

Processing the Pain

When the phone rang the next morning, I knew it would be Josh. And when it did—I knew this was it! I didn't even know where to begin, but I was soon into it, and I told him *everything*. The lump, the mammogram, the biopsy and then the diagnosis; without even coming up for air, I reminded him of the product I'd told him about months ago, telling him that the good news was I was already on it.

He wasn't saying anything—and I didn't hesitate long to see if he was going to. I went right into giving him more detailed information on what Protocel® was, how it worked and how effective it can be for a diagnosis like this—hoping it would help. It didn't. He was crushed. And I was devastated that he was!

He said he didn't even know what to say. With urgency in his voice he wanted to know what all this meant—and what would I do, and was I going to be okay? And he was crying.

I wasn't prepared for him to take it so hard. Somehow in my naïveté I thought he'd take it much better than this.

He said he wanted to come home. I told him he didn't need to—I would be fine. And *that's* when he really got upset!

"Mom!—of course I'm coming home. What do you think, Mom? You're going to get a diagnosis like this and I'm not going to fly *home?* Of course I'm coming!" And immediately I agreed.

After that I found myself in a pretty much one-sided conversation. I tried to reassure him with, "Protocel® has been known to work in as quickly as *three months* in getting rid of tumors, Josh, but even then, people stay on it much longer, to be certain all the cancer is gone."

But I could feel everything I said coming back at me—nothing was registering. And when he did finally speak, he said he couldn't talk anymore. He wanted to hang up and call back later—adding that this was the absolute *worst* and he *couldn't believe it!* And now I was crying as hard as he was.

I wasn't prepared for this reaction. I honestly didn't expect him to sink into such deep despair. And he was so far away in that big city, and I could literally feel him being swallowed up by it—were it not for one thing. His girlfriend, Randi! She's an absolute jewel! Because of her, I knew he'd be okay. He was in pain, and I knew he was traumatized. But he'd work through it. I just took great comfort in knowing he wouldn't have to work through it alone. I knew he had Randi!

The Art of Chasing Rainbows

Josh and I have been through many things in life together, and he knows—all too well—what can be accomplished in life when facing the impossible—with God's help and a little *tenacity!* It pulled him out of one unfathomable life-threatening situation when he was four.

He'd had a severe reaction to immunization shots (which the doctors tried to deny was possible). They told us that Josh was the worst case they had ever seen of a combination of eczema and psoriasis, and still being alive. (That meant children died from this. And I wouldn't even let myself go there!)

God only knows what other factors were thrown in the mix as we tried various products, in desperate attempts to help him get better. All any of them ever did was cause things to get worse, throwing his system completely out of balance.

Ninety percent of his little body was affected, and the only part that wasn't was where his underwear covered (one small comforting miracle in the midst of a tragedy). The doctors said they didn't dare hospitalize him . . . considering the bacteria, viruses and infections in that environment—he wouldn't survive it.

Josh lived in a sheet on our sofa, with no clothes, for six months. At night his skin would begin itching with what they called "excruciating itching." And it lasted until morning. It was vile, and as a parent I died inside watching him suffer, wishing it was me instead of him. *Praying* it was me instead of him!

The doctor cautioned, "Don't go chasing rainbows. There are no answers out there for this." And I didn't want to hear it.

I told that man: "The God I serve is bigger than that! I've spent the last ten years of my life helping people regain their health through nutrition and finding answers to life's issues. It's what I do. You can't tell me that God won't honor that by giving me answers for my own child! I'll *never* stop searching!"

I still have the before and after pictures of Josh. And, after sending them to his doctor, who by the way, was the head of the pediatric center at this very highly regarded clinic in Central Florida, I received a prompt reply stating he could only attribute Josh's full recovery to the tender loving care of his parents and the grace of God. He had no other explanation.

What finally ended up being Josh's lifesaving answer was a relatively new supplement on the market: an omega-3 fatty acid called EPA, being hailed as a nutrient with tremendous benefits to the heart. It appeared that the EPA more than likely changed his system by changing the prostaglandins from putting out serum that was burning his skin to serum that was healing it, which resulted in 90 percent of Josh's problem being gone in ten days. The doctors told us it was a combination of psoriasis and eczema, but it wasn't until years later that I discovered from my own online search it was really more than that. It was Steven's Johnson Syndrome: a potentially deadly skin disease that usually results from a drug reaction.

So if *anyone* knew, it was Josh, that if there was someone who had the iron-willed determination to search out answers to beat any disease—it was his Mom!

The Worst of the Worst

While all this was going on, I looked over at Kerri, who was sitting at the dining room table, to indicate to her that Josh was taking it *hard*—only to discover that she too was crying harder than I'd seen her cry in years.

My life was in complete and utter shambles! My kids in pain—the likes of which I'd never seen . . . and me, with nothing to offer—except to continue to tell them, "Your mom is going to be okay! I'm going to make it!" But even as the words I spoke fell on *my* ears, they sounded like nothing more than weak hollow flimsy clichés—especially this early in the fight. And if that was what I was getting, how were *they* supposed to buy into any of it with conviction or assurance?

This whole thing is insane. I'm living someone else's nightmare! This can't possibly be playing out in my life.

As Josh and I hung up, Kerri jumped out of her chair, grabbed the handset and headed downstairs—dialing as she went. I knew she was calling her brother: Like I said—*they're tight!*

What I didn't know, and wouldn't find out until Kerri emerged from downstairs almost an hour later, was that Josh had gotten a phone call only the day before from one of his friends. He called to say he'd lost his own mom that day. *She died of breast cancer.*

No wonder Josh was so torn up! What timing! He had to have felt like someone sucker-punched him. This only added to the list of "this can't be happening" moments.

My heart ached for him—for all of them! And all I knew to do was—*draw another line!*

"This is it!" I told myself. "They both finally know. And what's taking place today will be the absolute worst of it. No more! Once we get past this, it will all get better from here!" It *had* to!

I never knew what the rest of their conversation consisted of: neither one of them ever brought it up. Maybe Kerri called to reassure Josh about what she knew of Protocel®'s effectiveness. Or—maybe they were both scared out of their minds and were strategizing about how they'd handle the situation, discussing how it would affect their lives, or how they'd present themselves in front of me. I didn't ask—I didn't need to know. Because the one thing I *did* know was exactly how they felt. And I knew what they were going through. I'd already been there and got the T-shirt, which still hangs in my mind—in the closet of my past.

The Passion Runs Deep—*This Is Personal!*

I know what it's like to lose someone to cancer. I was supposed to go to my grave never hearing what these doctors were saying to me. And there I sat with "dummy lights" going off all over the place on the dashboard of my life, alerting me of the impending danger and the accompanying fact that I just *might* get there *sooner* than I'd planned if I didn't handle this right and make the right choices!

Let's face it . . . when you get the diagnosis you thought you were never going to get, it's also a signal that *other* things "lying in wait" might also be ahead—that you were convinced were never going to happen to you either. I was never going to do this to my husband and my kids. *I didn't even have grandchildren yet!*

I remember how devastated I was when my mom called to say she was diagnosed with breast cancer. And as much as she was determined to beat it, and as much as we believed and prayed with her that she would, after a five-year battle, my mom died. I'm sure they were both wondering—*would their mom die, too?*

I had lost my mother to breast cancer in 1987. She was sixty-four, and she was young and so full of life. Mom had battled breast cancer for five years and, on the surface, she lived a normal, quality life (as normal and qualitative as it can be with all the terror that accompanies this life-shattering diagnosis) up to just weeks before she passed away. That's when it got bad.

She had been going to Mexico for treatments all along and was doing remarkably well. They loved her out there. She lit the place up whenever she arrived; she just loved helping people and encouraging them, and gave so many of them hope. Her name was Marjune. She was an incredible woman—and she was *beautiful!*

People tell Kerri that the resemblance between the two of us is unmistakable. She hears, "You look *just* like your mother!" But what I heard all throughout high school from my friends was, "She looks more like your *sister* than your mom!" And it never did change. The bittersweet thing about losing someone so young is they always stay that way. In your mind its how they're always going to be. And so . . . Mom just never gets any older.

In Mexico, they had gotten the tumor down from the size of a lemon to the size of a quarter. They tried to talk her into a lumpectomy, but she would have no part of it. Then somewhere along the line, someone outside the clinic with another "alternative treatment" talked her into getting on it, promising it would break down the rest of what was there and carry it out through her lymph system. After battling this for five years, on a very strict regimented program, which also involved a very strict diet, Mom was weary of it all. And, losing patience, and probably focus, she decided to try it.

She had a way of doing things her way. She didn't even tell her doctors that she started on it. And neither Sally nor I knew anything about it either, until just two weeks before she passed away. She told me that after she'd gotten on it, her lymph nodes and ligaments under her arm became very swollen and painful, and she got scared and stopped the treatment. That had to have been when the cancer metastasized. And that's where I fault the medical industry and FDA: She was on the right path and she was winning!—But *one* decision that she was forced to make based on limited information due to a "lack of funding" is what cost her. *Her life! And I'm not supposed to get steamed over this?*

In light of the courageous battle I watched my mom wage against cancer (which she almost won!), I would never—*ever*—have consented to conventional treatment! This was more than just a bad diagnosis. *This* package had "PERSONAL" stamped all over it! My mom fought for five years to live, with many trips to Mexico. Had she known about Protocel®—she and Daddy would have only had to drive *to Detroit!*

Let the Affirmations Begin!

Just days later while out on tour, Josh called to say he was coming home! The band changed his flight so he could fly in for the weekend before returning to New York. We were all so excited! I knew he'd feel better after he saw me. And I already felt better just knowing he was coming! In fact, Kerri was right. Once I told Josh, got him through it and knew he was coming home, for me, there wasn't much of anything to cry over anymore. I had so much reassurance and faith that I was going to be okay; looking forward to that day I could begin telling the world about Protocel®, *so nobody else's mom had to die anymore!*

Willie was doing well with it, too, which meant a lot to me. It took a lot of pressure off. I didn't want him in pain over this either. We had a lot of private moments during the course of my recovery, personal to us and not pertinent to my story, but all in all we were adjusting. And now, just knowing the kids were coming home—all except for Glenn and Kathy—gave us something bright to look forward to.

We both wished Glenn and Kathy were coming, so we could all be together. But we knew they'd come another time. And having time alone with Josh and Kerri could be good, because we didn't know for sure how this was going to go. We had already seen how the hint of "death" has a way of throwing everything you know to be true and solid in life right out of sync.

It was just days earlier that Kerri was able to open up and share with me that on the day of my mammogram, with everything surrounding it, when Shawn walked through the door at five o'clock she said she was about to lose it. But Shawn told her, "Kerri—your mom is one of the strongest women I know! She is going to make it through this. She's going to be *just fine!*"

It was yet another reality check as to the degree of seriousness of it all. Like I didn't already know, or needed reminding, but when you hear your child say something to indicate how deeply they're being affected, it cuts to the quick, driving it home even harder. Yet, I distinctly remember the feeling of empowerment I felt at Shawn's "vote of confidence," as it reverberated throughout my spirit, solidified my convictions and strengthened my resolve! *It was exactly what I needed to hear, at a time when I needed to hear it!*

Dining in Five-Star Cuisine

When the day arrived that Josh flew in, it was so wonderful to have him home! On the two-hour drive Up North, he had a chance to ask a lot of questions. We talked all the way, and Kerri and Shawn were waiting for us when we arrived!

We played board games that night and had *more pizza,* which I wasn't supposed to be eating, but the Protocel® people said eating white flour or white sugar now and then wouldn't affect Protocel®'s effectiveness. "It's more powerful than what little damage a splurge now and then on white sugar or flour could do," they told me. But I had no plans to make a habit of it. (White sugar and white flour are not at all healthy to consume to begin with, but they also give cancer cells the glucose they need to feed on.)

What a memorable weekend. The kids prepared a wonderful dinner with all the trimmings. And Shawn even made homemade biscuits!

I had just gotten up from a nap, which was the only I nap I allowed myself all weekend. (And even then, they had to *make* me take it.) I had slept so hard and was so hungry. And that dinner was better than any I could remember eating—even in some of the finest five-star restaurants in the world!

Maybe it was because the kids made it, and Willie and I didn't have to do anything but sit down and enjoy it with them. And maybe it was because I had my family around me at a time of crisis in my life, and Josh in particular was hugging me long and squeezing me tight the whole time he was there. I think it was a combination of it all. All I know is—it was one sweet dinner I'll never forget. I have the most incredible family in the world!

And when the day came when it was time for Josh to fly back out, I so selfishly hated to see him leave. As much as I knew he loved it in New York, the parting was always bittersweet.

Tears trickled down his cheeks as he stood at the window overlooking the lake. I hugged him and asked him what he was thinking.

"I just want it to be *three months* from now, Mom."

"Oh, Josh—so do I!"

It gave us both something to hang onto as we held each other in tears of hope that day. A *lot* of healing began that weekend. I know it did. Just being surrounded by my family!

MAKING SENSE OF INSANITY

CHAPTER 9

Refusing to Take Ownership

You Must Have Me Confused With Someone
Who Could Possibly Have Cancer

I made the decision from day one that when I spoke about this diagnosis I would refer to it as just that, *"a diagnosis."* I vowed I would never say, "I *have* cancer" *to anyone!—Especially myself!*

This is NOT my cancer! This vile disease is from the pits of hell! It has no right to be here. It's here illegally. It's trespassing. And it has to go! I don't deny it exists—but I do deny its right to exist in <u>my</u> body!

I told my family if and when they felt the need to talk about it with a close friend, or even in conversations between themselves, I wanted them always to say, "My mom was *diagnosed* with breast cancer," never "My mom *has* breast cancer."

I could tell how relieved they were to know the only "owner-ship" I'd be taking in this was that of being given a diagnosis to beat, rather than a disease to live with—or worse yet—*die from!*

Tomorrow was my first appointment with the oncologist. I didn't like any of this. *Couldn't I just hug my bottle of Protocel® and go to bed—for about six months?*

Okay, so I'm supposed to be under the care of someone who knows what they are doing, so they can monitor this, right? But I knew the chances were pretty good that this could end up being a situation where some guy in a white coat with his name on a door was going to look at me like I was insane and orchestrating my own demise by not allowing them to do what they do to almost every other woman in my shoes. (In my *bra* is more like it.)

I was standing in the kitchen making dinner that evening when from the living room I heard Willie ask, "What time did you say your appointment is tomorrow with the . . . osha-cologist?"

I stopped what I was doing, peeked around the corner and looked at him with a smirk on my face, and said, "Osha-*what*?"—and we both laughed.

"My tongue got confused and I couldn't get it to come out right. Besides—how many times in life have *you* said the word? I don't even know if I've *ever* said it before. I don't think I've ever had reason to—before this."

Boy, wasn't that the truth! Just like all those other terms and even hospital "departments" that had never applied to our life before, either. It can really start to mess with your mind. But I knew it wasn't as much about what was going on around me as it was about what was going on *inside* me that was going to keep me from being sucked into the mire that comes with a diagnosis like this. I knew of women who had survived cancer using conventional therapy. But it was all of the ones I knew who *didn't*, and how they suffered from the side-effects of conventional treatments before passing, that made me so determined to stay completely out of mainstream medicine, taking what I felt, *for me,* was "the higher road."

Oh, how I wanted to bail out of this! Bail out and just run! But, then, so does anyone who finds themselves smack in the middle of what everything says is a "death watch!" It's a nightmare you can't wake up from. I was facing *the biggest test of my life!* And I knew it was imperative for me to develop a focused mindset (for the next however long) consisting of everything and anything it took for me to pass it! And not just by the skin of my teeth, either. *I intended to pass this thing with flying colors!*

I had looked over the books the surgeon had given me the day of the biopsy (eleven days ago now) regarding conventional treatment for breast cancer. After reading a few pages, the more I read, the more I knew I didn't want to read anymore. Ugh! I put those books in a place where I couldn't even *see* them! I told myself I'd hang onto them "just in case" there was something in them I wanted to look up later. (*Like that was ever gonna happen!* The content of those books was some of the most *depressing* stuff I'd ever read. It isn't any wonder why women think they don't have a choice. Well — I have one! And I choose to pass!)

I'll own the fact that they've given me a "diagnosis," but that's all I'll own. And when I beat this thing (and I *will* beat this thing!) it will be because I *overcame* it. I don't plan to "survive" anything. Because, to me . . . in order to survive something you first have to fall victim to it. Semantics to some, but while I'm in my "watch how I let myself view, think and speak about my recovery" mode — considering the vantage point I'm at and how diligently I've worked to get to it — I'll just stay right up here in overcomer mode with work to do, thank you very much!

Curio Curiosity

When we arrived for the appointment with the oncologist, we were the only ones in the waiting room. And I was glad. I didn't want to be sitting there looking at other women facing similar issues. (And I certainly didn't want anyone sitting there — *looking at me!*)

Sizing up my surroundings, I was intrigued by a tall thin cherry display case standing to the side of us.

A curio cabinet? In a doctor's office? That's odd, I thought. In the cabinet was a pretty hat, a scarf, and, on the shelf below it, something that looked like lingerie. I decided it was probably a local specialty shop doing a little advertising. (This was, after all, an office frequented by women.) Still, I found it odd that a clinic would let a store set up an advertising display. Then it hit me! *It was there to solicit business from women who would be losing their hair and their breasts!*

All I could think was, *Oh, dear Lord, please get me out of this place! I am NOT going to lose my hair — and I am certainly not going to lose my breasts!*

And just that quick, something inside me, in an almost audible voice, said, "You're right. You're not."

See! So for goodness' sake, snap out of it, and get a grip! I told myself as I sat back in the stiff uncomfortable waiting-room chair, positioning myself to look up at the ceiling (and *away* from the display). *That thing is in here as a service to women who need it, so you don't need to get all creeped out about it! And you don't need to be going off the deep end when these types of things present themselves! This is all going to be a part of it. It just doesn't have to pertain to you anymore than you want it to.*

Okay, I'm glad we got that straight—me, myself and I! I can do this! And with that I felt myself beginning to calm down.

If It Acts Like a Duck

When they finally called us, and we got in to see the oncologist, he seemed pleasant enough, so I was relieved. After telling him I wouldn't be doing anything conventional, and I would be using a product called Protocel® as my treatment of choice, he wanted to know what he could do for me.

Well, by the way he *didn't* respond, it could only mean the surgeon had already informed him of my situation (as he said he would), so my electing to refuse a lumpectomy, mastectomy or chemo, etc., came as no surprise to him.

I told him I wanted him to monitor my progress in the coming months. (And by monitor, I meant reading scans, blood tests, etc., to compare how things were going as my recovery progressed.) I didn't go into specific details—this was *his* expertise.

After examining me and taking a measurement of the lump, he commented that it was "pretty big." I knew it was. It was the size of an egg—and I was confused. I know with the way Protocel® works, over time, a mass can sometimes appear to be a little bigger before the tumor breaks down and goes away. But this was pretty fast. I had only been on it <u>eleven days</u>. And the lump had started out the size of a small grape (although flat—not round). I couldn't detect much depth before, but I certainly could now!

I told him that I agreed. It was big. But he didn't comment further, which I found strange. It was as if he wasn't interested. Like he was, for whatever reason, staying *detached*. (Go figure?)

(I just have to say right here, had he looked at what the surgeon had documented, regarding size, he would have seen the drastic increase in only eleven days. On the day of the biopsy, it was the size of a small grape. What the oncologist took a measurement of was now two inches in diameter! And still, he had nothing to say.)

I wasn't impressed so far. There was an obvious lack of enthusiasm on his part. You'd think he could at least *act* like he was interested, right?

He asked me a few other questions, did some reflex testing and checked high up inside my armpit area, on both sides, for anything that felt suspicious. He said there was nothing on either side and that it hadn't yet metastasized. That was the one *big* reassuring thing that happened during that visit. (And thinking back, it was the *only* reassuring thing that happened during that visit!)

After the exam there was an obvious change in his demeanor, and his tone of voice, as he sat down and proceeded to say, "I have absolutely no confidence at all in what you're doing, and, professionally, I have to tell you, you're making a terrible mistake!" And, in his *expert opinion,* he had to inform me there was nothing out there in the world of so-called "alternative treatments" that could possibly be effective against cancer, as in—"You're being taken in by some sort of *quackery."* (My translation.)

He then went on to say, "If you go ahead with what you have planned—I hope I'm wrong. But I don't think I am! I'd like to see you back in here in six weeks."

It was obvious he didn't want to hear anything about Protocel®, or why I'd chosen to use it. So I decided if he could so flippantly run down the world of alternative treatments, I wasn't leaving there without informing him why I wanted no part of chemotherapy or surgery. I wasn't as naïve as he obviously assumed I was—and finding myself in a classic situation of "push-push back," I probably said more than I normally would have. I didn't go in there for a confrontation, but I knew enough to be able to hold my own with him if that's where this was going. I thought, *Doc, if you start talking "quackery" you'll be opening doors to places you don't even want to go with me!*

We batted it around for a bit longer, but, even though he said he wanted to see me again in six weeks, he seemed to be keeping me at arm's length about helping me. So I guessed I'd have to "wait and see"—but I certainly didn't like playing this mind-game!

A Diagnosis of My Own

Thinking back over the appointment, I had been polite, but it was obvious I had ruffled his feathers, though, because he became defensive, and even *a little huffy.*

I don't imagine he's used to *informed* patients standing up to him—but I didn't care. This was *my* life on the line here. Not his! I wanted to leave no doubt in his mind as to where I stood on the matter. He *needed* to know—up front—how I felt, if we were going to work together and I was going to keep him in my "employ."

In a somewhat chastening tone of voice (like he was going to intimidate me with *that* tactic?) he informed me, "Thousands of people die from cancer every day in this country, and if there was *anything* out there that would treat cancer effectively the FDA and the NCI would have approved it long ago (you foolish mouthy little woman), because the market for it would be astronomical."

(No intimidation here, folks.) "Just because natural treatments can't be patented and, therefore, sold by big drug companies for thousands of dollars a month to a cancer patient doesn't mean they aren't scientific and they don't exist," I replied. "All someone has to do is read about Protocel® to understand and recognize that it doesn't get much more scientific than this formula."

I could see we were worlds apart on this, but if he was willing to work with me, maybe he'd change his tune after seeing the progress over time. (Boy, would I soon find out in *this* guy's case what a *pipe dream* that was!)

Seeing that the conversation was obviously going nowhere, I backed off. If he wanted to think, because he had all the degrees on the wall, that he had all the answers and that I was just the poor schmuck who couldn't possibly have a brain in her head if she bought into the idea that you could come at cancer from any other direction than what he'd been educated in, *and win*—then just let him go on in his ignorance.

Before we left he did try to smooth things over by saying, "Just because we don't agree on things doesn't mean we can't be friends—right?"

I agreed. But I think I wanted to say, "No, because I don't think I *like* you." Because it was clear he was still patronizing me. (You have to wonder how many times he's used that line?)

If he only knew he wasn't as smart as he thought he was. He may be the expert, but as the saying goes, "An 'expert' can be nothing more than a 'drip under pressure'!" (Which he probably *is* under a lot: I don't think that stuff he uses works so well.)

Okay—so that was rude, and maybe even a little disrespectful. But this is my book. And all things considered, in light of what I'm dealing with, and how I was treated, I'd say I'm allowed at least *three* of those throughout these pages. (*That* was two.)

So I left there that day disillusioned. No wonder the surgeon had indicated he wasn't certain the oncologist would agree to work with me. He knew this guy's personality, and from his remarks, I should have known what I might be in for. Oh, he had tried to act like he was there for me, but it was all about patronizing me at first, and then trying to intimidate me. I left there that day wondering how we were ever going to work together when it was clear he wasn't at all interested in (let alone supportive of) anything I'd be doing. He certainly was not at all what I expected, or wanted, in a doctor. (Why couldn't the surgeon have been the one to take up *oncology?*)

We no sooner got out of his office than Willie read my mind, saying, "That man wasn't interested in hearing anything you had to say."

"So, you picked up on it, too? To him there's only one way to look at this. And that's with tunnel vision—right through his *jaded* 'Conventional-Cancer-Treatment' colored glasses!"

Being Down on What You're Not Up On

What an experience! What the guy lacked in sincerity he thought he made up for in spin. Did I really have to deal with some opinionated, narrow-minded, egotistical oncologist—just so someone with a title behind his name could monitor my recovery? Especially when he was so convinced there wasn't even going to *be* one?

I decided I'd deal with it later. *If Protocel® is going to work,* I thought, *it isn't going to work any more or less effectively for me based on whether or not I keep this guy as my doctor. I may just have to go it alone. Just as soon as I went to bed for a while.*

I'd feel remiss in not qualifying those last remarks. Many people will tell you they've had wonderful, understanding, supportive oncologists. I just didn't happen to get one. And let me just say right here: Compassion?—definitely *not* one of his strong suits! Some people would put up with that. But then, again, some people would also follow their doctor right off a cliff. I just don't happen to be one of them.

Although it's true that in most states doctors can't legally prescribe Protocel®, they *can* be supportive in ordering scans and blood work to monitor their patient's progress, in order to advise them. And if your doctor won't help you, there's another who will. With the Internet, and the world it opens up being only a click away for anyone interested and motivated enough to do their own research, people today are in search of health care professionals who are smart enough to recognize that, in this age of information and technology, new discoveries are not only a reality, but a daily occurrence. And it's to a doctor's advantage to keep up on what's happening in the world they operate in. Being down on something just because they're not "up" on it is a sure giveaway that they haven't been. Many doctors today will tell you that they learn so much from their patients (which was *definitely* not happening with this guy!).

Unfortunately for him, though, he was defiantly *against* something he knew *nothing* about. And, the more I thought about it, the clearer it became: for him to get too involved with what I had chosen to do would be a complete waste of his precious time. And I know how precious he felt his time was, because I paid dearly for twenty minutes of it. His fee was more than twice the cost of the surgeon's— and the surgeon performed an *operative* procedure! (Don't tell me that cancer's not a "business.")

How sad for this guy, I thought to myself. *If I can't work with him, he'll miss the opportunity to be "wowed" by my recovery!*

Well, the jury's still out. I guess we'll just have to wait and see. I could be wrong about him. He could always have a change of heart. (Me—the eternal optimist.)

CHAPTER 10

My Yellow Brick Road

Surely You Jest?

Later that same evening, it occurred to me . . . the surgeon, on the day of the biopsy, had said he wanted me to have blood tests and a chest X-ray—to be certain the lump hadn't metastasized to the lungs. But the oncologist didn't even mention it during my appointment.

Now I was frustrated. And puzzled and confused. Why wouldn't he at least have ordered tests for me? How could he monitor my progress without them? Determined to figure this one out, I placed a call to the surgeon, going right to the source who first said I should have them. And, after explaining my situation, his assistant went to find him and then came back to say that the surgeon said he was sorry he couldn't help. He had already sent my *entire* file to the oncologist's office, and I should call there. So—I did.

The oncologist's assistant I spoke with had no idea what I was talking about. Now I was on hold. She'd gone to find the oncologist—to relay a message she didn't even understand.

After several minutes she came back on the line to say, "He said he wanted me to ask you—'What for?'"

What for? Did she just say, "What for?" I was speechless!

"He wants to know what you want them for."

Where do I even start? (Wouldn't you think the last thing I should have to do would be explain to my oncologist's nurse, or the oncologist himself, why I would want testing done?)

"So I have some type of test results now, you know ... to compare to testing *down the road—*so I can know how I'm doing?"

She was still at a loss—and this was beyond frustrating.

Could someone please give this woman a "program?" A schedule of events maybe? Honestly! It was like talking to the new gal in the donut factory who was clueless about all those holes!

I couldn't believe this conversation was even happening. Who ever heard of an oncologist who wouldn't order tests? This guy was just *mean!* And, I might add—*unprofessional!*

Well, one thing was crystal clear. The uneasiness I'd had about this guy was justified. I had left his office thinking he was a bit of a jerk. *Now I was convinced of it!*

And then I realized something else—*he hadn't told me what my actual diagnosis was!* The surgeon only had the word of the pathologist. My diagnosis would be in my file. *And I wanted it!*

So—I picked up the phone, and called back. (I could tell she was *really* glad to hear from me.)

I asked if I could speak with the oncologist and was told by his assistant that it was her job to see if she could help me first. So I explained: During my appointment he had failed to mention my diagnosis. And I wanted to know what it was.

She left to go get my file.

"It's not in your file."

Well, surprise—surprise! He had gone through the entire appointment with me *without* a lab report!

"I really need to speak with the doctor."

"I can get your diagnosis for you and call you right back."

I *wanted* to say: "I talk to God every morning—why can't I talk to *this guy?*"—but I just ... *let it go.* This was one picture that didn't require a "scan" to read what was going on! Either he *knew* it wasn't in there, and didn't care. *Or*—he didn't care to begin with—*so he never looked!* What other explanation was there? And it had to be the latter: The surgeon told him I'd be using an alternative treatment, why bother to read my file?

124

She called back to say the diagnosis was Ductile Invasive Positive Estrogen Driven Breast Cancer. You'd have thought they would advise their patient (*me*) to stay away from anything that would cause increased estrogen levels that could and *would* "drive" a positive estrogen diagnosis. But they probably don't make a practice of it because they remove the problem by removing the breast. *Except what about the other one?* Shouldn't it be protected from "estrogen dominance" now? Unreal. You have to be kidding! I couldn't believe how this "osha-cologist" thing was going!

Test Scans and Best Laid Plans

Now, being at a complete loss (having given up on comprehending how this oncologist could be so impossible), my next move was to find someone who *would* order scans. And I knew just the person to call—my nurse practitioner, Carol. (I don't know why I didn't think of her in the first place.)

I've doctored with Carol for years, monitoring my hormones and lipid levels, just staying on top of things regarding my overall health. (Which, again, is why I was so baffled by this diagnosis!)

Appalled by what I was telling her, she said she would be more than glad to order tests: except, although the chest X-ray wasn't a problem, she wouldn't know what else to order. "But," she said, "as soon as you find out what you need, give me a call and I'll write them up—and we'll learn together!"

So I started asking around. Everyone I spoke with advised that I should have testing done, but no one knew which I should start out with. A CT scan, an ultrasound, an MRI? I sure didn't know.

I went to a support group website where I read stories and testimonies of cancer recoveries, searching for something they might mention in the way of what tests they'd had done. I needed "tumor marker tests," but had no idea what kind. There were numerous codes, none of which meant anything to me. I called the blood labs, but they wouldn't give me any information. (Wasn't it so weird that I had to be doing my own research to determine what kind of scans or tests I needed to have done?) What it all came down to was that blood labs don't give out the kind of information I was looking for, because it was the job of any thorough oncologist to do the ordering.

Well, I didn't have one of those. (And I was beginning to think I didn't want one!)

I spent days on what amounted to my own personal "scavenger hunt." I knew I needed something, but every time I thought I was going to the right place to get it—*it wasn't there!*

I've got a "bit part" in The Wizard of Oz!—*I'm part of the cast of characters on a wild goose chase trying to get to the guy with the answers*—I thought! And we all know what happened to them . . . the guy had no capabilities or intentions of helping them either. *I'm in Oz'ville—and I need to get out!*

So, rather than waste more time, I decided I'd start by scheduling a breast MRI—until I hit another wall when I discovered out of the three hospitals in our area, and one very big well-known clinic—none of them could do one. A larger hospital three hours away said they could, but when I called the scheduling department I heard, "No, we don't do them here, but in this 'other hospital' (another hour farther away) they do."

Exasperated, I was starting to get the picture. None of these places knew what I was asking for because women diagnosed with breast cancer are few and far between who still have a lump or mass in their breast—or their *breast* for that matter!

What is it about breasts that make doctors so bent on cutting them off? Cut off a healthy breast—just because there's something in it *that's not?* (You can bet it was no woman that came up with that one!) Whacking off these "natural born beauties" as a means of saving lives makes about as much sense as blowing up all those "other" national treasures in this country to solve the terrorist problem! You don't destroy the good to get at the bad!

If there's a rat in your house you don't blow the whole house up to kill it. So why blow up my boob to crush a bug? Especially when I have the opportunity to choose something like Protocel®, which cuts off its energy source, rendering it completely unable to function, which in the end brings about eminent death, cell by cell. And without, I might add, disturbing or *damaging* as much as one healthy living cell surrounding it. Thus, allowing me to just keep right on living. (Which, excuse me, but isn't that *exactly* what I was doing when this whole ordeal started?)

Just Give Me Something to Write About

Now I was steamed. I had an oncologist with an "attitude," who, for whatever reason, was blocking me from getting the very things I'd need to determine in time if I was even recovering. I was *so* ready to go this alone. It was just hateful of him to do this to me. Like he didn't know what scans or markers to order—*please!*

From the beginning in my recovery, I had been documenting details, and I was glad I had, because I had an inkling there might one day be an article published about my experience. A testimonial, if nothing else, that I could do all on my own.

I try to think of myself as an artist, and I've thought of setting up a website where I could display some of my originals and prints. And then—since it would be *my* website, I could post my story where anyone who visited it could read about my recovery and how I used Protocel® to overcome a diagnosis of breast cancer. (What a plan!) When the "Cancer-*free*" day in my life came *(and it would!)*, I wanted a day-to-day, detailed, documented journal of my recovery, including everything I discovered (and uncovered) that made the difference. So others would know how I did it. (Remember—that's why I had the biopsy in the first place!)

Email and instant messages that I'd been saving really began to accumulate—creating great reference material, not to mention an accurate timeline. And now, as I looked it over, I felt a twinge of excitement! Because, although just days into my journey, considering what a spectacular full-on recovery we all *knew* was coming, I could see this already had all the makings of a book! And, to top it all off—I already had the title! I had the title the day I went to see the surgeon. All I could think about on the drive to his office was, *The breast stays put! No chemo, no radiation, no lumpectomy, no thank you. Put your scalpel back in your pocket and nobody gets hurt!* (With an "on-a-mission" statement like that in my head, chances were there had to be the makings of a book in there with it some-where, too.)

So, early on, just days into my Protocel® program, when I started to sense God was dealing with me on all of this, He also reminded me of one particular conversation He and I'd had, and not that long ago. I just have to share this with you.

What I *couldn't* seem to shake off, or deny, was the surprisingly strong sense of desire I felt when I first thought about writing a book. And it seemed to get stronger and stronger with each passing year. Even to the point where several times in prayer I told God that I was aware of it, I just didn't know what to *do* about it. But there was this one conversation in particular where I told Him, "I think the only thing stopping me from writing is . . . I don't think there's a novel in me. I don't think I'd be good at making stuff up. You know me, Lord. I'm more apt to be the 'true life story' kind of writer. You know—the *deep* stuff. "

(Do you believe that? Do you believe I *said* that? *To God?*—The Guy who *invented* 'deep'!" *What was I thinking?*)

"And," I went on to say, "since there's obviously nothing of any earth-shattering significance going on in my life—what would I write about?"

(If I'd had any idea *(at all)* that something like this was in the works, believe me, I'd have gotten creative long ago, *in short order*, and come up with a subject and a book title—all on my own. Long before this breast cancer fiasco! Christmas 2003 would have found me busy! *Writing something!*)

Note to Self #11 – Would you *please* rethink it the next time you decide to talk to *God* about something like getting "deep!"

Before you even go there, the answer is, "No, I don't believe for a moment that God put cancer on me so I would write a book!" But I do see it as another case of the Lord using for good what the devil meant for evil! That's *exactly* what was going on here!

They say, "If God calls a vision He supplies the provisions," and since "God can't steer a parked car," I decided I needed to get moving! For me it was like putting my foot in the Jordan and then watching the waters part. I was already in awe of what was starting to materialize, and even though I was only weeks into this horrible diagnosis, as ridiculous and off-the-wall as it sounds, I was also bursting with anticipation at times with the thought that I just might actually *get* to write that book!

Honey I just fired the "Osha-cologist"

Then there was this *other* little issue. As the weeks went by it was more and more evident that I wouldn't be able to keep up with the workout program I had signed up for at a local workout center.

Well, here's something my oncologist can handle. I'll have him write up a "script" saying I can't work out for a while.

(You're starting to write this for me, aren't you?)

I phoned his office and got the same woman. (I get her *every* time.) I told her why I was calling, and she said she would ask him and get back to me. *(Great! Something they can finally do!)*

To my absolute shock (which I don't know why, because I can tell it comes as no shock to *you*), she called back to say that he said he wouldn't do it. I couldn't believe what I was hearing, and this time I told her so! *(This was his idea of "helping" me?)*

She then added—"He wants to know—are you *sick?*"

(You want to run that by me again?) I kid you not! I did *not* make that up! The man wanted to know—*if I was sick!*

I wanted to pull the receiver about two feet away from my mouth and scream, "It's about this *egg-size* mass that's in my breast! So, now that you mention it, I guess I'd have to say, '*Yes, I am just a bit of a bubble off plumb!*'"

But—once again—I kept my cool and explained that the way Protocel® works it can cause extreme tiredness, as the body works so hard to rid itself of the dead cancer. And I also reminded her of "the lump"!

"What is Protocel®?" she wanted to know.

(Ugh! Like I want to go into that with you!)

"It's an alternative treatment."

"Did he prescribe it?"

(What difference does that make?)

"No. But it's a treatment he knows I'm using: I spoke with him about it when he agreed to monitor my progress."

"Well, if he didn't prescribe it, he won't do anything for you on this. I'm very sorry, but I know that's the stance he'll take."

I was speechless, and she knew it. I proceeded to thank her (wanting to kill something) and got off the phone.

This guy needs to get over himself! Would someone please tell me just WHAT I paid that man three hundred and twenty-four dollars for? He spent twenty minutes with us (not an hour and a half!) and took one measurement! And didn't even give me the actual diagnosis! No diagnosis, no testing, no note to get out of gym class! What a complete jerk!

Note to Self #12 – Fire osha-cologist in the morning! *The audacity of that man!*

Let Me Check "The List"

As I got further into my recovery, it became evident in hearing other people's stories that dealing with difficult, arrogant, know-it-all doctors is more of an occurrence than you'd think. When you've opened yourself to vulnerability in a doctor-patient relationship and they disrespect you in such a degrading way, you feel as though you've been violated. And you have. This oncologist made me feel like I was a joke to him, and that's just wrong!

My workout center was appalled an oncologist could be so insensitive! Another health care practitioner said, "Did you ask him if he makes his chemotherapy patients continue their workouts and obligations when they're puking their guts out?"

And then, (this one was good!) even my nurse practitioner's assistant had said to me, "Oh, Pam, don't you want to wait until you have another oncologist lined up before you fire this guy? So you won't feel like you are out there all alone in this?"

Now that was funny! Since "alone" in it is exactly how I've been all along—even *with* him!

Unfortunately so many doctors just don't get it. It is amazing that they can be so cold and heartless. (Not all doctors, of course—there are actually only about ten or twelve really bad ones out there. But you gotta watch out for 'em, because they tend to make the rounds.) (I know—*stop* already!)

But then again maybe it *is* being recognized as somewhat of a major problem, because one evening on cable news I heard a story featuring classes for doctors in "Bedside Manners." Educating them in how what they do and say affects their patients, in an effort to enlighten them that patients are, after all, real people, with real feelings. (And, because what I was hearing hit close to home — I took notes.)

"Research proves that the way patients are treated by their doctors affects them emotionally, which in turn affects their recovery as much, or sometimes even *more,* as anything they, as physicians, can prescribe or do to treat them physically."

It's hard to believe that type of thing even needs to be taught to someone like a doctor. You'd think it would have been part of basic training somewhere in med school just in case, in real life, they hadn't figured it out yet — *it matters how you treat people!*

A few weeks later the oncologist's office called to say they noticed I'd cancelled my appointment.

"Yes. I cancelled it."

(There was silence on the other end of the phone.)

"Would you like to reschedule it?"

"No."

(Silence.)

"Do you *ever* plan to call our office back to see the doctor again?"

(Well — I don't exactly have you on speed-dial, but, here — let me check my "To-Do" list. Whoops, here it is, and, sorry . . . nope — you're not on it!)

"No-o?" I said, as in *"perish the thought!"* (Like I was ever going to darken that guy's door again!)

She half laughed, didn't inquire why, said "Okay" and hung up.

So — that was it. I was through with him!

And, you know, I kind of hated to see the guy go. The material was great! *"Are you sick?"* You can't *make* that kind of stuff up!

Surgical Pathology Report
Pamela Hoeppner
Date of service 1-29-04

DIAGNOSIS:

Invasive ductal carcinoma, needle biopsy, right breast
Addendum: 2-2-04
Estrogen Receptor 2+
Progesterone Receptor 3+

MICROSCOPIC:
SIZE OF INVASIVE COMPONENT: cannot be determined
HISTOLOGIC TYPE: invasive ductile carcinoma
HISTOLOGIC GRADE: (Nottingham Histologic Score)
Tubule Formation
Minimal: less than 10% (score = 3)
Nuclear Pleomorphism
Marked variation in size, nucleoli, chromatin clumping, etc.
Score = 3.
Micotic Count (For a 40x objective with a field area of 0.152 mm2)
0-5 Mitotic per 10 HPF (score 1)
Total Nottingham Score
Grade II: 6-7 points

CHAPTER 11

The Ultrasound Shop

I Don't Think I Can Stay All Night

The days had now turned into weeks—and I continued to be tired. (You have to be getting tired *for* me by now.) I wondered sometimes if it was because I allowed myself to be. Or was I just that tired? I didn't have to get up to go to work every day, so I didn't have to force myself to keep going. I think I could have, but it would have been a real effort. Most people on Protocel® are able to continue work. So I had to be the exception. Life, for me, had become *way* too much of an effort!

At this point, the lump seemed to be stabilized. I was, however, beginning to see more and more signs of "lysing." My eyes became crusty with what people often describe as "sand in their eyes." I would wake up and hardly be able to open one of them. And it wasn't only at night; they became "crusty" during the day as well. I also began developing an excess amount of wax in my left ear.

So if there are no signs of lysing—it doesn't necessarily mean Protocel®'s *not* working. But when there *are* signs—it can be a great indicator that it is! Whether seeing evidence of lysing or not, it's vitally important to have tests done in the beginning. And so far – out of frustration – I still hadn't had any. Now a month into it, however, I knew I needed to have something done.

It was evident I wasn't going to get an MRI anytime soon, and I still needed the chest X-ray the surgeon recommended, so I decided

133

to start with an *ultrasound.* I phoned Carol, my nurse practitioner, and she faxed me two scripts. And on February 27, 2004, I had a chest X-ray and my first ultrasound—one month after I began taking Protocel® 23.

Arriving for the ultrasound appointment the next morning, I was still experiencing the anxiety I had felt the night before.

This could get messy. These people aren't used to seeing breasts with lumps still in them. But it really isn't any of their business <u>what</u> *is in my breast! Their job is to take scans. Period!*

I had a *really* strange feeling about this!

Upon arriving at the hospital, I reminded myself once again, *Even if they think you're crazy—it's still a non-issue! You only need them to run the test. What they think doesn't even enter into the equation—because "they" don't get to vote!*

Well—as you can imagine; the technician was full of questions. And I explained them as best I could. She took a lot of images. *A lot!* Then she said the words I did NOT want to hear!

"I'll be right back. I need to run these by the . . . (. . . *yada, yada, yada! —Of course you do!*)

(*Ugh! What exactly is it with these people that is so hard about ". . . get dressed and go?"*)

So here I am again. Only this time a diagnosis of cancer is involved. This time there could be a bomb coming! A real bomb! And here I lie—in this annoying perfect-for-counting-ceiling-tiles-position . . . waiting. It's like knowing there's a package coming and you'd rather not be here to sign for it. The only thing keeping me here is the "remote" possibility that they might actually need more films. Except the chances of that are slim to none. She's already taken a boatload. She <u>couldn't</u> *have missed.*

Oh brother, another holding pattern—just like before. She was gone so long. I was praying, "Dear God, please let me get out of here without any confrontations. Just let her come back in here and tell me, 'You can go get dressed and go *home* now.'"

But, ya' know—*the longer she was gone . . .*

And then I felt something inside me say, "It doesn't matter what they say to you *now*, it will be a different story the day you come back in here—*and it's gone!"* (Like I wanted to hear that! *Oh, man . . . that means . . . Ugh!)*

That's when I heard them. Footsteps in the hall. *Two* sets. Headed right for my room. The door flung open and wouldn't-cha know it. One *extremely* alarmed doctor *(my films in hand)* was about to invade my *personal* space! *Oh, Lord, I don't need this!"*

Not a Pretty Picture

The MD who just *burst* into my life had barely introduced himself when he went on to say, "After reading your ultrasound films I had to talk to you about what you are *doing!" (Not even first about what he was "seeing," but right for the jugular about what I was "doing!")* (I felt like I was in the principal's office, only worse—the principal had come looking for me!)

First he went into how serious my situation was (as if I needed to be briefed on that), and then he came down on me with, "I have to inform you: There is *nothing* out there in the way of 'homeopathic or alternative treatments' that could possibly kill cancer" (". . . you poor gullible naïve little thing").

He proceeded to hang my ultrasound images up on the light, pointing out the original tumor, and then asked me, "Do you see all these other black areas? That's where it has already spread to!"

He then *whipped* out my mammogram films and hung *them* up there, too—to further prove his point! "See? *Those* weren't there before! *Look at that! That is all cancer! This is one of the fastest growing, most aggressive cancers I have ever seen. And if you don't do something soon—you are facing a horrid death!"*

I tried to tell myself I wasn't, but the longer I stood there looking at those images and listening to this man (who obviously had never heard of "sugarcoating") I had to admit—I was in a world of hurt! I didn't know *what* to believe!

I knew what he was saying, and why he was saying it, but he just didn't understand how Protocel® worked. And since he already told me that whatever I was using didn't work, he'd already "cut me off at the knees" before I ever got started.

I had told the technician I had chosen not to have a lumpectomy or mastectomy, and I was using an alternative treatment. *That* was *my* choice! I didn't come there to ask their permission. And I didn't need someone to tell me that this thing in my breast was capable of causing death. *I already knew that!* And, now, by this doctor coming in and telling me nothing I could possibly be doing would work, it left me with nowhere to go.

It was easy to see that this kind compassionate man was scared to no end for me. I knew he was sincere, but he was also *sincerely wrong!* I just didn't have it in me to try to explain why. And it didn't really matter what he thought anyway.

I remember looking at the pitch-black spots shown on the images hanging on the light, wanting so much to see what was going on. Wanting to understand it, and yet wishing I didn't have to have that stuff *seared* into my memory!

Then I got this bright idea to point out to him how none of the "black" stuff he had pointed out to me seemed to have any "defined edges." (Which is what they say happens when Protocel® starts to work and the cells begin to fall apart)—but that swift little move on my part only fired him up *even more!*

"That's what makes this so *much worse!*" he said. "Because if it were still at a point where it had defined edges ("like it was a month ago when I first had the mammogram"—was what he was *really* getting at!) and all still one mass, it would be so much easier to remove."

Well, that train left the station *weeks* ago! *(Probably the same day that boat left the dock!)*

What he was saying was: at one time I could have had a lumpectomy (which I would have never done anyway); but now I knew it would be a mastectomy they'd be insisting on—and probably "a double"! And all I could think while I was standing there was, *I've done some really stupid things in life that I wished I'd never done, Doc, but you can bet what you're talkin' about here won't be added to the list!* All I could think of was, *I have to get out of this room! I have to get out of here and get away from this man!* Well, I might have been through, but he wasn't.

Double and Nothing Doing!

"This is all quite informative, but I think you should know, if it weren't for me, and my persistence in setting up this scan in the first

place (and all on my own, I might add), I wouldn't even be in here today for you to be getting so alarmed on my behalf! Lord knows the oncologist didn't see the urgency!"—is what I *wanted* to say to the guy! Instead, I heard myself blurt out the only thing I could think of—"I'll have to talk to my doctor about it."

(Ugh! What did you say that for?—Like you have one?)

Okay—so now I'm not only confused and losing control of the situation, but I'm also reduced to *making stuff up?*

"Yes, you have to do that. Don't put it off! *You don't have much time*. You have to do something *now!*"

(Oh, contraire! If it's one thing I do have a lot of, it's time, I thought, reminding myself that God invented time to process us back to Himself. And not only that, but He's the "Redeemer" of time! *Just like our moms used to redeem S & H Green Stamps, we spend time with God and He redeems ours for us—He makes it s-t-r-e-t-c-h. So don't try to scare me with this "time" thing, Doc, because that's one subject I'm totally clear on. All I have belongs to God, and because of that, He said all He has belongs to me—and that includes—His "time!"*) (I know it. I think I have an answer for everything! Don't you love it!)

Pulling myself back into the moment, I realized he was explaining about a little family friend who'd had to have a *double* mastectomy—when she was in her twenties. (So there it is. He knows now I'd be headed for a double! So much for the "nip and tuck" deal the surgeon spoke of.) "That was twenty years ago, and she's led a wonderful life. So there's hope for you, too!"

I'd be tempted to believe he's told that story before, except I don't think they're supposed to do this. But I also think both of them were so scared for me they couldn't help themselves. (Certainly rattling the cages of the hired help around here, aren't I?)

And, can I just say . . . It's a good thing this stuff comes in stages, because if the radiologist who read the mammogram had been the one to say these things to me—this doctor wouldn't have had to worry about me dying. I'd have already keeled over!

Seeing Doesn't Always Make It So

I so much wanted to tell this doctor about Protocel® and how I knew I'd be okay, but he wouldn't have wanted to hear it. He had already cleverly taken control of the situation by telling me in his "expert" opinion there was nothing out there in the way of alternative treatments that could go up against cancer and win.

The man stood there speaking death over me, and I allowed it. That's what was *really* ticking me off! Normally, I would never allow myself to be put in a position where someone had that kind of control. But there wasn't anything *normal* about the way any of this was going. *Everything* seemed out of my control when it came to dealing with the medical world and this "diagnosis." To try to convince him of something he had already made up his mind was a lie would have been futile and a waste of my time, effort and energy. All which could be better put to use! And I *didn't need* the stress. So once again I just . . . let it go.

I walked out of that room in a stupor—something was trying to suck the life out of me. Looking at the images on the screen had made me want to double over and vomit. I had tried so hard to see what I was looking at—*so I could comprehend it!* Now all I wanted to do was put it out of my mind—*so I could forget it!*

Well, this day certainly managed to spin right out of control! On a scale of one to ten, this one just went right in the toilet!

What was happening to me? Was Protocel® working, or wasn't it? And if this had spread, why had it spread so fast?

This was going from bad to worse. Nothing made any sense! I was seeing signs of lysing so I knew *something* was working. Surely there had to be an explanation.

Thoughts of people who had died of cancer within two or three months after being diagnosed came to mind. But I refused to be pulled in that direction of thought. Anyway, who was I kidding? I knew of people who on rare occasions found something and were gone in *weeks!* And that's where the battle comes in: By faith, in my heart, I knew I had all kinds of time—because I knew *why* I did. I had already settled that. But then comes the devil, planting seeds of fear and doubt and unbelief, trying to get me off center to focus on worst case scenarios. It's his job. Well! *It's my job to stay in the press!* I felt like if I let up, *for even a second,* at this critical juncture, I'd be crushed by the weight of it all.

I needed to clear my head and find another way to see this. I know you can be staring right at something, and it's not at all what it seems. And that's because things that are "seen" can be *changed* by things that are "unseen." *(Like the power of almighty God!)*

What a Revolting Development This Is!

I should never have gone in that ultrasound room without Willie. But who knew this was coming? And who would expect a doctor would be all over someone like that, telling me I was going to die. (And soon!) I knew going in there that I had this diagnosis, and I told them so. I knew they were trying to help, but they don't have any understanding of the path that I've chosen—and they don't want to listen, because they think they have all the answers!

And, as I made my way down the hall carrying on that one-sided conversation, there sat Willie in the Imaging Department waiting room. He probably took one look at me and went, *Oh, boy!* . . . I knew he could see the distress.

On the way out of the hospital I attempted to quietly talk through controlled tears, trying not to hyperventilate, while attempting to explain to my husband what had just happened.

"This is bad, Willie. The radiologist flew in the room and stuck those scans up on the light and showed me where this has already spread! He claims my breast is full of cancer and I don't have long." (I couldn't even believe I was saying the words that were coming out, let alone believe they were about me!)

"We'll go home and you can make some phone calls," he said, trying his best to encourage me. "They said a lot of times it looks like it's getting worse, when it's just how Protocel® works."

"Yes, but you didn't see what I saw. Something else is going on. There were black spots all through my breast on the ultrasound that didn't show up at all on the mammogram films a month ago. This is probably why it feels like it's gone to the size of an egg." (Another misconception on my part. And I'll clue you in now: What I would later find out is that I was actually dealing with two separate masses—the "grape" *and* the biopsy induced "egg.")

When we got home I went straight to the phone and called my friend. Surely he'd have some answers.

Well—he didn't! At least nothing like I had hoped to hear.

He was very concerned for me. I thought I'd already experienced my lowest possible moment—but this may have just replaced it. (I'm only going to have *one!* I figure if I stand firm on that they'll soon stop!) The idea that Protocel® might not be working for me was more than chilling; it was debilitating. This was wearing me down. And the scene with the doctor in the ultrasound room didn't help. How could this have gone from being a grape-size lump to an "egg-size" aggressively growing cancer—*in just four weeks*—after it had sat in my breast the whole month of January, doing nothing?

We spoke for the better part of an hour, going over everything.

"I don't want to steer you wrong, if this *is* such a fast growing cancer that Protocel® can't get on top of it," he said. "But, you know, if you *did* have a mastectomy, Protocel® would get any bad cells left anywhere else in the body."

"I know. But I don't want to have one."

"I know. I don't want you to have one either."

I told him I was seeing a lot of signs of lysing, and maybe all those satellite tumors were actually *there* in the beginning but were too small to get picked up on the mammogram (which Willie had suggested earlier). He agreed. It was certainly a possibility.

He finally said, "Well—if it were me, I'd go up to 1/3 teaspoonful of Protocel®, from the 1/4 you've been taking. Then see what happens within the next two weeks. Getting a little more aggressive with Protocel® could make all the difference!"

So that's how we ended it. Him puzzled—and me feeling like my head was in a vice. (This was going to be a *long* night!)

A Slight Chance of Drizzle

The next day—back to the hospital we went. I wanted that report! And I wanted my scans. I wanted to *see* those "things" again, for myself. The report was bleak:

Targeted ultrasound examination in the 10 o'clock area of the right breast in the area of palpable abnormality identified on prior screening mammographic examination dated 1/28/04, demonstrated multiple irregularly marginated hypoechoic lesions with posterior shadowing which are highly suspicious for carcinoma. The largest of these measures 17.2 x 15.4 x 17.6 mm in diameter with multiple surrounding smaller lesions. These findings are highly suspicious for breast cancer. IMPRESSION: Sonographic findings highly suspicious for aggressive, invasive breast cancer in the upper outer quadrant of the right breast. Consultation recommendations were discussed with the patient. BI-RADS category 5. Highly suggestive of malignancy. Appropriate action should be taken.

Unreal. What was once the size of a small grape had now possibly developed tumors at the end of all those "feeler-like looking gizmos." Okay, so how could this possibly get much worse? Not only did I have the original one to get rid of, now all these others had sprung up in less than a month. Could it really be spreading *that* fast?

I was going to have a battle over the weekend keeping my head on straight. All I knew was that I had God's promise that everything was going to be okay, and the Bible says, "After having done all to stand—just stand!"[12] And that's what I purposed in my heart to do—and continue to have an ultrasound every other month.

Healing scripture CDs in hand, I went to bed. I'd sleep hard, and, when I woke up, I'd look for God to find some way to reassure me that He was on top of this, and everything was going to be okay. Storm clouds had definitely rained on my parade today. I wanted to go to sleep. I loved it that I slept so hard—what an amazing feeling, that gift of escape. (*If only I could sleep through the whole weekend!*)

THERE WILL BE NO WHITE FLAG

CHAPTER 12

Whatever Happened to My So-Called Life

Lead, Follow or Get Out of the Way!

Proclaimed authoritatively into my life were the words: "You have cancer! You are going to die! You don't have much time!" The ramifications of that are off the charts!

So many times I've thought about all the people who have heard those words spoken over them by a doctor and what it must have done to them. What it does to you inside—to you and your mind—is nothing short of crushing! And that's *after* you finally get to the place where you can even begin to accept that it's actually *you* they're talking about. But I had enough knowledge in the arena of "words" and "declarations" to know that just because something is spoken into my life—doesn't make it so! And I don't just *allow* any *"thing"* to come into my life. Especially words! They have to first "sign in"—and if they aren't on "The List" they don't even get their foot in the door—let alone get to move in and set up housekeeping!

Awakened by the first rays of early morning sunlight to peek into our second floor windows, my first thoughts of the day confirmed that it was all still there. The paralyzing feelings created, once again, by the showing I'd been forced to sit through at the "Ultrasound Theater" were not letting up easily.

It would have helped if something . . . anything . . . had turned up by now to help rewrite the script. But it hadn't.

I could still hear the radiologist flipping out on me, going, "You're going to die!" . . . accompanied by the sinking feeling of hearing the one person I was *certain* would tell me it was going to be okay, practically say to me, *"You just might."*

That one-month "mile-marker" was the first stop in the time-line I had looked forward to reaching, to be able to at least begin to breathe a little easier and feel better about things. Now, instead . . . *just when I had . . .* my whole world had come crashing in. Now, rather than making *progress*, everything pointed to the fact that if anything, I might actually be worse!

Well, I've heard other people say doctors told them they were going to die — and they just decided not to!

Note to Self #13 – Take out a lifetime membership in the "I Fully Intend to Continue to Live Club."

(Hey! If I became a member of "The Doctor Said You're Going to Die Club" *without having any say in the matter*, I can certainly cancel my membership in it, without notice, and start a more "user-friendly" one of my own — right?)

I kept going over things in my mind. I knew if I had a mastectomy, whatever renegade cells that were left lurking, Protocel® would get them. So dying still was a non-issue. Unless, of course, it had already spread throughout my body, being the type of cancer that was *so* aggressively out of control Protocel® wouldn't be able to stop it. But, then, if it was *that* aggressive, what good would a mastectomy (and whatever else they'd want to throw at it) do? There are some strains of cancer that are very aggressive and multi-drug resistant. But I'd heard that's usually a problem for someone who has been through courses of chemotherapy, where the chemo promoted the development of drug-resistant cancer cells and their immune system was compromised because of it. And that sure didn't apply to me.

What was behind all this explosive growth? None of the testimonials I'd read had ever indicated anything like this: where a biopsy caused explosive growth in a tumor in just days. So why just mine? (Another error in assumption on my part — I wasn't as alone in this as I had thought. I just hadn't talked to enough women yet with regard to "exploding growth" from a biopsy.) (See Chapter 18—Putting It in Perspective.)

Something had happened when I had the biopsy that was like pouring gasoline on a fire. And, as fast as it had grown in the first two weeks, Protocel® had to be shutting it down or it would have continued to grow, wouldn't it? It wouldn't have gone to ten times the size in two weeks and then just *stopped*. And because I can *feel* this thing, I know that is *exactly* what it did.

You know the old saying, "Good things come to those who wait?" Well, the guy who said it got *run over* by the people who decided to get up off their *duffs* and get out there and get what they needed and wanted in life! And the Bible also states, "The kingdom of heaven suffereth violence, and the violent take it by force."[13] (Which I had every intention of doing!) I was convinced Protocel® was working, and maybe by going up to 1/3 teaspoonful five times a day, things would start going in the other direction.

Well—one thing was evident! This wasn't going to be any *"Three Months on Protocel®—Tumor Gone"* story. There was some worst-case scenario stuff going on, and things needed to be documented so that, as time went on, I had something to look back on.

Ya' gotta love that journaling! It helps you see patterns, and even if it only brings one thing to mind, to help you make better choices, it's so worth the time it takes. (And, besides, you never know when it could one day turn into *a book!*)

Peace Rules!

So, as bleak as this looked, I knew I was still okay—and I still had time. Time to think this through, and time for God to open doors that would reveal "insight, concepts and ideas," things I hadn't even considered yet—the "treasures of darkness"—"hidden riches in secret places" kind of stuff![14]

I'd had the whole weekend to mull this over in my mind and do some serious soul-searching, and I was able to come to a very big conclusion, which in turn allowed my thought process to clear just enough for one big eye-opening breakthrough! (I love it when I get those!)

At a time when it seemed all I had to work with was uncertainties, two things I was alive-certain of (as opposed to *dead*-certain of) were: The decision I was about to make was life-altering. And I didn't plan on making it alone! I needed *Rock-solid* answers. I was looking for God *everywhere* in this!

Okay, so let's reason this out, I thought. *Protocel® without a mastectomy—the ideal! A mastectomy with Protocel®—a last resort! In fact, okay—out of the question!* Just the thought of it made me nauseous.

Every time I tried to "go there" and envision having a breast cut off, the images were so much scarier than what was staring me in the face at the moment—I vowed there wasn't even a remote possibility I'd have one. It really was, for me, *out of the question!*

They say when you are walking through the fire, draw as close to God as you can by getting on your knees—staying under the inferno that's blazing above you. And if you can't physically get on your knees, you can get on your knees in your heart. So I decided it was time to go to bed—to do just that. Talk to my Father!

As I climbed the stairs, I felt like I was walking through mud. *I'm like an eighty-year-old woman,* I thought. *Except I know some eighty-year-old women, and, right now, any one of them could whip me with one arm tied!* I knew all this fatigue was a result of lysing, as the body uses energy stores to rid itself of broken down cells, so I just went with it and told myself, *I can handle three months of tired.* (Wouldn't *that* have been nice?)

So there I lay. Contemplating where I was going, where I'd been, and all that was yet to come—including how to deal with this so-called "out-of-control" *raging* diagnosis, when suddenly, just that quick, I remembered something I heard Gloria Copeland say a long time ago. And, let me tell you, I got excited! It was my answer to this whole decision-making dilemma, in a nutshell!

"When making life-altering choices and decisions," she said, "first of all—*never* be in a hurry! And then, one determining factor that can help you choose what to do, when you don't know what to do, is . . . *always* follow peace!" Wow! Talk about a word fitly spoken—*for such a time as this!*

Amazing! I'd already purposed in my heart not to be rushed into anything. And I certainly knew where my peace *was,* and even more so, where it *wasn't!* Wow! With this new light shed on it I had such a peace about *following peace!*

And with that peace came the knowing: there *had* to be other answers for me, too. With the way this timely revelation had just "come to me," I was now more convinced of it than ever: God would not have brought me this far, shown up for me with answers in the way He had, for everything to fall apart on me now! No, this was a journey, and if I trusted Him, just as everything else had already showed up (right when I needed it), others would show up, too! This "peace" thing, for me, was the tiebreaker!

Walk in Love

Oh, but then, by the way—there was also this other little matter of "walking in love." It's kind of a precursor to the "follow peace" thing. And, from what I understand, it's not a *choice.* It's a *command.*[15] In fact, the *ultimate* command! The one that everything we ask God for hinges on. We have to forgive *everybody!* It doesn't matter what they did to us. It doesn't matter what we went through. It doesn't matter how wrong they are—or were. And it doesn't matter if they won't admit it. We have to forgive. And it's for our own benefit that we do, because unforgiveness is a package deal. You can't harbor it without bitterness, resentment, hatred and the like setting up camp in your heart, too. And that's one "killer package!" Any of those things causes *dis*-ease in the body, so the one who gets hurt by unforgiveness is the one carrying it. Not to mention unforgiveness compromises our relationship with God.

If God offers us forgiveness for the mistakes we make, no matter how big or how small, I don't believe we can *see God* if we don't forgive the people who hurt us. And that also means "see Him" in our *circumstances.* I want God in my circumstances! I *need* Him in my circumstances!

When you don't forgive, when you hold on to past hurts and offenses, it's like you're eating off a dead carcass. (I remember the first time I heard Joyce Meyer say that one.)

I have work to do here.

Note to Self #14 – Forgive oshacologist immediately! *(Ugh! Like I feel like doing that!)*

Well, thank goodness forgiveness isn't a "feeling." It's a decision. A choice! I first make the decision to forgive, and the feelings change later. But in the meantime I get to go free.

If healing hinges on forgiveness (and it does) and I don't forgive, not only did the jerk do me wrong, but now I'm going to risk *dying* over it?

Why would I want to waste that kind of negative energy on this guy, when he's probably never even given me a second thought? (Well, maybe one. Okay, maybe two. But that's it! Two! *Max!*)

No, if I want God's best I have to let the oshacologist go free—to bring God on the scene in my life so my blessings don't get blocked—*including my healing!* And I even feel better about this already, just being able to release it and get rid of it.

In the Greek forgiveness translates as "exhale." (I first heard Paula White say that.) It literally means, "To breathe someone right out of you." Because if you're "holding" a grudge—(are you ready for this)—they're "in there!" (Yuck!)

So how does it feel to know that if you resent someone, you're actually carrying him or her around with you? Explore that scenario for a while. Nice, huh? Thus the adage, "To err is human; to forgive divine!" And I say *divine indeed!*

The Lord Leads—the Devil *Pushes*

And that thing about "never be in a hurry"? Did you ever notice, as desperate as things get in life, that God is never in one? It's like sometimes you want to say, "*G—od . . . ?* Don't You see what's going on down here? Don't You think maybe You could be *doing* something?" (And *He's* probably "up there" going, "So. Would you like a little cheese with that *whine?*")

Then you pull out your itemized list of suggestions you think He'd do well to consider. (Like He'd never thought of any of them.) But He's never in a hurry. Because that's just how God is! So—if *He's* never in a hurry—*why should I be?*

Okay—He wants me at rest:[16] walking in love;[17] following peace.[18] That way I can hear from Him. I can't if my inner man is all in turmoil with my mind flooded with fear, doubt and unbelief. You follow peace by getting quiet before God, contemplating all the facts and circumstances, and then picture yourself in each scenario.

So—okay, never be in a hurry, walk in love and follow peace! I can do that.

I then began to allow myself to do almost the "thinkable." I started to envision having a mastectomy *in depth!* (Let's just see how long it takes before *peace* flies out the window on this deal!) The hospital room. The operating room. The instruments. The monitors, IVs and tubes. The doctors. The nurses. The operating room. Being sedated. The gurney—the anesthesia—*the operating room—the instruments!* Okay! I've seen enough. What am I? *Nuts?* Like I would *ever* subject myself to *any* of that mess!

And I know you don't want to hear this, but I don't care—I wanna know! Just *what* would they do with my boob? I'm serious! That bothers me! *Haven't you ever thought about that?* They cut it off and do what? Dispose of it? I'm sure. But where? The "Boob Graveyard?" Or would mine be the luck-of-the-draw "bodacious ta-ta" that wound up marinating in a glass jar on a shelf on some college campus? Okay, so maybe they don't do that. But I'd want to know! *What would happen to it?*

'Nough said. Case closed! This was still such a no-brainer. Ugh! Alarms; flashing red lights; bells and whistles, like none other, going off at the mere thought of going in what I now knew was the *wrong* direction. This was amazing! Standing at this fork in the road, and I just confirmed I was right all along. There was no way I would *ever* put myself in a situation where I'd be setting myself up for such trauma! I was now clear on what path was in the direction of my best interest. And it wasn't the one down "Surgery Alley." I was beginning to feel so much better.

After all those years of reminding God that I trusted Him to "order my steps, direct my paths and establish my thoughts"—and, once again, He just had. I *love* that about Him!

So—I had work to do! God had just given me the "green light" to press on and start seeing this situation turn around. And the first place to start? Right here at home. It was time to have a talk with "the girls."

Talk to the Breast—the Boob's Not Listening

And talk I did! And the first one I talked to was the one *without* the problem.

"Listen, Lady!" I said. "*We*—have a problem, and we are *not* going to continue in the direction we've been going! And if you have any interest at all in continuing to look good and retaining your 'standing' in life, you best get on the stick and start talking to your twin! Because without it, life for you will certainly lose its luster!"

Well, that lit a fire under her, because the next thing I heard was, "Okay, Lady Mc-B! Let's just *stop* the madness! All this talk about 'cutting' is hitting just way too close to home. *Way* too close! They finish you off, and the next thing ya' know they'll be lookin' in *my* direction! And since there's no way I will *ever* be taken *alive,* I'll wind up stuck here next to some cheesy imposter. *Then* who am I going to talk to? Ya' can't talk to something that isn't even alive let alone *real*. So...since you're the one causing all the ruckus, you deal with it, and get rid of whatever it is they want to cut you off for: 'Cuz, ain't nobody touchin' the 'real estate!' Trust me on this! We came into this world together—and one day we'll go out that way. *But it won't be anytime soon!"*

The whole thing was a stitch! Really hysterical. I'd finally stop laughing, only to get tickled all over again at the thought of it. (Which, by the way, is what I was supposed to be doing to recover— laugh and "think on good things!"[19])

This *brilliant* concept came from one of my dearest friends, Barb, at church that I had chosen to tell about myself, because I felt comfortable confiding in her. She felt led to call me to tell me a story about a relative of hers whose leg had been crushed in an automobile accident. The doctors had insisted they had no recourse but to amputate. *(How horrible!)*

Barb said that after hearing the "stand" I had taken, it reminded her so much of how her aunt had also taken charge in a similar *dismal* situation of her own. In the end, she turned the entire situation around with what she applied, much to the disbelief of the doctors. Barb thought the technique would come in handy in the war I was waging to keep them from "amputating" in my case, too!

As the story goes, the thought of having one of her legs cut off just didn't compute. (Much like having a mastectomy didn't compute with me either!) So—being fed up with the gloom and doom of the doctors—insisting there was "no hope" for her leg, she said she finally "put her *other* foot down" and informed the doctors they were *never* to say anything *bad* about her leg "in front of it" ever again!

Then she started getting her good leg to talk to the one they wanted to take. Long story short, Barb said, "When my aunt walks today you really can't tell she ever had a problem. The only time you notice anything is when she climbs steps: her one foot tends to lag a little." *And this was a crushed leg!*

That's what I'm talking about, people! *Don't try to tell me this stuff doesn't work!*

(And, for the handful of skeptics who think this sounds a little far-fetched or bizarre, or even a little above you to ever talk to your body—just think back on all those times you've smacked your dash-board, or hit the steering wheel, when your car wouldn't start! (And the times that it *did* when you did!) Who (or more like *what*) exactly were you talking to when you were going, "You sorry thing—*start!*"? Words carry authority—and we're the only creatures on earth who get to use them. At least a body part has *life*. How much life is there in a car part?

Affirmations, Pacts and Self-Fulfilling Prophecies

And, speaking of words, have you ever noticed how many people have their very own personal "finish" line? We've all heard them. I used to do it myself. (An easy habit to slide into—that you don't even realize you're doing!) When I heard the reasoning behind it, I made the decision to go to work and get rid of it years ago. Who needs "death statements" in their life? And there is no one who has as much of a "programming" effect on us as we do—in what we hear ourselves say about ourselves, by unknowingly speaking covenants into existence.

"Why would I want to stop all my bad habits when I'll probably never even see forty?"

"With my luck, I'll be the one to drop over dead of a heart attack before I hit fifty."

"Mom died of breast cancer, so did Aunt Kate; I *know* I'm going to die of it, too."

Then there are the ones who start this when they've been given a bad report about their health:

"I knew one day I'd die of cancer."

"I want to see the mountains before I go."

(Go *where?* How 'bout: I want to see *the rest of my life* before I go *anywhere!*)

Do you hear some of the things people say with regard to death? What if everything that came out of your mouth came to pass? Like, "I knew it! I'm losing my mind!" or "That made my blood boil!" (Eeeoowch!) They're all covenants, pacts and self-fulfilling prophecies and we don't even realize we're making them.

It was easy to turn it around. Like anything else, it just took time and a little effort. (Okay—at times, a lot!) I just started "listening" to myself and began saying what I *wanted* to see happen, instead of what I didn't. I asked forgiveness for doing it (out of ignorance), renounced it and got rid of it. And then I started speaking LIFE over myself and my situations. And now it's become a way of life. I miss it sometimes, but when I do, I cancel out what I just said, and I move on.

My Green Card

In my early teens, I had this knowing about myself. If there was a situation that needed a solution, and I didn't have one, one way or another, I'd figure it out. I got it from my dad. He was awesome at figuring things out and inventing whatever he needed to get things accomplished. This "fact" that I knew to be true about myself has helped me in so many situations in life, I can't even begin to tell you. It was my "pass" in life to get into places where I never would have otherwise tread!

Then, in the '90s, I had the opportunity to take a life-changing secular self-awareness/self-development course. So much of it paralleled the teachings of the Bible—and *all* of it applied to the laws of life. It was an eye-opening experience, and afterward I made a genuine effort to apply as much as possible to transforming my life and re-inventing my outlook on it. So, in addition to Scripture, much of what I speak about in this book, and what I applied in my recovery, came from what I learned in that class, and from listening to programs like *The Believer's Voice of Victory, Changing Your World, Changing Your Life, Enjoying Everyday Life and The Potter's Touch* on TBN and Daystar—*just to name a few!*

But one thing I have to tell you that I feel was so instrumental in my recovery stems from one particular assignment we were given to write up several "affirmations" on index cards, read them out loud several times daily and "envision" them coming to pass in our lives. (Just like the people who affirm every day that things are going to go wrong for them—only just the opposite. The affirmations just help to change the software and replace the tapes that once caused you to dwell on the wrong stuff—attracting things into your life that work *for* you, rather than *against* you.)

One particular affirmation I wrote up on a bright fluorescent lime green index card (for me, the brighter the better!) stood out to me as my favorite. And I put it in a place where I would see it every day, but no one else would. (After all—it *was* lime green!) So I wedged a corner of it in the edge of the molding in our walk-in closet—where I would stand by it as I selected my clothes every morning, and where I changed out of them every night, and, of course, many times in between. That card hung there (and I "hung onto it!") for years. Seven to be exact! Sometimes I read it aloud, sometimes not; but just looking up at it on a regular basis gave me a good feeling about doing something to keep my life "on track" every day, positioning me for success. I mean, when the rubber meets the road, what better "blessing generating assets" can you have than answers, solutions and keys?

Well, it has served me well throughout this recovery. And I'm certain it was also instrumental in my finding Protocel® before I ever knew I'd need it! No one will *ever* convince me otherwise.

I am highly skilled at finding
answers to questions, solutions to challenges,
and keys to unlocking doors that move me
swiftly to my goals.

I can't tell you how many answers I found to questions regarding my recovery when, in the natural, it looked as though there were no answers for them; or how many solutions I discovered to challenges where the issues were life-threatening; or when I just needed answers for peace of mind. And most of the time the distance between "I need it!" and "There it is!" was the time it took me to pick up a phone, read a book or open an email. I saw that card come to life in my recovery, as if it were drawing things in like a magnet, based on my faith about what I knew to be true about myself, and what I believed in, and the God who is the basis for all of it! Just like healing, all true answers come from God, but answers don't necessarily come without listening and expecting. Two of the things in life that I purposed in my life to get good at—*for such a time as this!*

CHAPTER 13

Everything to Live For

"Complete Recovery" Takes on a Whole New Meaning

It was Friday night and I had only been doing exactly what I wanted. If I felt like reading, I read. If I felt like a movie, I did that, too. But, whatever I did, I ended up falling asleep. I slept so much. Kerri would call and as we spoke I would lose my train of thought. At times, it was a royal effort to even project my voice. My body was working overtime to rid itself of this intruder. All I knew to do was stay on schedule with my dosing *and rest*. I *knew* Protocel® was hard at work! It was shutting down whatever was inside me that was so bent on killing me that it was willing to kill itself in the process.

(Cancer is not only vile ... if you ask me, it's also deranged and just plain dumb! Anything so obsessed with death that it would create its own suicide would have to be!)

Well, it was going to die long before it ever died of starvation because it killed me! A full recovery was all I was focused on. It was all I thought about! I had so much to live for, and lo and behold, I was about to find out just *how* much!

We had just stepped in the door from having dinner out. After getting the kind of news I received at the "Ultrasound Shop" that day, I didn't feel much like cooking. The phone rang, and it was Kerri calling to say she'd sent me an instant message, telling me

157

to be sure to check my email. She wondered if I'd seen it. Since I hadn't, I stepped into my office to pull up my messages. And there it was. "Check this out. We think this is pretty cool!" it read.

Right about then Willie walked into my office, which he rarely does in the evening. As Kerri and Shawn's email was slowly opening up, it was obvious that it was a picture of "something." Right away Shawn was suspect. He's always up to something! And there was this rabbit he had been stalking. It had been eating their shrubs. It kept outsmarting him, and he was so mad at that rabbit! We, of course, all kidded him about it. And this had gone on for days!

"Take the bunny somewhere and let him go when you catch him," I told Shawn.

But Shawn was like, "No! *This rabbit is going down!*" (Wanting me to *think* the poor thing's days were numbered!)

So, as the picture opened, I looked over my shoulder at Willie and said, "This better not be a picture of a dead rabbit!"

Whatever was opening up, it was full screen and taupe in color. And then I could see what looked to be—some type of lettering.

As I sat waiting, leaning on my elbows—quite close to the monitor, waiting for it to open—suddenly these huge letters started to appear. They spelled—PREGNANT! *I nearly went airborne!*

It was a pregnancy test strip, and Shawn had taken a close-up of it. I couldn't believe what I was reading! I started flipping out as I grabbed the phone and dialed.

When they answered I was up out of my chair all over the place in my office: laughing, crying, trying to talk and hyperventilating—all at the same time.

I could hear Kerri on the other end of the line going, *"Mom—breathe! Breathe, Mom—breathe!"*

They were rolling with laughter, and so was Willie behind me! He told them later they really blew it: if he'd had a camcorder they'd have made a lot of money off "Grammy" that night!

And the most wonderful part of all? In an instant, it was as if the *new life* in my daughter had just cancelled out any *death* the doctors were convinced was in me!

I knew there was no way that Kerri and Shawn were finally going to be pregnant, after being married seven years, and me not be here to love and help raise that precious little life. Another awesome confirmation from God that He was in control and everything was going to be just fine—the evidence was mounting!

If you thought I was determined to beat this thing before, well, let me tell you—*"full recovery" just got taken to a whole new level!* A baby! A real tiny new little person. A new little "nose" and ten more "tiny toes!"—*in our family!* Her PopPop and I were ecstatic! I just knew she was going to be a little girl. For years every time I thought of Kerri with a baby it was a little girl. I just knew she would be! And I told everyone so!

What an amazing gift they'd just given me to visualize and plan for. Talk about living in the future! Nope. I wasn't going anywhere. This little "baby-gram" had just sealed the fate of a disease!

Being able to picture a little baby here with us all the time was simply the best! I knew the second she was born it would be as though she had always been right here. After all, she was already a little person. We just couldn't see her. She existed: she was like a little bun in the oven, a little pea in a pod—gently maturing. And now, when things got too overwhelming—when it got too hard to be where I was—I'd just close my eyes and go to a place where I could hold my grandbaby. She started out as an infant, but it didn't take long for her to become a "little girl" in my heart!

I could see her running toward me with outstretched arms. Her soft hair flying in the breeze. And that beautiful smile! I could feel her baby-soft arms around my neck as she hugged me tight! Talk about healing endorphins! It was like magic! So how heavenly will it be when she's finally here? Grammy Pammy and PopPop Willie—with our very own "little Munchkin"! PopPop will be like her very own personal big Teddy Bear—and I couldn't wait to be her Grammy! How awesome! I had the answer to cancer and a new grandbaby on the way! *What a way to give the devil a nervous breakdown!*

Speak to Your Mountain—It Talks to You!

Stop talking to God about how big your mountains are,
and start talking to your mountains about how big your God is!
Joel Osteen

Waking up Saturday morning, I checked like I always do (forty times a day) to see what was happening in that area. With the baby coming, the already high stakes had become so much higher! There was no margin for error—I had to do this right! This had to be a recovery *for the books.* And I knew I had to be the one to see to it that it was!

Last night, after the ultrasound, with all the talk of explosive growth I had done the same thing. I examined that area with my fingertips. And—*to my disgust* I detected small BB-like growths, little pea shaped lumps right at the top of the initial mass. They definitely weren't there at the time of the biopsy: I didn't notice them even a week ago. But they were easily detectible now.

And then I noticed something else. There was a small water-spot-like red dot on my breast with a tiny pinpoint darker red spot, right in the middle of it. There was no denying it. *This thing was still growing!* Those new BB-shaped growths I had detected were very close to the surface. And the startling significance of this red-dot-discovery? It had materialized in the very same area—directly above them!

As the facts systematically pieced themselves together, I felt that same *cold chill.* This time I knew what this was. I knew exactly what I was looking at . . . because I'd seen it before! My heart sank. Just when I thought things couldn't get any worse—*they just had!*

This was cancer trying to eat through my skin. I had seen this on my mom—right before she passed away. I became livid! This thing had just gotten on my *last* nerve!

Without hesitation I stood there in front of that mirror, pointed at it and said, "No! You will *not* come out through my breast. You will *not* eat through my skin. You!—are going to die! So you back off, shrivel and dry up—and go back where you came from, because I refuse to let you advance one step farther! This is *my body*—and *you* are trespassing! I'm a child of the living God! Everything in me is *life* because God Himself lives in me, and I live in Him—and He is *all* Life, Light and Love! And you cannot live in His presence! So *you* will be the one to die. And this is me—*commanding* you to do it! *In Jesus' name!*"

Well—that took care of that! I thought!

I felt very authoritative when I spoke those words and fully expected the red things to immediately back off and disappear. But it didn't. And soon after I stopped speaking, other *feelings* started settling in—which, incidentally, is why you never base your faith and decisions *on feelings*. Feelings are way too fickle. We don't walk *by feelings*. We walk *"by faith."* Feelings tell you to look at your situation and circumstances—and limit you to thinking they're never going to change. Faith tells you to keep your eyes on God—*so they can!* I had been so ecstatic last night learning about our new grandbaby that was on the way . . . and now *this?* Could a new baby be coming into our lives and me not get to be here for her throughout hers? There was just way too much *drama* going on, and I wanted it *to stop!* And the only way I knew how to see to it that it did was stay *totally focused* on what God *already* had to say about my life and situation *in His Word!*

Life is certainly full of peaks and valleys. And, you know . . . at times—*the peaks are definitely greased!*

What If I Died?

Me, me, me! Well, this "all about me" business was getting old. Which is another really creepy thing about a disease like cancer: It causes you to turn inward—constantly focusing all your energy on yourself.

Blindsided once again, and not at all happy about it, I recognized there was a dirt-bag that needed to be set out with the trash!

I had never let myself contemplate this before, but since death kept rearing its ugly head, threatening me with all it had to offer, I decided to allow myself to think about it. I decided to think about, *What if I died?*

I know—I don't believe it either, but I decided it was time to come to terms with it. A "shoot-out" was in order! (When you confront persistent fears it robs them of their power.) This was a "stronghold" I was dealing with, and it was about to lose its grip!

Practically everyone in the medical world told me I was deceived, except for the surgeon—he just seemed sad and disappointed and told me in his opinion I should have a mastectomy followed by some chemo. But I knew he thought I was deceived, too. And with these new developments (like this creepy stuff eating through my skin) even the Protocel® people had no real answers, so I began to allow myself to think about the "sliver" of possibility . . . that I might be wrong.

Ouch! Like I wanted to go there. Thinking about death and dying. Ugh! But it was like something was telling me if I allowed myself to, I might be surprised. So I did.

So off I went to find my "chair." My prayer chair. More has been wrought in my life in *that* chair than I can even begin to tell you! It's because it's saturated with the presence of God! If I want to get something done—I head for that chair!

"Okay, God, we're going to talk about this. And You show me what I need to see. Because I will attest to the fact, and even admit, that I've known a lot of Christians who were determined to live, who I thought were going to—*and they didn't*. And I was floored that they didn't. So where does that leave me?

"You said Your thoughts are higher than ours and so are Your ways,[20] so maybe You can shed some light on where all this is going. I have no intention of dying—but everything else keeps trying to tell me I *have* to. So I'm going to contemplate it happening, and I need You with me to walk me through it." And so it began.

First of all, for me it would be "Graduation Day." I've heard of people who died and went to heaven, and they didn't want to come back! My family would be devastated and brokenhearted, just like we were when we lost Mom, but for them life would go on. There would be more babies and marriages, and missing them is what I'd hate. I wanted to make Christmas cookies with my grandbabies— teach them how to paint and encourage them to write. They'd miss a lot if I wasn't around. But my kids missed a lot after we lost Mom. It's just the way that sort of thing goes . . . In the end, life does go on.

Then there was Willie. Willie would do just fine without me. He'd have my portrait blown up sitting right next to his recliner, go on eating his popcorn at night, and continue to design and build homes, working from sunup to sundown with no time for much else, and he'd go on enjoying life all by himself! And what little time he did have left over, Mike would find ways to fill it by starting projects and then playing dumb so Willie would end up doing all his work for him, just like always. Bill would be helping Willie build, like he always does, and keep him busy walking the Pointe morning and night. Rocky would buy more land to have Willie help him clear, and when he wasn't doing that he'd be showing Willie real estate, or taking him for ice cream. And Butch would keep Willie busy filling the gas cans in "our" garage for "their" pontoon; Lord knows Willie wouldn't be using our deck-boat anymore. Nobody would. They couldn't bear to go out on the lake without me. They'd probably just sell it.

Willie had been alone for seven years raising Glenn and not dating before I met him. Why should anything be any different if I were to leave? Nope. We're good! If I was actually forced to "check out" before I was ready to, Willie would go on to spend the rest of his years biding his time doing everything he's always done—until the day came when we met up with each other again in eternity. What a guy! It was as simple as that!

So—if I died . . . I could live with it!

"Live with it" indeed! I had come to terms with death. O death, where is thy sting? O grave, where is thy victory?[21] Now I could get on with life, liberty and the pursuit . . . ! Not only did this whole thing just backfire on hell, but I'd have many a laugh over it in the months to come. (God has such a sense of humor!)

Dot to Dot

And if that wasn't the end of the fear factor—it was sure the end of the terror! I had taken back all the power. So, once again, just to remind myself as to where I stood: I began sorting through all the proof I had—that a turnaround was coming. Something I'd done from the very first day in that "Bad News Room." Plead your case. It works every time. Evidence—just connect the dots!

- I had an answer before I knew I had a problem
- I knew God had been there for me the day of the mammogram by having me take the little book along.
- Delaying the mammogram gave me time to learn of Protocel®.
- I felt safe and had a peace about the path I was on.

- I could have a mastectomy as a last resort and still use Protocel® without needing chemo or radiation.
- It takes time for tumors to disappear—I had only been on Protocel® for one month!
- People with worse diagnoses than mine have overcome cancer with Protocel® and even other alternative treatments.
- Time was on my side to discover even more answers.
- If God really did call me to be a part of keeping Jim Sheridan's dream alive, I had to be "alive" to do it.

So I was still holding steady, but this, without question, had rocked my world! It's both sobering and chilling to see something you think is "cancer" start *eating* through your skin! But this was getting way too ridiculous (to the point of weird)—and the devil was really blowing his cover with such radical maneuvers in this last-ditch attempt to get me to fold. (He is so stupid. Like I was going to fall for any of it.)

Did I mention that I'd also noticed I wasn't having to battle the "terror thing" anymore? Not like I had over those "meltdowns" with the two radiologists anyway. So how cool is that? Not signing for the package anymore! Some mighty impressive headway goin' on here. And I also had this *knowing* in my "knower"—God was about to show up for me yet one more time!

I'm Glad He Picked You!

So I took this as yet another confirmation that things were going to be okay. Because just when I thought things couldn't get any worse—*they had!* And it's become my "cue" to look for God to show up with another one of His "over-the-top" indicators that everything's going to be okay!

But have you noticed that it was like the devil not only wanted me dead bad—he wanted me dead *fast?* I hadn't had any conventional treatment. My immune system was strong and I had everything going for me for Protocel® to work. So what was all this craziness about? It had to be that the devil wanted more than just me dead. He wanted my testimony dead with me. He knew by putting this on me how bad he'd messed up!

Barb had even said to me, "Pam, I wouldn't wish this diagnosis on anyone, but I can't tell you how glad I am the devil made the mistake of picking you to do it to! 'Cause—*I know you!* When you beat this thing, you're going to tell *everybody* how you did it!"

Then she asked me if I was journaling, because she felt strongly that I should be writing a book. (Her and everybody else on the planet. It was coming at me from everywhere now.) It would definitely be informative. And you have to admit, it wouldn't be boring with all this "drama" going on. I mean, if you think about it, the way things were unfolding, it seemed like every step of the way if something could go wrong—it did. And I don't even live like that. I *expect* things to go my way. It isn't at all like me to be on a collision course with destruction!

It was like one minute the devil was saying, "Look here. See how horrible and hopeless this is?" Then no sooner would that happen than God would lift my head up and say, "But look over here. Take a gander at this, would ya'!" And every time it was something that counteracted and cancelled out the horror enough to put me back on top of my circumstances. The signs were clear from both sides: God was telling me everything was going to be okay—and the devil was *lying* as usual!

Note to Self #15 – Even when the devil attempts one of his pathetic half-gainers in my life—he still ends up being a total *loser!*

CHAPTER 14

Dethroning the Beast

Kicking Things Up a Notch

I made it through the weekend, only to wake up Monday morning to find another tiny reddish pink water spot, about one-half inch away from the first one. I just stood there . . . staring at it. (This was starting to get old.)

"That is so pathetic," I said. "Is this really the best you can do? Well, if it is—*if this is the best you've got*—then you are *so* being shut down!"

I had gone up to 1/3 teaspoonful of Protocel®, from 1/4 teaspoonful, and intended to stay on it until I saw some kind of indicator that Protocel® was on top of things. Then it occurred to me. *Now I had one!* If Protocel® was close to stopping it, when it did, there would be no more breakouts. Right? Yet another situation where what the devil meant to use to do me in would serve a purpose for my good.

This diagnosis decided to just barge right into my life, doing everything in its power to take over by throwing one wretched pathetic situation at me after another—all designed to get me to cave! It just picked the wrong person to do it to. And that's not arrogance, that's confidence! And not in myself. In something, or I should say, *Someone,* a whole lot bigger than me!

So the jig was up! This was about to come full circle—and I knew it!

It was February 28, 2004. A landmark day! The day I stared cancer square in the face and said:

Note to Self #16 – *"One of us is about to die—and it's NOT going to be ME!"*

Today was Monday, one month after I'd started Protocel®. I was supposed to be feeling good about reaching this thirty-day point, but seeing what I believe was cancer come through my skin was enough to give anybody the "heebie-jeebies." As strong as your faith is (and mine was *strong*), it takes some kinda intestinal fortitude to look at something as vile as this and not *stay* rattled.

But I knew—that I <u>knew</u>—that *"by faith"* I *was healed!*

And as long as I could keep the upper hand *in my spirit,* and keep moving forward, I knew the manifestation would soon show up! More information and answers were out there, the likes of which I knew I needed to make it my business to find!

I remember not being able to get interested in doing much of anything that morning. I just wanted to let go and *let God!* But there were things I needed to be doing in "the natural." (I'd already done everything I knew to do in "the spirit"!) Just sitting around waiting for this thing to die wouldn't cut it. After all, (remember?) God can't steer a parked car! What I wanted more than anything right now was for time to pass and some kind of *proof* that I was doing the right thing. But something kept telling me there was another answer to this critical moment.

Willie was gone, the TV was off and the room was silent. It was just me and my thoughts. Knowing there had to be more I could be doing, but not knowing what, I closed my eyes and started talking to God—and then sat there. In silence.

Rarely have I heard what I felt was God's audible voice, but always when I get quiet and seek conversation with God, He communicates to me in all sorts of different ways. Maybe not right then, but eventually, somewhere throughout the day, I would clearly "hear" His voice come in the way of an idea, or prompting, or a phone call with someone who had something to say that stood out to me. (And today was no different.)

I noticed the *Outsmart Your Cancer E-Booklet* sitting on the coffee table. I picked it up and started leafing through it. (Again, the book was not yet in print.) I flipped to the second section on Women's Hormones (a pre-released copy, at the time, of Chapter 19 of *Outsmart Your Cancer*, by Tanya Harter Pierce that Kerri had also purchased with the Protocel® e-booklet).

I was already familiar with the benefits of progesterone cream from having read the books *What Your Doctor May Not Tell You About Menopause*, by John Lee, MD, and Virginia Hopkins, and *What Your Doctor May Not Tell You About Breast Cancer*, by John Lee, MD, David Zava, PhD, and Virginia Hopkins, and had used progesterone cream and even other plant-based phyto-estrogens through doctoring with my nurse practitioner, Carol, for several years. But since being diagnosed with breast cancer, I had stopped using the cream and was so glad that I had, because not only was my diagnosis Positive Estrogen Driven, it was also Positive *Progesterone* Driven. (Which is another reason why my oncologist should have given me my diagnosis the day I was in his office!) So although I knew how beneficial progesterone cream is with regard to breast cancer prevention and treatment, I wasn't sure if that was true in my case anymore. Maybe someone else would know.

I picked up the phone to call one of my Protocel® friends. After asking the "progesterone question" (to which they said they agreed, at this stage of the game for me it was too early yet to start any of these measures) I brought up the hardcore ultrasound room experience from the day before, the spots that had come through my skin and my decision to increase my doses of Protocel®. Apparently there was a term for this, because she then began talking about "power-dosing." And after explaining what power-dosing was to me, she also suggested, in addition to going up to 1/3 teaspoonful, that I *might* want to think about going to "a dose in the middle of the night."

"A dose in the middle of the night?" That got my attention!

They said that Ed Sopcak, the man who helped countless people successfully use Jim Sheridan's formula for cancer in the late '80s and early '90s, insisted people should never go more than six hours without it, and that included *during the night*. Okay, now we were getting somewhere! This made so much sense.

Something that had always puzzled me was the dosing instructions. Maybe they were fine. But I could never figure out why, if it was so crucial to get the doses on schedule and not miss them during the day, getting them every four hours, it was presumably okay to go eight hours overnight without one (which was what the directions were at the time).

Well, it was time to regroup and attack this situation head on with a little "oomph" and "gusto!" This could be my answer, and it was time to pull out all the stops! We were gonna get a little crazy here with some "power-dosing" and that "dose in the middle of the night" deal. And this time I wouldn't be the one feeling like I was being pushed over the edge. This time *I'd* be the one doing the pushing, because one of the reasons for power-doing is that it causes the cancer to break down faster!

Launching Out Into the Deep

I had been taking my doses at 7 a.m., 11 a.m., 3 p.m., 7 p.m. and 11 p.m. every day. I thought the idea of going up to 1/3 teaspoonful of Protocel® was an excellent plan, but I really liked this idea of going no more than six hours without it. Now those rotten little "traitor" cells (*internal* terrorists is what they amounted to!) were going to start getting a hit of "what for" in the *night,* too!

It made so much sense. W*hat could it hurt to error on the side of caution? If all I'd be doing was inconveniencing myself a little— what's to lose?* Maybe I didn't need to, but after being told I was dealing with "a raging, out-of-control, aggressive cancer," I decided a little "raging, out-of-control aggressiveness" on my part might be exactly what the situation called for!

I talked with Willie about it. He thought it sounded like an excellent plan, too—so it was decided. I would start that night. My ending dose would be midnight and my beginning dose the next day would be at six a.m. The other three doses would all remain the same: 1/3 teaspoonful at 11 a.m., 3 p.m. and 7 p.m.

In less than forty-eight hours of being on 1/3 teaspoonful of Protocel® 23, and not going more than six hours without it, praise God—the breakouts stopped!

The next day, not only were there no more new ones, but by the day after, the two that were there previously had lost their redness. I could tell they were fading. By that evening the newest one to come out was no longer visible, and in the next two days the spot that had been the first to show up was now also completely gone!

I had done it! Protocel® had *visibly* taken the lead and those rotten "cancer boogers" were out of business! A crisis had passed!

Maybe it was the 1/3 teaspoonful; maybe it was going to a dosing schedule that kept a saturation of Protocel® in my bloodstream at all times. Or maybe it was that I was at the thirty-day mark and Protocel® would have shut it down by now anyway.

I don't believe it was the latter. Those breakouts were coming on strong. They looked red, mad, angry and threatening. But, within hours of getting aggressive with Protocel®, you could just *see* the life being sucked right out of them!

Yes-sir-ee! I told myself, *This here's Protocel® Country! And on a quiet night—you can hear bad cells beg for mercy—as they whimper, fall apart, shrivel-up—and die!*

Walking Through Mud

As time wore on, not only was I very tired, I also ached all over. I was experiencing tiny burning electrical pains randomly shooting throughout my body, and in the strangest spots. I'd get one on the top of my hand, on the outside of my wrist, and one really strange place was the outer cartilage of my ear. (Looking back, all significant "warning signs" of a pending severe "healing crisis" that I was oblivious to.) It continued in the days to come and even became more intense.

I not only felt like I was walking through mud, now I was walking through *deep* mud! And I was experiencing neuralgia-type pains on the top right side of my head, near the surface, accompanied by cold flashes.

Willie came home and I explained what was happening. He said he would fix dinner while I went up to bed. (Music to my ears!)

I practically had to pull myself up the stairs using the handrail, but I slept for two hours again—and it felt wonderful.

When I awoke I felt somewhat better; still tired and achy, but better. I went downstairs and ate dinner, but my stomach felt so "unsettled." And to make matters worse, the shooting electrical pain in my head had intensified. I felt like I was coming down with a bad case of the flu. (Except while you're on Protocel®, because of its anti-viral properties—you just don't *get* "the flu.")

I went back to bed, thinking it would subside, but it only got worse. My stomach felt as though it was ready to explode. I had never experienced anything like this in my life! No matter what I did, I couldn't get comfortable. I was dizzier than I ever remember being, and I detest being dizzy because I am prone to motion sickness. So now I was really a mess! I was so dizzy I could hardly walk and all of a sudden I realized—I was about to throw up.

Except, how was I going to get to the bathroom? The room was spinning so violently—I didn't think I could make it.

Kodak Moments

I could have called for Willie but chose not to. I had a feeling this was going to be pretty unpleasant.

I managed to get up off the bed, grabbed the wall, and I hung onto it all the way into the bathroom. And—I just made it! It was like a "fire hose" opened up. I vomited a toilet full of what looked like six-dozen *raw egg whites. A toilet full of slime!* And I mean it looked *exactly* like raw egg whites. This was crazy! I was looking into a toilet bowl full of—*dead cancer pieces and parts!*

I just sat there on the floor by the wall—letting myself recover. This was rough. *Really rough!* I was having cold chills one minute, hot flashes the next; I was dizzy beyond comprehension and yet stunned by indescribable proportions at what had just taken place. Could that mess really be dead *cancer?* But I knew it had to be —because one of the most common things people talk about seeing when they take Protocel® for cancer is "egg-white-like" stuff coming out of their bodies. It can be in the bowel movements, in the urine or even drain out of the nose! It's the basic protein parts of the cancer cells, I'd been told. But I'd never heard of an episode like this!

I wonder if anybody from the FDA, or any of those "We report— you decide" people, are in the neighborhood. I could ask 'em in, let them take a gander at this stuff and let them tell me what they think they're lookin' at. If Protocel® doesn't kill cancer, then what is this "stuff"?

This is dead cancer! Deader than dead. Dead to the 10th power, dead. Deader than a doornail, dead. Just plain dead. This is dead cancer! I think I just made history. Shouldn't somebody be here to document this?

I sat there. For a long time. The floor was cool and the wall felt good, too, cool against my back. I needed to recover more before I tried to move. Still, I couldn't keep from thinking about the significance of what had just occurred. Talk about a "hospital by-pass!" . . . I single-handedly took on cancer with a bottle of brown liquid—climbed the stairs to our bedroom and went to bed—and just flushed away a toiletful of dead cancer parts and pieces.

It's a pure travesty that none of the white coat people are here to see this with their Petri dishes and high-powered microscopes. Wouldn't this resonate right up there with "The shot heard 'round the world" kind of significance?

Well, it did with me! If people could see this with their own eyes—they'd have to believe it. And it would be life-altering! Here *they're* looking for the "answer to cancer"—and *I've* got it? *Right here in my house? Unbelievable!*

So alternative treatments don't work, huh? I thought to myself. *Well, tell that to those billions of shell-shocked, once out-of-control, positioned-to-kill-me, drowning, slimy cancer parts and pieces Protocel® just sent packin'!*

The Spin Cycle

Usually after you have a stomachache and throw up you feel better, and if you were dizzy, the dizziness subsides. *Right?* Well, not this time. And, as the minutes passed, with me expecting it to get better, it didn't. In fact, it started getting worse. The dizziness only escalated. And now I was flat on my back again—with everything spinning *violently!*

They say "Truth is stranger than fiction," and that certainly categorizes it for me. This is like a nail-biting "whodunit." Except there's no mystery to it. "Miss Pamela did it in the comfort of her own home—with *Life in a bottle!*" How hard is that?

The secrets and answers this formula holds could change the face of how cancer is thought of and treated. Because the fear it instills could be drastically weakened—worldwide—if people could have just seen that toilet full of dead cancer!

Another radically off-the-wall moment that had left me in an emotional freefall—yet it gave me hope that it was all a part of a process that could only end in my full triumphant recovery!

I had my cordless on the bed and dialed one of my knowledge-able Protocel® friends, to see what he thought.

He told me that, although vomiting is not a common lysing symptom, when it happens, in most cases the body waits until the food is digested, and only the "egg-white-like substance" is thrown up—the dead cancer cell debris. He said, "If it looked like all egg whites with no food in it, it's definitely lysed cancer cells."

"Well, then, it definitely is—cause that's all there was."

Then he mentioned that a "brain tumor" can act this way, and he wanted to know—was I sure that at the time I was diagnosed with breast cancer it hadn't already spread to my brain? *(Nice—something else to lie here and try not to obsess about!)*

But he then said that, more than likely, rather than the dizziness being due to a brain tumor, I had probably just stayed on 1/3 teaspoonful a little too long, and my system was backed up with lysed dead cell parts and debris. He suggested I drop back down to 1/4 teaspoonful or even 1/8th for a while. So I agreed, but I went to 1/4 teaspoonful doses—I didn't want to lose any ground.

That evening, later that night, and into the next morning, I still vomited egg-white-like substance every three or four hours—although it was less and less every time.

It's a good thing I own my own business—and my time is my own—because I was still so dizzy I couldn't walk, and I had no clue as to how many days this might go on. (I tried not to let myself even *think* about how I'd survive it if this were to continue for *weeks!*)

Just Take Me Out in the Backyard and Shoot Me!

After twenty-four hours the vomiting stopped, but the dizziness didn't. I was miserable. I lay flat on my back, and I just prayed that it would only be a day or two until this subsided, *and please—dear God, not weeks . . . I don't think I could handle it!*

What if this has metastasized to my brain and now I really am also dealing with a brain tumor? Talk about drama! This better just start to all settle down soon, I thought, *or I can forget writing any book. Who'd read it? Nobody's gonna believe all this . . . I'm "living it" and I don't even believe it!* The craziness of the last six weeks was just out of control! It reminded me of being on Mr. Toad's Wild Ride at Disney.

You were in this rickety old Model T and it took you around hairpin curves; there were signs all around warning of danger ahead—to turn around and go back! And you'd come through a door and go crashing through a barn with chickens flying everywhere, and then the last swing you made was through a door where you heard a train engine whistle, with you right in the path of this huge, blinding, rocking light that you just *knew* was mounted on the front of the engine, putting you square in the path of a head-on collision; and as you were just about to collide with it, and you just *knew* you were about to die—all you could do was—*grab the top of your head—close your eyes—and duck! And then!* —*The doors flew open—and you were outside in daylight!*

I felt like I was on Mr. Toad's Wild Ride—and I wanted to get to the part where *I saw daylight!*

Every Time I Wake Up—There I Am Again

The severe dizziness lasted for three days. I spent them upstairs in our master bedroom—in the dark, with the television off, unable to tolerate light *or sound.* I could only listen to soft radio. And I listened to it play softly for hours on end. It kept me calm, and it kept my sanity!

"Cold flashes" and "night sweats" were raging! I would go to sleep freezing, buried under quilts—with little cold, electrical pulsing sensations running up and down my spine, only to wake up ringing wet, especially the décolleté area. I took a lot of showers, went through a lot of nightclothes and bedding, and my hair would feel so (for lack of a better word) "greasy," even though I was constantly taking showers!

Some massive, intensive lysing was going on—over and above what I was throwing up—including bowel movements that were thick, pasty and in such amounts I'd find myself saying repeatedly, *"Where is all this stuff coming from?"*

Fortunately, I still slept *a lot*. Hour by hour I dozed on and off. After two days of it, I started waking up disappointed that I had, thinking I had to be all out of the capacity to sleep anymore—right before I dozed off again.

I had a lot of time to think and pray—*and reflect*. I remember lying there thinking:

Note to Self #17 – I'm spending way too much time with *me*.

You Run the Universe—Don't Mind Me

As I lay there, an old song, "Wasted Days and Wasted Nights," by Freddie Fender, started running through my mind. When I realized I was singing it in my head (for the umpteenth time), I turned the radio back on. I knew I wasn't wasting anything. It just *felt* like it. I thought about all the good things I had going for me.

For starters, you're far better off at home, lying in your own bed, dealing with a little discomfort and dizziness, than being in a hospital room, with "whatever" missing—all bandaged up, tubes coming out of you . . . Okay, well, that about sums it! *I'm good!*

I also listened to Scripture tapes that were overflowing with God's promises of healing and comfort. I talked to God a lot during that time, thanking Him for life and trusting what I was going through would be over very soon.

One thing I loved to do, when I felt like I was going to lose it, because I was so tired of lying flat on my back, would be to picture myself as a little girl, curled up in God's lap.

I'd lie there in the softness of His robe, snug and secure, and I'd see myself resting in His arms, in a deep healing sleep while He ran the entire universe! It was great! What awesome images. I could *feel* healing surging throughout my body when I did it. So I did it a lot! Deliberately envisioning and experiencing surging healing power being drawn out of Him into my body as I lay there.

I'd see myself turning over, and He would tip His head down to glance at me—as any father would whose child was so sick. Those moments shared with God were priceless! I remember asking Him, "How will I know how long this dizziness will last?"

176

I felt something inside me say, "Trust Me. You'll know."

Biding My Time

Kerri called a lot during those days. So did Josh, and so did my friend Barb. After the first intense day of lysing I could sense with each passing hour I was gaining ground and coming back to the land of the living. I soon knew that this was only a temporary situation, and the only thing going on in my brain was an overload of all the lysed dead cancer cells, the result of power dosing—*for too long!* The stuff just couldn't get out of my body fast enough.

I practically had no appetite during that time. The only thing that appealed to me was noodle soup and crackers (not something I would otherwise reach for) and plenty of water—much of which I laced with Willard Water, a "catalyst altered water" product that makes water wetter and could possibly help the body eliminate toxins and waste. (I used the "clear" version. The mineral content in the dark version could contain selenium.) And I managed to never miss one dose of Protocel®. (The day I vomited so intensely I took Protocel® rectally.) I also used a peppermint/ginger herb combination that settled and soothed my stomach—and an herbal bowel-normalizer combination containing senna leaf, licorice root, buckthorn bark, alfalfa leaf and fennel seed, etc. powders that prevented me from becoming constipated, *which you never want to let happen while on Protocel®.* It's important for the body to be able to eliminate and not become backed up. And I also used a yummy sport drink that contained fructose rather than refined sugar to replace electrolytes in the system lost due to vomiting, which also takes that "yuck" flu-like feeling away.

I couldn't go downstairs and fix any of this myself, so I had Willie bring me the cordless. I would call him on the *business line* so it would ring downstairs on the *home line*—sort of my own personal servant's bell. It was awesome! And oh he loved it. *(Just ask him.)* I had him up and down those stairs so many times in those three days he felt like he was *catching himself* on the "turnaround!" It got pretty funny after a while, and he was great about it. I don't know what I'd have done without him.

God's Lap—the Next Best Thing to His Heart

That very morning lying in bed—still dizzy—once again I saw myself in the lap of the Almighty. Only this time I was seeing the vision from *the back* of the throne. And all I could see of myself (as the *little me* curled up in God's lap) was the top of my hair—as my head lay on the billowy arm of His robe. I saw myself changing positions—as if I was getting restless.

Soon I saw myself with one arm hanging out of the side of the throne. Then with my feet sticking up over His shoulder. And this time it was my other arm that was dangling out of the side of the throne. So I was obviously lying on my back—on God's *lap*, with my feet pointed straight up in the air! (And it was getting pretty amusing!)

Then I saw myself peeking out from under the layers of His sleeve. All I could see were my eyes and nose, and my eyes were blinking. I started laughing out loud because, I'm telling you, it was *really* cute. I was *so* enjoying this!

(If you can't find a good movie to watch, you can always spend time with *"The Great I Am"* and create one of your own!)

The next thing I knew, I was up with my arms around His neck giving Him a hug. And then the last vision I saw was *me* walking *toward myself,* quite some distance from the throne. (Which I now couldn't see anymore, because *the vision* of me walking toward me—was blocking me from being able to see it.)

Then the little girl (the little me) turned to look back, and when she did, she stepped to the side. And there in the distance I could see God. *Standing* next to His throne, now turned around—facing me—with His hand held high in the air . . . softly, slowly *waving goodbye to me!* Suddenly, this wasn't cute or funny anymore—and I started to tremble. That couldn't have come from my imagination. I wasn't even thinking in that direction.

God, in all His glory and majesty, had gotten up out of His throne, and, for a moment, He had *turned His back on the entire universe*—just so He could wave goodbye to me, as if He were sad to see me go. I was more than overwhelmed. It was as though time had stopped. And—maybe . . . just maybe—it had.

And in that same instant, there was a "knowing" . . . when I sat up this time, I knew all the dizziness would be gone! And it was! I could feel God winking at me as what He had said to me earlier came back to me: "Trust Me. You'll know!" *It was over!*

Here I thought I'd been playing in an imaginary place, with my Best Friend, to pass the time—when in reality what I was really experiencing all along was a *visitation* from God. *No one will ever convince me otherwise!*

Crazy as it sounds, at that moment, still in the moment—everything I'd been through (and I say this with trepidation) was almost worth the diagnosis to have experienced the encounter.

Back to the Land of the Living

It felt incredible to be normal again. I was so grateful that the dizziness was gone. After three intense days of lysing and whatever else was going on, it took another four or five to feel like myself again. The good news was that I knew for sure Protocel® was kicking butt against this diagnosis! Those rotten little cancer boogers were being slaughtered by the billions!

I also went back through some notes that Elonna McKibben had written up and discovered the reason the man I had been speaking with had suggested I stay on 1/3 teaspoonful for "a week." In her notes on "Power-dosing," it said right there—"You only power-dose for 5 days." (I had done it for 14! Pretty hardcore, huh?) And then you wait at least two weeks before doing it again. *Yikes!* No wonder that stuff was coming out with such force. That was some serious waste my body was being asked to deal with.

It's important to note, however, that taking 1/3 teaspoonful doses is not necessarily power-dosing for all people. Some people can take 1/3 teaspoonful of Protocel®, or even more, as a regular dose over an extended period of time, showing no signs of too-rapid lysing, experiencing little or no discomfort. However, if lysed cells begin to come out too fast, from all directions, the process can be very uncomfortable.

But, on the other hand, if that happens, it's a great feeling to know something in there is *dying*, and it's not you!

(Visit www.thebreaststaysput.com for more detailed information on optimum Protocel® usage.)

Radiation and Chemotherapy and Protocel®

Radiation is known to be compatible with Protocel®. But those who choose to use it may do well to locate a facility that offers cutting-edge "CyberKnife Radiation Technology" known for its pinpoint accuracy of radiating only the exact targeted spot to avoid damage to surrounding tissues or organs – rather than men with prostate cancer risking urinary and/or sexual dysfunction and women with breast cancer risking heart damage.

Chemotherapy, however, can seriously interfere with Protocel®'s action on the cellular level. In a 1992 journal article Jim Sheridan even stated, "Chemotherapy can bring the percentage of success down, because chemotherapy changes the level on the oxidation-reduction ladder where Entelev/Cancell works."

Today, two anti-metabolite chemo drugs that are thought to be compatible with Protocel® are Xeloda and 5FU. Any other type of chemo could possibly interfere with Protocel®, rendering it ineffective at controlling the cancer growth. Even if one particular type of chemo were to work with Protocel® – another type might not. A risk people should not take lightly since chemo is rarely curative by itself.

Some want to use Protocel® to compliment chemo as it will often lessen the side effects of the chemo while not interfering with the chemo. Protocel® used in this manner would be considered CAM ("Complimentary Alternative Medicine") therapy. When used in this role it is my understanding that Protocel® should no longer be considered a cancer treatment.

Tamoxifen, Raloxifene and Protocel®

It is unclear at this point as to the compatibility of these types of hormone-blocking drugs with Protocel®. Breast cancer expert, Dr. John R. Lee, said Tamoxifen puts cancer cells into a sort of "sleep" state, and that may change their metabolism in ways that could make Protocel® less effective. As a rule, throughout the years, whether estrogen receptor positive or not, most Protocel® breast cancer recoveries are known to have been achieved without the use of hormone-blocking drugs.

CHAPTER 15

The 7th Inning Stretch

Going to Bed in February—Waking Up in May

As the coldness of winter made a valiant attempt to give way to the signs of spring, much of March and April still found themselves draped in a shroud of the same icy, windy, snowy conditions. Although I don't remember much of it . . . I slept most of it away.

I had been keeping a very low profile around the Pointe and had even temporarily stopped going to church, because I *thought* others wouldn't be able to help but notice that I wasn't quite myself. And then, for sure, they'd want to know what was wrong. (Never realizing exactly *how* noticeable it really was.)

One day we ventured out so that I could shop for our new soon-to-arrive grandbaby. While walking around in the baby department, I caught a glimpse of a woman that I thought looked like she didn't feel very well. It took a few seconds to register that what I was looking at was a mirror—and the woman in it *was me!*

Well, if I'd had any second thoughts or feelings of guilt about things like not going to church, and laying low around the Pointe, I'm here to tell you, "They evaporated in that reflection!" *I looked rough!* I not only looked tired, but the slow but steady weight gain I was experiencing was becoming evident. I needed to stay out of the pubic eye. Period! I couldn't wait to get out of that store. I was just grateful we'd found all the baby things we wanted before I caught sight of myself—or we'd have left that store before we ever got started! (And, again, chronic exhaustion is not typically one of the signs of lysing. At least not to the degree I experienced. Weight gain is also typically not something people experience from being on Protocel®. I've only heard one other person say they did.)

By mid-April I noticed that the chronic fatigue finally began to let up. But "tired," for me, on the other hand—went on and on. It was time to have another ultrasound taken. I wished that I'd had a CT scan back in February when I had my first ultrasound, but decided to have one now. So just shy of three months after starting on Protocel®, on April 20, 2004, and one week before having my second ultrasound, I had my first CT scan.

[In light of recent media reports regarding the exorbitant amount of radiation in CT scans possibly causing cancer, I would like to take this opportunity to say that had I been aware of this information at the time, I would never have had the first CT scan, let alone a second one a year later. There are other ways of determining how a recovery is progressing without setting yourself up for a diagnosis of cancer in later years because of a diagnostic test. For more information on different types of scans, tumor markers and alternative testing, visit www.thebreaststaysput.com.]

A Welcomed Refreshing Change

With a CT scan, I was told, like an X-ray, they take the image and you go home, because it takes at least a day for them to read it and issue a report. Nice. A scene without much cause for confrontation. I could get into this.

I had gone into the CT scan room with my "soap-box" speech all prepared. But to my amazement, not only was the technician in awe of what I told her had been my choice of treatment, but the radiologist was also there and understood what I was requesting in a density reading, and assured me that getting one was not a problem.

(With the effect that Protocel® has on a tumor, as the tumor begins to deteriorate and fall apart—it is said to "lose density." It can look the same size on scans, or sometimes even appear to be larger, when it is actually not as solid as it started out and is losing density.)

The CT scan didn't take anywhere near as long as the ultrasound did. And as I was leaving the Imaging Department that day, the technician walked me back to the waiting room where Willie was.

"This is so exciting that you've found something like this to recover with!" she said. "I can't tell you how happy I am for you, and if you only knew how encouraging this is. We deal on a daily basis with people who come in for CT scans because they have cancer, and most of the time—in fact, almost all of the time—it is either a very dire or 'no hope' situation. The same people come for scans over a period of months. Then, all of a sudden, we don't see them again . . . and then we realize—they aren't coming anymore. We know what's happened. And it seems like it's always the *nicest* people who get cancer! It's very hard to watch this day in and day out. So when someone like you comes in all excited about 'beating' a bad diagnosis like this with something other than what everyone else uses, I gotta tell you—you've made my day!"

The last thing she did when she dropped me off where Willie was waiting was turn to me, look me in the eye and say, "You just have to make it! And I want to read your book one day!" I assured her I'd be getting back to her.

They told me at the scheduling desk that the report would be ready for pick-up in twenty-four hours—along with films and a CD of the CT scan. Well, I'd be there with "bells on" to get them. I wanted to see what was on those films! I slept well that night.

The CD they provided us with the next day, plain and simple, didn't show us much of anything. At least, *we* couldn't see anything. Even the report seemed vague:

Definite mediastinal adenopathy was not confirmed. Central pulmonary vessels appear normal. There is increased radiopaque density within the right breast laterally. This may be secondary to prior biopsy or parenchymal asymmetry. The liver appears to be homogeneous in its overall CT density. Spleen is not enlarged. Adrenal gland enlargement was not identified. The lungs appear adequately ventilated with no pulmonary infiltrate, pleural effusion, or pneumothorax. I do not see definite pulmonary nodules or clearly defined metastatic disease. IMPRESSION: Increased breast parenchymal density is identified on the right as discussed. There is no CT confirmation of pulmonary nodule or abnormal mediastinal adenopathy.

And the radiologist who read it didn't do a density reading, which I found confusing and very disappointing. But I'd read online and heard from others how unpredictable and inaccurate scans can be, so that's what I attributed it to. It was obvious that ultrasounds were painting a much clearer picture of what was happening. And now that I was about to have a second one, we'd see how it compared to the one I'd had two months earlier.

The Best Defense—a Well Thought Out Offense

On April 27—three months from when I started Protocel®—and one week after my first CT scan, I had my second ultrasound.

On the drive to the hospital that morning, I had that same sick feeling in my stomach again, thinking about what was coming. Some of the most stress-filled moments in my recovery occurred when I had to deal with those in the medical world. (Which is why some opt to wait a few months after beginning a Protocel® program to have follow-up testing—to give Protocel® time to work and things time to improve, and then see what decisions and choices need to be made. But I feel that (like Oprah says) "knowledge is power", and as much as I didn't like going in and chancing that I'd have to deal with the "white coats," I had them taken anyway.)

Just as we arrived at the hospital, my cell phone rang. It was Kerri. "Mom," she said, "I just called to remind you, those people have no way of knowing how this treatment you're using even works, and you need to *tell* them that!" My thoughts exactly! This time I was prepared. This time Willie went in with me. And this time I was even more candid with the technician.

"Before we start today, I want you to know something. I am not doing anything conventional. That's *my* choice! I'm sure you probably remember from my last visit how the doctor, or whoever read my films, came in extremely alarmed, stating that if I didn't have a mastectomy, and *soon,* I was going to die. Well, while I know he meant well, I don't expect him, or you, or anyone else who reads these films today to understand anything about what I'm doing, and I don't want any more confrontations. I know exactly what it is I'm dealing with, I'm well aware of the risks involved—and it's not as if mastectomies, lumpectomies and chemotherapy are risk free either! So I don't want anyone coming in here freaking out on me today, like last time. All I want is the ultrasound and the report."

This time the only thing she had to say was when she finally stood up and said she had to go see if she'd gotten what he needed. Well, this time Willie was there, and I had already drawn a line. I was ready, either way, for what was coming!

She was gone a long time. Long time! Longer than the last time. And when she finally came back, to my surprise, she said, "He needs me to take more images."

Well, the second time around, she'd gotten enough and that took care of that! No one said a peep to me that day, and we were out of there. We could pick up the report in the morning.

PDH—Licensed CBM

After the intense bout of lysing I'd been through, I was expecting this ultrasound to show some *royal* progress had been made! I had been so in hopes that the CT scan would give us more insight as to what was happening. But since that didn't happen, I couldn't wait to get to the hospital to pick up the ultrasound report.

The report wasn't exactly what I had hoped for, but when you take into consideration that I had only been on Protocel® for three months, there were some definite indicators that progress was being made! What was once an "extremely aggressive, rapidly spreading cancer" now seemed to not be going anywhere very fast. In fact, it almost appeared as though it just might be *fizzling out*. The report read:

Ultrasound of the right breast was performed and reveals evidence of a hypoechoic mass in the 10 o'clock position. When compared to a February 27 study, this has increased in size and now measures 2 x 1.6 x 2.3 cm, increased from 1.7 x 1.5 x 1.7. IMPRESSION: Increasing right breast mass consistent with the patient's previously diagnosed invasive Intraductal carcinoma.

Two things were significant here. I'd been on Protocel® three months and was told that tumors usually appear to increase in size for the first few months while on it. And since this was said to be an aggressive, fast-growing cancer three months ago (for something that went nuts with growth within eleven days after the biopsy, it sure didn't appear like there was a "hot fire in the old town tonight" kind-of-a-thing going on *now*. And, even more importantly—what about all those "multiple lesions"? There was no mention of them. I found this report very encouraging and decided I was making progress. And I was right—two months later (five months after starting on Protocel®) my third ultrasound read:

Ultrasound of the right breast was performed and was compared to a prior study of 4/27/04, and once again, reveals a hypoechoic nodule in the 10 o'clock position of the right breast. This appears to have decreased slightly in size, now measuring 1.8 x 1.7 x 1.9 cm, decreased from 2 x 1.6 x 2.3 cm. No additional masses are identified. IMPRESSION: Slight interval decrease in size of nodular mass in the 10 o'clock position of the right breast.

"Decreased from 3/4" x 1" to 2/3" x 3/4"." *Love* that shrinkage! *I knew it was a "poor excuse of its former self"!* I thought as I read how the situation had gone from one of "multiple lesions surrounding the tumor" five months ago to "original tumor slightly *smaller* in size—*no additional masses detected."*

WooooHooooo! How's that for a little "non-invasive, no-sharp-instruments-involved, home-grown, righteous boob overhaul"? This was *over the top!* How awesome was that? In just five months, all those "rotten little tumor wannabes"—all those black spots the doctor had pointed out to be screaming, "aggressively spreading cancer" were now "no longer identifiable!"

But the one thing that bugged me was—where was the mention of the "multiple lesions" that were on the ultrasound films of April

27 and in the written report? If they had been detectible, you *know* he would have made a big production out of it—which can only mean—they weren't! But, regardless, since they *were* mentioned in the *first* report, shouldn't he have commented on them, one way or another?

It makes you wonder whose side these guys are on. He obviously couldn't see them—or he would have <u>stated</u> on the report that he could! So, *why* didn't he report on them, either way? I wondered if perhaps it was because he knew I was using an alternative treatment, because on the work orders the technicians had stated, "Patient is using an alternative treatment" and "Patient isn't doing anything." To wit I thought to myself: *That's what you think!* So was he biased and didn't want to encourage the patient by mentioning they weren't detectable? Can the closed-minded attitudes of those against alternative vs. conventional cancer treatment even spill over into the accuracy of how they report what they read on scans? And, why did he send the technician back to get more images that day? And why did she take so many? Was it because he found it hard to believe that they were nowhere to be found? Or maybe he wasn't so great at writing up reports. Even with what was staring him right in the face—or rather *what wasn't!*

So you can just go right ahead and call me Pamela D. Hoeppner, CBM—*Certified Breast Mechanic*. Licensed by God and powered by the "Big 'P.'" The Formula with the clout. The "clout" it takes—to make cancer "cut and run"!

The only way it could have been any better was if it had said the original tumor was "missing," because the significance of "original tumor is slightly smaller" is this: Protocel® can cause tumors to appear larger at first, while what it is actually happening is the tumor is losing density and falling apart. Which it seems is exactly what was happening in my case. To read that this tumor was actually smaller, and all the others were now MIA, was outstanding! Glory to God!—*I was in a full-blown recovery!*

Willie was thrilled, the kids were ecstatic and we were all *so very relieved!* Not only were there no "new ones," indicating it was no longer spreading, but the additional tumors they said my breast was "full of"—were now undetectable! Not even *smaller*—but outright *undetectable!* Out of the picture—*as in outright gone!*

In hindsight, I should have paid more attention to what that CT scan report *wasn't* saying. But with the ultrasound reports giving measurements of the original small tumor—which now was said to be shrinking!—It's no wonder I gave more credence to the ultrasound reports. *They* always had *something* to say!

Instant Replay—in Fast Forward

Right after my first CT scan and second ultrasound, and six weeks to the day from my dance with dizziness—another "same-time same-station" scenario occurred where I, as my kids would say, "hurled up" more lysed matter.

It's just so weird that this stuff seems to "build" and then all of a sudden I have a bout of vomiting. According to everyone else, vomiting is not that common. So, then—why me? Well, who needs "dead benign proteinous material" backed up in their system! What a relief to know that it's still dying in there—and at such a rate that, at times, my body can't get it out fast enough! Progress!

Progress? Now there's a thought. Making progress, while I'm at a complete standstill—feeling like the only direction I'm going at times is backwards? I'm still tired; I'm gaining weight; the lump is still there—it's a poor excuse of its former self, but it's still there. It's squishier; it feels more like a "hardboiled" egg rather than an egg in a shell. Some days it feels bigger, and then some days it is definitely smaller. But, hey—who am I to complain? Those multiple, multiplying lesions are history and the "original" culprit is on its way out. So "progress" it is! And that's my story—and I'm stickin'!

Elonna McKibben had a dog whose tumor did that when she gave her Protocel®. "Fair Dinkham" was her name and they called her "Dink" for short. The tumor could be seen on the outside of her body: they were able to witness it as it would shrink in size, and then it would get bigger. Then it would shrink again. And every time it got smaller, *it got smaller than it was the time before.* (Maybe that's what mine is doing. Right? I'm sure of it!) Incidentally, Dink made it on Protocel®. She lived to be over 14. They ended up having to put to her to sleep, and hated to because being on Protocel® had made her like a younger dog on the inside—but her bones on the outside could no longer support her and she was having too much difficulty getting up and walking once she got up. (You can also read about Elonna's horse, Ladd, too, and his recovery from melanoma in *Outsmart Your Cancer*, by Tanya Harter Pierce.)

I have to tell you: In my five months of being on Protocel®, I kept thinking about one particular conversation I'd had with my friend when he made the remark about how sometimes tumors can "encapsulate," as the body sometimes "walls it off." Or they can also deteriorate from the inside out as they lyse away. An encapsulated tumor can even work its way to the surface—coming out through the skin. He said there is a product you can put on the skin to assist the body in that situation, making it much easier.

(I was sitting there thinking, *Sir, if that thing in my breast ever starts to surface, trying to come out through the skin? I'll be headed for the surgeon's office, scalpel in hand myself—begging the guy to use it!*)

The Things in Life That Go Right Over Your Head

I would in time look back on all of these developments. And the one statement, in particular, that my friend had made was: "You know, Pam, there may not even be any live cancer cell activity in it anymore. Sometimes the cancer can be dead as early as four or five months after being on Protocel®—and sometimes even three." (According to my notes, it was May—I'd been on Protocel® just a little over three months when he said it.)

I had even read a story online at a Protocel® support website of a girl who had been diagnosed with cancer, with a large tumor on her cervix. After being on Protocel® three months she reported that the tumor was gone. That was astounding! The CT scan showed nothing where there had once been a significant size tumor.

Well, wouldn't that have just been *"the berries"*? Reminding myself that the day the Lord was passing out "speedy recoveries" I must have been talking—so I didn't raise my hand to get one!

What a blessing it would have been if it had happened in *my* situation, though. Couldn't you just read the headlines? "Out of control cancer diagnosis shut down in three months!" What a spectacular read that would have been! Maybe I should have given more thought to that "thought." (Me—the one who had been building myself up in my most holy faith, riding so high and trusting God and this "gift" called Protocel® for a quick, full and complete recovery.) But I was resigned to the fact that this lump was large and it was taking its time going away. So I was content to *not* think outside the box. Protocel® was taking it down, little by little, one day at a time. I was just satisfied and grateful the thing was going away.

What a shock I was in for! My *"epiphany,"* however, would be more than a *year* in coming.

(**Epiphany:** A comprehension or perception of reality by means of sudden intuitive realization.)

Looking back now, I never really asked God what was going on with my recovery! I assumed I knew. I should have known better. (And that "assume" stuff? You know what they say about "assuming" anything. It makes a *"behiny"* out of *u* and *me!*)

In October 2007, Dr. Isadore Rosenfeld was addressing breast cancer issues on Fox News, and—I start taking notes! "Seventy-five percent of the time," he stated, "mastectomies are not necessary. There are extenuating circumstances of course, but on the whole, it's a practice that's largely been abandoned." (Because it's barbaric, maybe?) It may be that there is a new way of thinking going on, but I don't see where the practice of performing mastectomies is being "largely abandoned" in favor of lumpectomies and other procedures. And when you read what *Life Extension* magazine has to say about it in an article in their November 2007 issue, it's not only still happening, it's happening in assembly line fashion.

(Visit www.lef.org for the article, "How Much Abuse Should Cancer Patients Have to Take?")

CHAPTER 16

The Summer of 2004

I Think I'll Just Stay in the Boat

Summer of 2004 rolled in right on schedule. And, as the season unfolded, it would prove to be, for many reasons, a very different summer. And, I know you're getting tired of hearing it, but, I, of course, was tired.

I was apprehensive about summer coming, since foremost on my mind was how I would get out of being around people. Because as far as summers in Northern Michigan go, you wait all year for them, and if the weather's great, no one stays inside.

There would be rendezvous at our favorite beaches and swimming holes, barbeques, campfires and the daily walks around the Pointe—where everyone would be expecting to see Pam. I couldn't see any way I could possibly avoid the inevitable. But I knew I had to find one. And, since, in the natural, I couldn't seem to invent any great plan I could put in place, I decided I'd just have to trust God to figure things out for me on a day-to-day basis, which is the way we're supposed to live anyway. But how He was going to pull this one off was beyond me! (Is that "Oh Ye of Little Faith" music I'm hearing in the background?)

I wasn't ready to tell people about myself, and it had been months since anyone had seen me, so I knew if they did, the first thing I would hear was, "You look so tired, Pam! *What* is wrong?"

But on the other hand, we had Glenn and Kathy driving up to spend weekends with us to look forward to—and I could finally tell them about me. So *that* was a good thing! And by this time Kerri was *very* pregnant—but they, too, would be up as often as they could. And this time, when Josh would come home, he'd be bringing Randi, which would be so much fun. Summer at the lake is the best! And this year proved to be no different.

We cruised the rivers with all those "friendly waving people," playing lazy, hazy, crazy days of summer songs right along with the best of them. And with the mesmerizing cry of the loon, the eagles soaring overhead, fish jumping and sun-tanned skiers and people tubing behind gorgeous boats—*it was awesome!* I was so happy to be there (actually, I was just—well . . . you know) in the midst of all the fun. *Enjoying life!* It truly was great to be alive!

Although still tired a lot, I felt much more like myself and had finally been able to tell Sally. And although she too was shocked that I could wind up with a diagnosis like this, considering how we had lost Mom, she was really glad to hear that I was on Protocel®. And for her, knowing how she also knew all about the phenomenal results the grandchild of our mutual family friends had experienced, it went without saying why I had chosen to use it.

And when Glenn and Kathy came up one weekend, I was finally able to tell them also, and both of them were glad I had found something to use other than conventional treatment. Kathy shared with me that after seeing what friends of hers went through watching family members use chemotherapy and other conventional methods, and the suffering that accompanied it, only to see them die anyway—she was just glad that I had found something like Protocel®. I assured them I knew I would recover and explained why we hadn't told them sooner. And they completely understood. They were just glad I was doing so well.

It was a cool summer that year, but the bonus to the coolness was, coincidentally (or not), our friends and neighbors weren't out and about as much. Everyone seemed to have other things going on in their lives this particular summer—which for me was great. No one would be missing "the Pamster"! God knew how much I wanted this secret kept, and this had "supernatural intervention" written all over it. I could feel God winking at me on another one!

A Promise to a Promise

One Sunday morning, the first weekend in June, I felt good enough, and thought I looked well enough, to go to church. It was wonderful to be back in the house of the Lord, among my friends. And since we do live in a resort area with people coming and going (gone for sometimes weeks and months at a time), no one really questioned where I had been for the last several months. (I *love* that about our church—everyone is just so glad to see you when you *do* get to come!)

Pastor Dave was giving the sermon this particular Sunday, and as much as I was into the sermon, I found myself thinking of the baby. Being preoccupied with thoughts of the baby was nothing new—I thought about the baby constantly. But this was my *first* Sunday back, and I wanted to hear the message! So I tried to jerk what I thought was the *slack* out of myself, telling myself, "You can think about the baby later—*listen* to the sermon."

But the thoughts not only kept coming—they intensified and were also *coming together.* I soon realized this was some incredibly *remarkable* stuff; there were such beautiful thoughts and expressions, personal things I'd want to say to the baby! And—so outstanding in nature, in fact, that it didn't take long to figure out—they weren't all necessarily coming from me. This was coming from *deep* down in my spirit, as in "God's whispers to my heart." And it had all the makings of a poem.

(Deciding I'd "decide" later if it was *legal* to be doing this in church)—these were words I had to get on paper before I lost them. Still fully aware it was the pastor's words I should be focused on, but now determined to get on paper what was coming to me, I started scrambling for anything I could find to write on. All I could come up with was the church program and a deposit slip that I tried desperately to tear *quietly* out of my checkbook.

Frantically scribbling on every inch of blank space I could find, I managed to get the words all down. And I was soon back into the sermon. (Okay—*somewhat.*) So precious were the words, I couldn't wait to put them together to see where they were going! All I knew was that while Pastor Dave was up there talking about heaven—*I had just heard from it!*

(And, incidentally, that was the first and last time that ever happened in church. But! Looking back now—with the way this "one-of-a-kind" turned out, hearing from heaven in that setting makes the memory of it just that much sweeter!)

Upon arriving home, as soon as I could get squared away I took my journal and those *scribbles* and headed for the lake . . . under the cool shade of our big cedar. A perfect setting on a summer day for getting creative.

I spent a lot of time out by the lake journaling and sketching for the baby's nursery. But what I wrote that day was nothing short of a gift. God was saying, "This is for you, for the baby and for your family. A promise of what's in your heart. A promise for the future. One with *you* in it!" And in a few hours a poem had come together. And this is how it read:

Grammy's Promise

A tiny pea in a pod
Is gently maturing,
In my own firstborn's tummy
A little "angel" is stirring.

Will your name be Connor?
Or will we call you Ellie?
It's a secret tucked safe
Inside your Mommy's belly.

One thing's for certain,
There'll be no greater joy
Than Mommy & Daddy's first glimpse
Of their precious baby girl or maybe boy.

No parents could love a baby
More than yours already love you.
When you take your first breath,
You'll take theirs away, too.

You'll call me Grammy,
And just so you know,
I promise to be here for you
Through the years, as you grow!

Wait 'til you meet PopPop,
He's a trip and a half!
He'll give you horsy-back rides
And make you giggle and laugh!

A Grandma has a special role
And very soon you'll see
Exactly what that will mean to you,
And just how much it means to me!

We'll make yummy frosted cookies
And angels in the snow—
And when we bake cupcakes to send to Uncle Josh
I'll let you lick the bowl!

We'll paint watercolor pictures
Mommy will hang proudly on her fridge . . .
And I'll tell you about Jesus,
And all He does, and all He is.

You'll notice the world's a little crazy—
Some things just are not right.
But it hasn't stopped the birdies from their singing,
And the stars still twinkle and wink at the night.

It's in this time of such uncertainty
Where so many things have gone so wrong
We know you're God's Covenant Promise of
Just how much He wants life to go on.

So rest assured Sweet Little Bumpkin
As your arrival day draws near—
At the moment you make your grand entrance
It will be as though you've always been right here!

All my love,
Grammy Pammy

Under the Umbrella of Friendship

Later that afternoon, Berneda (who had noticed I was out sitting under the umbrella on our deck) decided to walk over. I was so glad to see her, and as we talked, I'd forgotten that my manuscript lay off to my side on our patio table where I'd laid it when, as a change of pace, I had gotten out my pastels to work on a sketch for the nursery. I'd completely forgotten that the manuscript lay there—right out in the open. The next thing I knew, Berneda picked up the title page, glanced at me—and then back at the manuscript, and quietly said, "Does this mean what I think it does?" (I know my heart skipped a beat.)

"Yes," I said. "In late January I was diagnosed with breast cancer." Berneda sat down. I talked. And she listened.

She told me she admired what I was doing and didn't know how I could "rattle all that stuff off" when it came to nutrition and health conditions. And she told me that she and Noel had often spoken of how amazed they were at the gift I had for it. So she wasn't at all surprised I'd found and chosen something other than chemo or surgery.

I was able to tell her about the various recoveries I knew of, and about Jim Sheridan being the inventor—how it was practically in my backyard where he developed the formula. She was genuinely impressed and happy for me. And hopeful I'd truly found an answer in a treatment that sounded so promising.

196

I read her the poem I'd written for the baby, and we both welled up with tears. She's such a dear friend. I *knew* I could expect her to be totally supportive, and she was. She clearly saw the sensitivity of the issue and assured me she would tell no one. She also encouraged me to think about keeping my recovery to myself for a while longer—feeling, as I did, that it would serve no purpose for others to know—at least, not yet.

We've been so blessed to have such precious people for neighbors all these years. It was a relief to know someone else now knew, and I knew Noel would understand, too. They were a part of that special group of friends I wished I could have told all along. Now Valerie would no longer be the first, but it was okay because she'd certainly be the *next*—her and Annette *both!*

Summer seemed to fly by. You could already sense that fall was in the air. And, this year for a change, for me anyway, it was a relief to see it go. Come Labor Day, the mile-long loop around the Pointe would roll up. The foot traffic and golf carts full of friends would be gone. All the boats would be tucked safely away in storage, and the docks and boat hoists would be up on land out of the way of piled-up ice caused by the relentless winds of winter. The majority of the cabins and cottages would be empty, and all the kids would be back in school. And I'd have another winter to settle in by the warmth of the fireplace—to hunker down and recover. I was glad Berneda had encouraged me to "stay in the boat" a little longer, and I knew as soon as she told me to lay low yet, it was good advice. I could *jump in* and "test the waters" next summer. But for one more winter I could still recover in silence and solitude. How God ever got me through the summer of '04 without me being found out by anyone other than Berneda was just one more miraculous way I saw God's hand in my life during the course of my recovery. And I knew by the time summer rolled around next year—I'd be just fine!

February—March—April—Maybe Not

When fall arrived, I'd been on Protocel® eight months. *So much for that "three months to cancer free" idea Josh and I had rallied around in the beginning.* I had started on Protocel® 23 on January 28, 2004, and was looking for the beginning of May, the three-month mark, to bring with it evidence of some significant progress. But, as I felt the mass in my breast, although it had diminished significantly in size—it was still far from gone.

Glad I didn't know then what I know now, and *sometimes it really is better when you don't know some of these things are coming*—were two thoughts I contemplated a lot during the months since the three-month mark had come and gone.

"You always expect to do things that are over-the-top, anyway," I told myself. "Others say they don't want to get their hopes up, while you *live* with yours there!" And I do.

> "You don't get what you want. You don't get
> what you need. You get what you expect."
> Mike Murdock

Even something as devastating as a diagnosis of breast cancer could never discourage me from living this way. And, since I believe we *do* get what we "expect," my *"expecter"* is always just as far out there as I can get it. It's a much more exciting way to live. Living in the Word is "living life in style!" and it's second nature to me now. I *like* living by design!

But how do you deal with the things you *didn't* expect—the things for which there is no rhyme or reason? Like losing Mom—and so young? It's not like we are exempt from devastation, no matter how much we believe and pray—because we live in a flawed world. And I guess sometimes there are those "secret things" that God says belong to Him.

One such thing I could not understand was when the teenager from whom I learned about Protocel®—did not make it. It came as such a heartbreaking, unbelievable shock! Because, not only was it his story that was instrumental in my having an answer to turn to when I needed one, but it was the dramatic turnaround in the child's first months on Protocel® that made it clear to me how powerful this formula could be, and part of the reason why I had so much confidence going into it that it might work for me for a full recovery. So, because of all this, it was unfathomable that I was going to get to live—and the child wasn't.

But I had heard that an infection set in, and with such a compromised immune system from all the years of chemotherapy the body had nothing with which to fight back. I had also heard there were things done, medically, during the normal course of the conventional treatment used for leukemia that made the situation worse. When this child didn't make it, I was devastated. I couldn't understand how something like this could happen, especially in light of what had been, in the beginning, such a dramatically miraculous turnaround! Talk about something not being fair! But I had to turn it over to God and move forward. The only way I knew to come to terms with the loss was to see it as even more of a reason to recover. The world needed to know about Protocel®!

So, in my case, even when the five-month mark came and went, I at least knew from the third ultrasound report that the tumor had actually shrunk! It was so clear that Protocel® was doing what it was supposed to do, and it was only a matter of time before this thing became history! Now the only unknown I was dealing with was this significant sized "something-or-other"—thanks to the biopsy! (I *knew* those things could be trouble!)

There came a point when I wasn't that focused on *what* the reports said anymore. I knew it was only a matter of time for the rest of it to go away completely. And for me it was enough—just knowing I'd get to live. Because there for a while anyway—when I looked at it in *the natural* (which wasn't often) with all the "close encounters of the weirdest kind" I experienced—a full recovery did, at times, look questionable! With the new baby coming, if I had to stay on Protocel® forever, I'd just do it. The baby shower was coming soon, and we decided to start telling some of the relatives about me now that we were certain I was going to be okay. And even at this point, eight months into it, we still didn't know *how* okay!

The Newness of Life

One month later, our little granddaughter, Ella, was born. A beautiful healthy little baby girl! Is this where I get to say "I told you so"? (I just threw the name Connor in the poem to humor them.)

What a day it was! We were busy in Kerri and Shawn's kitchen preparing a variety of entrées and desserts for them for the coming week when they called to tell us they had a little girl! (Isn't that just the coolest experience? It's not like you don't know it's going to be one or the other, right? But when they said "little girl" it was like we were hearing the words for the very first time in life. Because we were! Because of the *new* life to whom those words pertained—they just took on a completely new ultra-incredible meaning.)

Then I heard on the line, "Yup—little Ella Marjune!"

"What?" I said!

"You didn't know? I thought we told you. She's going to be Ella Marjune."

I had no idea. "Marjune"—I had never heard of anyone else having my mom's name, except for Ella's mommy, of course, Kerri Marjune.

In all her life, my mom never had heard of anyone having her name either—and now there were three of them—right in a row! What a touching surprise. Mom would have loved it. She and Daddy would have both been so proud!

What a sweetheart "Baby Ella" was! And holding her was the one event I had most purposed in my heart to live for—but not the *only* one. There will even come the day when I will get to hold *Ella's* first baby, too! And all the other babies yet to be born into our family in between. Because, although I said it was this moment that I lived for, *I never once limited my future to it.*

Because of a few complications, Kerri had to stay off her feet for three weeks. So I stayed with them, in their downstairs living area, where I could be near in order to help. What a gift it was to be with this little "doll-baby" so much, but some of the most precious memories I'll ever have were the special times—when Grammy got to hold her in the night. Breathing in that new little life was amazing! Sometimes she didn't sleep at night, so I held her on my chest keeping her quiet, so Shawn and Kerri could. Sometimes I held her when I didn't have to hold her. *For hours.* Just so I could watch her sleep. Doing what I'd been told I wouldn't be *around* to do. My heart singing *"If they could see me now . . ."*

I knew I needed sleep, and I knew it wasn't good to stay awake until two and three in the morning. But, after all, there *are* those "color outside the lines moments" in life—and this was one of 'em!

Irreplaceable moments. Moments I knew I could never get back. So I also saw to it they were moments no one could ever take away. Besides, enough healing hormones were being produced by just holding this baby to compensate for what few were lost due to a little lost shut-eye.

What an amazing gift: the "Gift of Life"—for *both* of us! She was, without a doubt, the most beautiful baby in the world!

Shrinkage—*Sa-weeet!*

Now about ten months into my recovery, I knew this diagnosis was going nowhere. It was just going nowhere pretty slowly. But then—even slowly was a gift . . . considering.

I'd been having ultrasound scans done regularly. The last two reports said pretty much the same thing: "Distal acoustic shadowing," showing signs of spreading out toward the right underarm (my words).

Oh, it was "shadowing" all right, but, contrary to what *they* thought they were seeing, those "shadows" were cast by dead cells—*with marching orders!*

The original tumor was now squishy, soft and flattened. The puzzling thing was that the egg-shaped mass that had sprung up after the biopsy was still there. Albeit softer and a bit smaller—but the thing was still there.

In the beginning, before the original smaller tumor started to get softer and squishier, I had thought that the lump and the mass (that had exploded with growth from the biopsy) *were one and the same.* I discovered later that I was wrong: The flatter and more insignificant the *original* tumor became, the *clearer* it became that there were actually *two* of them! And, as time went on, the more neither of them felt anything alike.

The size of the egg-shaped one was at least 2" x 3." And the ultrasounds never did pick it up. Even with the first ultrasound, and every ultrasound thereafter, the "stuff" (mass) that I could actually wrap my fingers around did not show up at all.

With the first ultrasound, "multiple lesions" did. But I wasn't feeling "multiple lesions." What I was feeling was an "organized mass." A mass that, in the beginning, felt like a very hard tumor, and as it became softer I became more convinced that, rather than cancer, it was some type of fluid-like area. And, as the radiologist tried to interpret each additional ultrasound, it actually started to become quite amusing to read their reports—which were now finally saying it had gotten smaller. (And, again, remember, the "it" here was *the original grape-size tumor* (*not* the 2" x 3" "organized mass") they were referring to.) But eventually this sweeping "distal acoustic shadowing" they were seeing was *all* they were seeing. "Something" was headed out through the lymph system under my right arm. They said "Cancer." I said *"Pfffft!"*

Seeing the Light of Day

But it had become even more humorous when I went for ultrasounds right around my seventh-month mark for being on Protocel®–which was my third ultrasound.

The technician took the images and was gone, as usual—*forever*. When she came back she said she needed to get more images. (*I'll bet you do*, I thought.) (Remember—she's trying to "find" a tumor 2/3" x 3/4" in size, and I'm lying there knowing there is an even more significant 2" x 3" area they weren't even detecting.)

As she pulled her stool up to the ultrasound machine, to get situated to take more, she held the films up to a ceiling light with one eye closed so she could see better and said under her breath, "How do they expect us to get images of something we can't even see?" I was able to suppress a laugh (but not a Cheshire grin!).

Just like with the second ultrasound when the technician was gone for so long, once again, and then came back saying the radiologist wanted more images—this radiologist probably couldn't believe it had not only shrunk but that all those "multiple lesions" were gone. It had to be frustrating him to no end.

Locating any "defined edges" on the original tumor had become impossible anymore, and I think they were blaming the technician for not getting accurate enough shots—when she was *exasperated* trying to even *find* what they were talking about, let alone get any images of it! I was convinced this was what had to be happening—*and it was great!* I could just "hear" this guy's thoughts as he read and compared what he was seeing to the prior reports: *Something is definitely "spreading out" and going "somewhere." But this makes no sense. I can't even see the edges of the tumor itself anymore. Oh, what the heck! It's just all cancer now!*

But they weren't kidding me. For something that they said had been "aggressive" in the beginning and then continued to insist was "spreading" *for a year*, you know they had to be scratching their heads thinking, *But where is it going?* No other lymph nodes ever became involved—and now, incredibly, I could actually see daylight through the mass that had once been solid black, as I hung the films in the sunlight on our front windows.

So what was once solid black in each ultrasound shot was now charcoal-gray in color—and see-through. You'd think this would all be something they would question. But all they said on the ultrasound reports was (and I translate)—first there was an obvious tumor with several additional smaller lesions (tumors); then two months later the "tumor" got just a tad "bigger"—but the smaller lesions weren't mentioned; but then, on the third ultrasound, two months later, in addition to them finally acknowledging the fact that "no further masses were detected," it got just a tad "smaller"! And *that* was what I was waiting for!

How could something that had gotten "bigger" in just sixty days—and now was smaller than it was *five months earlier—be spreading?*

Especially when the "multiple lesions" were gone? Does cancer do all of the above, if it's spreading? Why would "multiple lesions" disappear practically overnight—*unless they were dying?*

So then—when all this "distal acoustic shadowing" began to show up on the ultrasounds they decided it was:

"Distal acoustic shadowing indicative of malignancy with progressive infiltration of the tumor into the adjacent tissues suspected. This finding should be correlated with conventional mammography."

Yeah, right! I don't think so. Not on my watch! And it shouldn't have been on *their* watch either—if they had just looked at *all* the facts and what I was trying to tell them. And, I should note, even if they didn't pick up on the "egg-shaped (presumably) fluid-filled mass" they still should have noted the significance of the multiple lesions disappearing along with the 2/3" x 3/4" tumor decreasing in size. But they didn't.

And, looking back, the ultrasound report that *claimed* it got even bigger within all the "distal acoustic shadowing" was done in August of 2005 — two years ago at this writing, and eighteen months *after* that radiologist burst through the door telling me I was going to die — *and very soon!* So not only has this "distal acoustic shadowing" strangely been going on for two years now, but what happened to the original "aggressive-raging" part of it that they said was occurring in February of 2004? — *if Protocel® doesn't "kill" anything?*

Then, as time went on, the original "grape-sized mass" became less and less detectible to the touch, and I knew it was going away — even if they couldn't "find it" anymore — for all the "distal acoustic shadowing" that was getting in the way of them seeing what no longer existed in its original state! — because *it had become* the "distal acoustic shadowing"! They just didn't know it — or perhaps they didn't want to see it. Once again proving — it was just another case of them looking at something with tunnel vision through their conventional cancer treatment colored glasses!

(And to prove the existence of this "mass" I made an appointment with a woman physician solely to ask her to please take a measurement of it. I explained what I was dealing with and how it was not showing up on any scans. Amazed at this mass, and even more amazed that it didn't show up on an ultrasound or a CT scan, she recorded the measurement as 3" x 4." Thankfully, she "got" the concept of Protocel®, and it wasn't a "stretch" for her to believe it could be working this effectively for me.

So I now have the initial measurement the surgeon took of the tumor, including the circumference of the area where it had made inroads that was the size of a "small tangerine," which all clearly shows up on the mammogram; the original measurement taken by the oncologist of the "egg-shaped" mass; and now a measurement of it being a larger 3" x 4," but much softer and fluid-filled feeling, rather than solid. And I can no longer find the original tumor

I discovered while showering on Christmas Day of '03 that started this whole saga!

So it had definitely fluctuated in size during these times. Sometimes it felt swollen and fluid filled, and sometimes it felt smaller. At times it felt *much* smaller. Not only was this fluctuation in size typical, it also seemed to be a "cyclical" thing.

I've heard it said that the body eliminates the lysed waste in cycles. And although the cycles themselves seem to be the "common thread" among Protocel® users, the cycles, intensity and the duration of them tend to differ with each person.

But as the months continued to drag on—even knowing this thing was deteriorated and fading fast—*I was so ready for this to be over!*

The Amazing Patience of God

Doesn't it just amaze you how God operates? You know full well, if you or I were running the universe, with the same limitless power He has, we'd be zapping this and zinging that and have things wrapped up in short order! *But not God.* He has amazing self-control. You know He wants to! Think about it. He *has* to have a *gazillion* things pending in just this world alone! Wouldn't you think He'd want to get a few of them off His plate? Clear out His "IN" basket maybe, and shorten that "To-Do List"?

Even during those times when He does show up with the provisions, like He did for me in the beginning *(every time I turned around there was a solution or an answer)*, He still has that way about Him where it appears like He is totally ignoring you.

You're thinking, *Okay, we are going to wrap this up in short order!*—but it's like He never even noticed you were poised for the grand finale. He goes right on about His schedule—leaving you hanging there in mid-air—ready to land the whole thing and "stick it" so you can take your bow, while He's still waiting for things to line up. All in good time. All in good time! (It has to be because He knows the end from the beginning—and we don't. We only see in part—while He sees the whole picture!) And, I guess if we had everything we wanted, when we wanted it, and we knew everything that was happening at all times, it wouldn't take faith to believe or trust God for anything. It has to be why He invented "walking by faith." *He* knew what was coming!

We're supposed to look in His Word for the promises and the conditions that activate them, and live like we already have them (because, by faith—we already *do!*) by lifting them off the pages of His Word and claiming them for our very own—while we wait for the manifestation to show up. It's that simple. It really is *that* simple! So why does it seem so hard a lot of times? Well—the secret is—the longer you do it, *it's not.*

But, still, haven't you had that sensation go through you when you are in dire straits, and here comes God?—All the answers you need show up, and you just know you're on a roll! Then you start looking around, like—*Where is it?* And then you begin to feel as though you should be holding your breath as you begin *reaching* and *stretching* (as if *that's* going to help get you to the end of the thing!) for the finish line, if you will—because you've been on a roll in times past when you thought you had it; you thought you were there and then something showed up to bring everything to a halt—a *screeching* halt! And you don't want that to happen this time!—You just don't want it to happen *again!* Please—not this time! And there it is again. *Hurry up and wait!*

Couldn't we just please go through *one* episode in life that's a one-act play! I have a need—You show up with the answer. *Bam!*—miracle manifested—mission accomplished! I kick back, put my feet up, have a cold glass of iced green tea and bask in the winner's circle—giving You all the glory. (You *know* I will!) Now wouldn't you think He'd recognize that as the *ideal* plan? (Maybe it's just me.)

THEN CAME THE MORNING

CHAPTER 17

What a Difference a Day Makes

Second Opinion Power

Throughout the course of my recovery, I kept one eye on myself and one on Willie. And, even though it appeared that we were on top of the situation, by the end of summer 2005 it was becoming evident—Willie wasn't doing so well. He seemed confused at times, he was gaining weight, he couldn't remember simple things and, worst of all, he was withdrawing. As I talked to him about it, I found out the situation was even worse than I had thought—Willie was becoming very depressed. And, as I searched the Internet, I found a website with a thread where people who were on some of the same heart meds Willie's cardiac doctor *insisted* he be on (which were not even keeping his blood pressure regulated, and, if anything, they seemed to be making it worse) posted that they had the very same symptoms: unexplained weight gain, foggy thinking, depression and memory loss—just to name a few. Several commented how relieved they were to hear that others were experiencing the same thing, because now they knew they weren't crazy! As they reported, their doctors all insisted "There are no side effects to these drugs." In other words, "It's all in your head!"

I'd seen enough! I made an appointment with the cardiac doctor who had started Willie on the meds in the hospital—and not that you would be shocked to hear this, but I came close to getting into it with the guy.

He walked in the room and never said a word. He just sat looking at Willie's chart. Finally, I asked him who he was. (So how was I supposed to know he was Willie's cardiac doctor? Willie had only met him once in the hospital, without me being there, and after that we always saw a nurse practitioner.) He knew who I was though—I had explained to his assistant why we were coming when I called to schedule.

So he had just walked in the room and never felt the need to say "Hello" let alone tell me who he was. So obviously he wasn't happy with me, and he decided to send a very strong deliberate message— that he was ticked! (Actually, *livid* would be more like it!)—as he looked up at me over his glasses and finally told me who he was. (And, of course, we all *know* how much effect that tactic was gonna have on me, right?) So now that I knew who he was—I went right on to explaining why we were there.

And that's when he looked up across the desk at me, this time with *daggers*—and said, "This is *death* we are talking about here!" (A bit testy there, don't you think?)

"Well, *life* is what I came in here to talk about!"—the one my husband's *not living!*—is what I wanted to say! But Willie's BP was already something like 197/104 (which I knew the doctor was shocked over since he had Willie on *three* meds—and it had only made him worse! 'Course I don't think he knew that Willie tends to have "white coat" blood pressure—just walking into a doctor's office causes it to elevate) and so I figured if I *really* got into it with this guy, Willie being the non-confrontational type person that he is, it might send him right over the edge. So I held my peace. (There's power in doing that, you know.)

The doctor then pulled him off one of the meds—cold turkey! Which you are never supposed to do. You are supposed to "gradually" come off *any* blood pressure medication! And, needless to say, we've never been back! We found and took another path that offered better options—and yielded much better results!

In calling several well-established local health and wellness businesses in the area, I kept hearing the name of one particular woman, a naturopath with some sort of "bio-feedback" machine who some said had a remarkable, even uncanny, ability to pinpoint issues doctors had not only misdiagnosed, but in most cases completely overlooked. One even said, "Now that I think about it, no one has had anything to say about her but *good!*"

Well—it was time to give this naturopath's office a call. And Dr. "Bird," as her patients fondly refer to her, as it turns out, was just forty minutes away. And the machine she used in her office was called a "Quantum Xxriod Conciousness Interface."

Dr. Bird was extremely knowledgeable in holistic medicine, and from the very first session with her not only was the machine giving accurate feedback regarding Willie, but it was clear that she was knowledgeable and very highly skilled in her field. Wellness and prevention avenues were her approach—and she was extremely dedicated. By our follow-up visit, thank goodness, Willie was doing so much better!

After getting to the bottom of many issues for Willie and moving him toward becoming medication-free, I decided I would make an appointment and share my diagnosis, situation and beliefs regarding conventional medicine with this doctor by having a reading done on the QXCI machine—and tell her about Protocel®.

(You will also find online the pros and cons of QXCI machine screening. The QXCI machine is a tool that should be used "in conjunction" with other methods of testing during your recovery as only a *piece* of the puzzle. Some even say if you have cancer you should steer clear of this machine. And—if people use it as their sole testing and reference source on which they base their decision-making, I have to say, "I agree. Stay away from it!" Even Dr. Bird herself cautions that not everyone who has a QXCI machine is sufficiently skilled to use it.)

Diligence Starts With Me

Proof and confidence as to whether I am actually progressing (or not) with the treatment I've chosen can be gained by me, first of all, being *aware* of what is going on with my own body.

Pain, for instance, is always a concern. In the early stages of cancer, there usually is no pain. It's like a parasite. It doesn't want you to know it's there. It's like that's its "job." But when an actual diagnosis *has* been established, pain can mean many things—all of which anyone should definitely discuss with their physician. Pain can be caused by things such as simply overdoing it. However, one significant clue as to what might be happening when a person is on Protocel® and experiences *constant* pain is that "constant pain" can be a sign the cancer is progressing. Intermittent pain, however, can be a sign the cancer is *dying*, which is what I experienced in the area of my diagnosis—especially in the second to fourth week after I started Protocel®. I experienced stinging, pulsating, needle-like, sharp shooting pains that lasted anywhere from a few seconds to several minutes, on and off, sometimes with hours in between episodes. After the first few weeks, the pains completely stopped. So it helps to keep a journal of what you're experiencing, especially regarding significant developments, such as episodes of pain.

But to take any indicator, such as pain, and think you know what it means is nothing more than presumption, especially if you aren't having regular testing. Pain should be taken as an indicator that you need to be even *more* on top of what is happening to you. You must be able to compare the base line of numbers you start out with when you begin something like Protocel® to the numbers you receive with follow-up testing in months to come, to know where you stand— for your own peace of mind. And you must be able to determine whether or not the treatment you've chosen to use is working. Pain or any types of bodily changes are warning signs. And, again—pain in the area where you've been diagnosed with cancer (when you are on Protocel®) is either warning you that things are getting worse, or warning your diagnosis that its days are numbered.

Diligence on your part in gathering information, to stay on top of your situation, is the only way you can know if you truly are making progress in your recovery, or whether, in your situation, you need to look elsewhere for another treatment. *Nothing is guaranteed when you are using any type of treatment.* To go on Protocel® and not be diligent and vigilant about regular testing to know if you are making prog-ress—is foolishness. And, like my neighborhood compounding phar-macist Mike tells people, "No one knows your body like you do—and no one's as concerned about your health as you are. Get involved!"

The big picture is what you want to look at. If there is a large amount of cancer you are dealing with (as opposed to already having had a tumor removed through lumpectomy or mastectomy—or even a slow-growing tumor where cancer cells die off at a much slower rate), tiredness, to some degree, is usually experienced for the first few months, as are signs of lysing. But, again, it can vary with each individual when it comes to the tiredness and lysing phenomena. So, again—keeping a journal of anything you experience can be helpful in seeing the overall picture of what is taking place in your recovery—even from one day to the next when you look back at what you've recorded!

(Visit www.thebreaststaysput.com for more information on scans, tumor markers and alternative testing.)

Are You Talkin' to Me?

On my first appointment with Dr. Bird, I indicated to her that she should brace herself for what the machine was about to pick up. She said she'd seen it all before, and she'd be fine.

While waiting for the machine to warm up, I took the time to share more of my story with her. Particularly the part where after being on Protocel® for eighteen months, I had fully *expected* for this to be over by now, but I was still dealing with something significant.

From our first appointment with her for Willie, with her wit, humor and laid-back caring attitude, a visit to her office was an experience to look forward to—which, of course, was in direct contrast to anything I'd experienced on the other side of the aisle. (With the exception of the caring surgeon and the staff in the CT scan room.) It was good to be somewhere someone understood—and in more ways than one.

After she fastened the little Velcro straps around my wrists, ankles and forehead, we sat there for what seemed like *forever*. All she did was type and wait, type and wait. She was obviously checking for breast cancer, and I was becoming very apprehensive.

Suddenly she stopped, put her pen down, sat back in her chair, looked at me and said, "I don't believe this. I've scanned your entire body, and I cannot find *one* live cancer cell!"

We both just sat there. Looking at each other. (This was making up for that radiologist stare-down in the mammogram room—

big-time!) Once again, I was dazed—but this situation called for tears of sheer joy! Could it really be?

"I'm speechless, Pam. Believe me—I don't see stuff like this," she said. "In fact, I don't know if I've ever seen this before where there is nothing to be found anywhere. Even people who come in here who don't *have* a diagnosis of cancer have a bad cell or two I can find here and there—*somewhere!*—because everyone has them . . . everyone except *you* that is. It's when they become out of control that we get the diagnosis of cancer. But you don't have any! Anywhere! And, believe me, I just finished checking and rechecking all the systems of the body. What a testament to Protocel®! It obviously has done what you were told it would. It has systematically wiped your body clean of any cancer cells! Whatever is left in there [pointing to my breast] *is dead!* And not only that, but you also don't have anything else I can find that's wrong. This is amazing! You and your husband are two of the healthiest people I've ever had walk into my office!"

What affirmations and confirmations! (*I wrote this whole book up to this point—in anticipation of writing that line!*) Proof that what we had been doing all these years truly *was* paying off. We weren't falling apart after all! *And now I was "cancer-free"?*

And we were doing the right thing getting Willie off the meds. The only thing she picked up on the QXCI machine was that his liver and kidneys were being stressed—all side effects of the medication. (Meds he didn't even need, because his arteries were clean!) All he needed was the support of nutritional supplements that would keep his heart strong and his vitals solid.

But the cancer-free thing? *That* was just over the top! So much so, in fact, I found it difficult to even grasp! She was talking to me, and this time the numbness that I felt came from hearing the words *"Pam"* and *"cancer-free"*—in the same sentence!

And then thoughts like: *How long have I been cancer-free? How can I be cancer-free when there is still a significant size "thing" in my breast? Why am I still so tired if Protocel® isn't still dealing with cancer?* started going off in my head. But I shut it all down, because "Hello-o-o-o? Someone just said, 'You're cancer-free!' Would you *stop* already!—and just *savor* the moment!"

214

All the Density Wasn't in the Lump

Dr. Bird did say there was a reading on the machine for breast cancer of 82, but when she went to look for live cells it kept telling her it couldn't find what she was asking for, which meant that the machine was aware there was an issue of breast cancer, but there were still no live cells it could detect. And she added, "When a woman comes in here with a very tiny pea-size mass or smaller in her breast, if it's cancer, the machine will give a reading somewhere in the vicinity of 380 to 400. With the size you described yours to be and the reading on it being only 82, it just shows how much it's deteriorated. You, my dear, have done it!" she said, once again. "*You are cancer-free!*"

I probably didn't even need my cell phone to call Willie and the kids! The whole world could have heard me! I was *"cancer-free"*! They were as speechless as I was and elated beyond words—and *so* relieved!

In the weeks to come I continued to be monitored, and the count continued to drop. And it was falling fast!

Week by week I would have a fifteen to thirty-minute visit with Dr. Bird, just to check that number. It went from 82 to 53; then 53 to 32; 32 to 41 (which was the only time it went up); and the next time it was 13. Then it went to 3 and it never did register at 0. It just wouldn't even talk about breast cancer anymore. Yet it seemed that every time I came into the office Dr. Bird commented on how *tired* I looked. And I was. It was the story of my life.

Finally, the day came when Dr. Bird said she had consulted with two of her naturopath friends, with regard to my exhaustion, and they both felt that perhaps I had been on Protocel® so long my system was tired from working overtime to rid itself of what was left of the dead lysed cells, and it just needed a break. The more I thought about it, the more I felt she was right. (Have you noticed that going with an alternative treatment *requires a lot of thought?*)

The decision was made that I would stop the Protocel® and continue to go in weekly to be monitored with a quick check on the QXCI machine. It continued to show that I was still cancer-free. And then one day we couldn't even get a reading—the machine wouldn't even talk about cancer. The beast was beyond dead. According to her machine, it didn't even exist. But I sure had a mass in my breast that begged to differ! I knew one thing: I needed to get in and have some more tests run!

Time to Scan Another Cat

Dr. Bird encouraged me to have another CT scan, which I had planned to do. (And can I just say, "I have *yet* to see that 'cat!'") And, again, I specifically told the radiologist who would read it that I wanted a "density reading."

Anytime you can get a density reading done on a scan of a tumor or mass you have a great opportunity to know exactly what is going on with regard to deterioration, as it changes from scan to scan. However, not all radiologists will do them. Either they aren't capable or the clinic/hospital may lack the equipment. But it is definitely something to request. Because if you *can* get one, so much the better!

So on August 7, 2005, I had my second CT scan. Once again, they were great in there and so excited for me. But when I picked up the report it said nothing of density. And I couldn't understand *why*. I knew Carol, my nurse practitioner, had been faxed a copy of my report, so I called her, and as she read it, she said, "Pam, what this doctor is saying is that he sees *'no change.'*"

Well—that was a disappointment! Was I now getting conflicting reports—was this in direct contradiction to what the QXCI machine was saying?

"Pam," she went on, "he's saying there is 'no change' *because he didn't see cancer in April of last year when you had the first CT scan, and he doesn't see cancer now.* All he is seeing is a small amount of scar tissue. And we know the scar tissue is from the biopsy. He's saying there is *no cancer*, Pam. And there *wasn't any* on the CT scan you had in April of last year either!"

Okay, now I'm stunned again! Because not only does this back up Dr. Bird's findings, but the real significance of it was that he didn't see cancer a year ago, in April of 2004—just one week shy of three *months* after I'd started on Protocel®!

Could it be? Could it really be that Josh and I'd had our "Three Months to Cancer-Free" one-act-play prayer answered after all? Talk about something rocking your world! I was numb, I was speechless, I was dumbfounded—I was praising God all over the place! Not only was I cancer-free—but I may have been for over a year and not even known it!

The two reports read:

CT scan report dated 4/20/2004:
Mediastinal and lung windows are reviewed. The heart was not enlarged. There is no pericardial effusion. Definite Mediastinal adenopathy was not confirmed. Central pulmonary vessels appear normal. There is increased radiopaque density within the right breast laterally. This may be secondary to prior biopsy or parenchymal asymmetry. The liver appears homogeneous in its overall CT density. Spleen is not enlarged. Adrenal gland is not enlarged. The lungs appear adequately ventilated with no pulmonary infiltrate, pleural effusion, or pneumothorax. I do not see definite pulmonary nodules or clearly defined metastatic disease. IMPRESSION: Increased breast parenchymal density is identified on the right as discussed. There is no CT confirmation of pulmonary nodule or abnormal mediastinal adenopathy.

CT scan report dated 8/09/2005:
Scans taken at two different window settings are compared with the last study of 4/20/2004. There has been no interval change. The lungs have remained well expanded and clear for an acute infiltrate or a mass and there is no hilar or mediastinal lymphadenopathy. No pleural effusion is demonstrated. Once again, there is increased parenchymal density within the right breast which is unchanged and most likely on the basis of scarring from previous surgery. CONCLUSION: The CT of the thorax has remained negative for evidence of pulmonary mass or lymphadenopathy and there has been no change since the previous study of 4/20/2004.

In comparing the two reports, it actually does state that neither doctor reading the CT scans saw any evidence of breast cancer. And, interestingly, another technician we asked to read the two reports, who is skilled in reading scans, also commented, "Are you sure the patient was correctly diagnosed? Are you sure she *even* had breast cancer to begin with? Because both of these reports indicate she didn't."

(Important to note is that just because a scan can't "see" tumors doesn't necessarily mean a person is completely cancer-free. "Free-floating" microscopic cancer cells, or even very "tiny tumors," won't necessarily be picked up on a scan, being invisible to the human eye—which is exactly why, in my estimation, when people reach this point they would always want to continue to take Protocel® for at least another year.)

So to "assume" I was free of cancer within three months after beginning Protocel® will always remain questionable. But it's enough to say they couldn't <u>find</u> any cancer on the first CT scan. And that added to the fact that Dr. Bird was now detecting no sign of cancer anywhere in my body, in addition to all tumor marker blood tests showing to be low and in the normal range, told me without question—*I was winning!*

(Also important to note is that a person being deemed "cancer-free" is *not* typically something that is pronounced by a doctor at any one specific time. Tumor regression and tumors disappearing are all indicators the cancer-free day is *coming*—but since cancer cells, and cancer cell clusters, can still exist and yet be undetectable, the cancer-free status of an individual needs to be thought of as *a goal to reach for* in an ongoing process of treatment. Which is why staying on an alternative treatment like Protocel® is the ideal. With chemotherapy a person can only be on it for so long, or it would kill them. It's poison. Which is why it has to be administered in "courses." And while a person is off of it, it often gives cancer cells a chance to make a comeback, and they can come back *stronger*. By being on a product like Protocel®, a person can stay on it indefinitely until blood tests, such as the AMAS Test, CAProfile and/or tumor marker testing, or something like a breast thermograph or QXCI testing, show the person to be well into the safe range. After that point is reached, many people still stay on Protocel® for six months to a year, and then continue to use one bottle of Protocel® per year as *insurance* against a recurrence. All the while knowing the process they are in can be "thought of" as *cancer-free and intending to remain so.*)

The Plot Thickens

So—time went on, and I continued to have ultrasounds because the stubborn, persistent, difficult to explain mass was still in my breast. And if you're thinking, *Why not just be done with it—and have a lumpectomy?* I didn't think that even if I had wanted to have one *(which I didn't)* I could have.

When I had the biopsy that caused the *explosive* growth of the tumor, I knew Protocel® was already working on the whole of it. And in light of what had developed after the biopsy, having a lumpectomy would have been a *disaster.* Even as far back as just days after the surgeon had recommended surgery, if I *had* opted for a lumpectomy (we all know I would never have opted for the other), by the time they performed it, even if it had been done within days after the biopsy, they would have undoubtedly run into the "egg-shaped mass." And then what?

One doctor I spoke with agreed and said, "If you'd had a lumpectomy after the biopsy, because of what this second 'mass' did within days (which was *created* by it) you'd have wound up with a severe deformity. And as fast as this grew, the mastectomy they would have insisted on would have probably been a double!" (Which I'd already figured out—just *days* into it.)

The ultrasounds continued to read in the same vein, "distal acoustic shadowing"—all moving outward toward the lymph system. And now these *befuddled* radiologists (who had to be *clueless*), since they couldn't get an actual measurement on it (see?—intermingled tissue, just like I said), seemed to just throw up their hands and say, "Oh, what the heck—it's just *all* cancer!" (I knew better!)

Now my recovery began going much smoother, and Willie and I decided to sell our home on the lake, purchase another lot and build again, perhaps in the spring, and move close to Shawn and Kerri for the winter. If we were selling our home and going to have to rent *somewhere* until we built, I mean, hey—why not temporarily move closer to our grandbaby? What a bonus!

Naturally, the move was hard on me, but we managed. I was still *struggling* with "struggling." But I told myself that in time I would find answers—to *all* of it. And, besides, I did, after all, have that cancer-free stamp on my forehead and "in my heart" going for me—so how much better could things be?

After packing up our entire home, selling much of what was in it with plans to buy new and moving to where we'd be renting, in the process, once again, from out of nowhere—I found them! Two very distinct, hard, pea-shaped lumps! And in the same area! And here it was—Christmas . . . *two years later.* Deja vu all over again? *This was insane!*

I went into a hole on this one. A *big* one! A very quiet one. And I stayed there. It was like I didn't have the wherewithal anymore to muster up any faith to even *want* to fight. I just prayed, put it on auto-pilot and didn't even try to make sense out of what appeared to be *more* insanity! (Sometimes you can do that. You can just say, *"Ya' know God—you gotta fix this. So You take it. According to and based on everything* I've been standing on—I say, 'Ditto and amen,' please get me out of this—*in the name of Jesus!"* And, *especially* in *that* situation, invoking that *name—it's <u>more</u> than enough!)*

When I finally told Willie what I had discovered, he had me call Dr. Bird's office and she worked us in the next day. And as we made the early morning drive, I found I was still in a hole—and I was also again in "Fog City." This was so disappointing. If this had come back it was going to be *horrible*—on *all* of us! I was just so tired of everything being about *me!*

As it turned out, when we got to Dr. Bird's office and I was put on the QXCI machine, after doing an overall check of the body, and then specifically checking the breast, Dr. Bird sat back and said, "Well! There's no sign of cancer cells anywhere, including the breasts. But let me tell you—you have a *screamin'* case of fibroid cysts going on!" And I was relieved beyond description. A recurrence after having had such an outstanding recovery would have been the worst. And what got me was—*these things in my breast felt so much more like cancer than the original malignant tumor ever thought of!* Could this recovery get much crazier or more bizarre? But what a relief! Except I think my book just got longer. How much more information did God want found out for the reader? Now I'd be working on fibroids?

Iodine—the Missing Element

At Dr. Bird's suggestion we decided to seek out a medical doctor locally for Willie, one who might also treat nutritionally. And we found one that we both liked. He spent time with us and focused on treating *the whole person*—which is exactly what we'd been looking for!

Just as Willie's first visit was winding down, I mentioned to the doctor the facts in my situation in what I had been dealing with and where I stood. And I told him that during the move more lumps had developed, which our naturopath said were cysts.

I told him I was convinced they were, because up till then everything else she had said had been right on, and they also changed periodically in size. And sometimes there were two and sometimes three.

"She said they're *fibroid* cysts," I told him. And when I said "fibroid" he said, "Iodine"—stood up and said he'd be right back. ". . . I want to get you a sheet on Lugol's Iodine Solution and Iodoral Tablets before you leave. *You* need iodine!"

And, with that—he sent us to a compounding pharmacy, which is when we first met Mike. And the first thing Mike did when I said "Iodine" was hand me a book that was sitting on the counter in his pharmacy titled *Iodine—Why You Need IT and Why You Can't Live Without It,* by David Brownstein, M.D.

"According to Dr. Brownstein's findings," he said, "not only are women getting rid of fibroid cysts when their iodine levels are met, but some are even recovering from breast cancer with iodine alone! And his latest revised edition has a new chapter in it called—*Iodine, Hypothyroidism, Fibrocystic Disease and Breast Cancer.*" I couldn't wait to get it, and I immediately started the drops of Lugol's Iodine Solution the doctor had ordered.

(With what I know now, I can say, in all probability, this one element alone could have possibly prevented me from ever getting this diagnosis to begin with—and my mother, and millions of other women like her. Iodine is one of the most crucial elements there is

to preventing breast cancer. And two decades ago they took a large amount of it out of our food supply when they replaced iodine in baked goods with bromine, which is a <u>known toxin</u>. And it was at that time, incidentally, when breast cancer diagnoses skyrocketed! According to Dr. Brownstein, the breast is the largest storage area for iodine in the body. And the thyroid and the breast both compete for it. If there is an iodine deficiency present, it's the perfect setting for either thyroid or breast cancer to develop. And if someone is on thyroid medication for hypothyroidism, and iodine deficient at the same time—it creates even more *of an iodine deficiency, causing even greater breast cancer risk.)*

Iodine: one simple and inexpensive way to prevent thyroid, prostate or breast cancer. And who out there is telling us about it?

(Visit <u>www.DrBrownstein.com</u> for more information on iodine.)

CHAPTER 18

Putting It in Perspective

When You Know That You Know

When I found the lump on Christmas Day of '03—as much as I knew I didn't want any part of anything involving conventional medicine (which is probably part of why I waited a month to do anything), I *still* succumbed to two diagnostic procedures that I was certain were troublesome and could be problematic because of the complications that mammograms and biopsies can both pose. And yet I had them anyway—because *I thought I had <u>no</u> choice.* Which just shows you can know *a lot* and still not know everything about how to protect yourself from questionable medical practices! (And now I find the decision to have CT scans also turned out to be a poor choice on my part, to say the least.)

Well—let me tell you . . . less than two weeks into the diagnosis, I was wishing I had found my way around those two tests and come up with another way to get a handle on what was going on, because they weren't worth the risk. And the one I wasn't even that suspicious of for creating problems—the biopsy—turned out to be the one that created my biggest headache!

If cancer spreads cell by cell, and the bloodstream is its sought-out, preferred method of transportation to infiltrate the systems of the body—why wouldn't a procedure that involved bleeding—even with something as small as the tip of a surgical needle tearing into tissue, snipping out even a miniscule amount of it—not pose a serious risk? (The special needle used in a biopsy has a type of little "hook" at the tip. And the reason my surgeon called it a "gun" is because it has a trigger that causes the hook to take a snippet of tissue. Which is also why the surgeon could say that I need not worry—the needle may be "eight inches long," but to get what he needed, he would only be using "the tip.")

So, finding myself in dire straits after my own biopsy, I had to ask myself the question—over and over: "Why do women even have to have this procedure when, for me, the results of it turned out to be so ghastly?"

And I also asked others, with considerable knowledge in alternative medicine, for their opinions on biopsies, because I now knew firsthand how the procedure posed *definite* risks. (I said early in the book that my decision to go ahead with one was for proof! I just didn't know at the time that there were other ways of getting that "proof" that were much safer. And had I known about them, I would have gone an entirely different route.) And I wanted to know—was I really the only one who saw the inherent danger? So I kept asking and I kept searching. I wanted answers; I *knew* they were out there and I continually revisited the fact that I didn't believe in mammograms, I thought biopsies were questionable—*and yet I still had both*. And that irritated me!

I knew I made an informed choice to have a biopsy, so I knew why I had it. But *why* it's a given—that all women have to have one, if they find a lump, is *still* a huge "burr" under my bra-strap! There had to be other ways!

They don't "biopsy" pancreatic cancer, stomach cancer and the like, and yet people are still somehow diagnosed, so obviously there *are* other ways! In fact, when you think about it—they *only* biopsy what they can get at with a needle. And since I was writing a book about a recovery that was so adversely affected by one *(mine!)* and these nagging thoughts wouldn't go away, I took the time to research the subject—for you and me both! The following article speaks for itself.

Yes sir—the lump, the mammogram, the biopsy, the oncologist—your "all-inclusive" starter package deal for a ticket on the "Breast Cancer Express"! Just as American as baseball, hot dogs, apple pie and Chevrolet in this country—and the programming they've done to get us to accept it has been relentless! You find a lump, you get a mammogram (and not necessarily in that order), you have a biopsy and you see an oncologist. Because that's just the way it's done—right? Well, once again—*not so fast!*

The Simple Harmless Biopsy—or Not

From an article at www.breastcancerchoices.org, I quote the following:

> In June 2004, the results of the bombshell Hansen study, "Manipulation of The Primary Breast Tumor and The Incidence of Sentinel Node Metastases From Invasive Breast Cancer," were published in the American Medical Association's prestigious journal, Archives of Surgery, revealing that **patients undergoing fine needle biopsies were 50% more likely to have micro-metastases spread to the sentinel lymph node than those patients having the entire tumor removed for biopsy.**
>
> The implication of this discovery is that a woman without lymph node involvement, who would have been staged at a low level, **now will be staged higher, her disease considered more advanced, and more aggressive treatment might be recommended.**
>
> Over the years, several researchers have voiced serious reservations about routine needle biopsies, but they were mostly ignored by their colleagues. Hansen's research team cited their predecessors, and the research path leads back several decades. It's hard to understand why The Archives of Surgery study, which embodies all of these reservations about needle biopsies, didn't make the front page of the New York Times.
>
> Cancer authority, Ralph Moss, comments in his February 6th, 2005 *Moss Reports* newsletter: "Imagine the outrage these patients will feel when they learn that many of these sentinel node metastases were caused not by the natural progression of their disease but directly by the actions of

well-intentioned (but ill informed) doctors. Imagine, further, what will happen when patients find out that questions have been raised about the safety and advisability of needle biopsies for a number of years by some of the finest minds in oncology. Imagine the disruption of the smooth functioning of the 'cancer industry' when patients start demanding less invasive ways of diagnosing tumors. And imagine the class action lawsuits."

Well—imagine and go figure!

Okay, so *now* let's analyze that little piece of jaw-dropping insight into the world of conventional cancer treatment.

Since it's been proven that the technique used by conventional medicine to determine malignancy—*the needle biopsy*—actually leaves a "seeded trail" that causes metastasis to the sentinel node in one out of every two women who have the procedure (see www. breastcancerchoices.org for the full article), they have decided—the solution is not to commit to find a safer way of determining the malignancies and stop this debacle. But to instead just treat the patient as though they have a *more advanced stage of cancer*, with a treatment protocol that is even *more aggressive* (which is code for: "Bombard their body with radiation and chemo, and insist on a mastectomy rather than a lumpectomy)—to compensate for the pending metastasis *occurrence* that they know they themselves, in all probability, *have just caused!*

The cancer industry is out of control, and they are killing women and getting away with it. What a wretchedly unprofessional and unforgivably deadly practice. How convenient, how profitable and how *ludicrous!* How do these people sleep? And people wonder why I see *red* over their "pink ribbon" campaigns! *And*, as I add the findings of this horrifying Hansen study to my own personal experience, the reality of "Wish I knew then what I know now" bites hard! There were other ways I could have determined whether I was looking at a diagnosis of breast cancer. But even the people surrounding Protocel® advised me that they, too, didn't feel a biopsy would pose a problem. They said, "You need a biopsy, because you need a 'diagnosis.'"

I say, *"What for?"*

If I found a lump, I would get on Protocel® or whatever treatment I'd chosen. I would have a blood panel done, a chest X-ray, testing on the QXCI machine, an ultrasound, MRI and/or a PET scan, and a breast thermograph (a heat sensitive test that detects breast cancer). And I would stay on top of how I was progressing.

It's important to note that there are choices to be made when deciding not only what type of testing a person wants to have done, but also *when* they want to schedule the scans and tests.

In the first and second month when using Protocel® against cancer, tumors tend to appear larger on scans because of the way Protocel® works, as was true in my case. And it's usually after the fourth or fifth month of being on Protocel® when tumor regression starts to become evident, which also proved to be true in my case.

In my particular situation, although it was very difficult to overcome the terror I was subjected to by the doctor's "take" on what he read on my scans, I later realized that had I not had the ultrasound done after being on Protocel® one month, I would have never known the "multiple surrounding lesions" had even developed (or maybe a better term in my case would be "appeared"—because they may have already been there and just hadn't shown up until Protocel® caused them to start to lyse). And although it's true that I would have been spared the trauma of wondering what all of it meant, I would also have missed out on the joy and reassurance of seeing the things disappear two or three months later. Which was a huge turning point and a celebratory moment in my recovery—clear evidence that Protocel® was working!

So it's important to monitor progress. But it's also hard to hear a doctor tell you, "You are getting worse." Because it's easy to get discouraged and be misled and, so to speak, feel "forced" into treatment by their conventional white coats! The bottom line is that for me it was important to have initial scanning done (which, remember— my oncologist refused to do, so I had to look elsewhere). Everyone has to determine when to schedule an ultrasound, breast thermography, PET scan or MRI, but it's important to begin somewhere in those first months so you have a clear picture as to whether the lumps, tumor or masses you are suspiciously monitoring are truly going away and not continuing to grow.

In the situation where I might have chosen to opt out of having the biopsy (for reasons I've already stated), I would have just gone with the assumption that I *had* been diagnosed with breast cancer, started on Protocel® 23, and then followed through with everything one must do in the way of conventional diagnostics (ultrasounds, MRI's and blood work), and alternative diagnostic testing (thermograph, AMAS and CAProfile blood-work, QXCI machine, etc.) to monitor my progress. So, again, why was it that a biopsy was so necessary (as everyone today still seems to think) when with or without one I would have done everything I did anyway?

(Except, as I said, earlier, I would have never had CT scans done. I'd have continued to have ultrasounds, which is the only non-toxic diagnostic test. And I would also have pursued having MRIs, which are even being talked about more and more as an option to mammograms.)

(Visit www.thebreaststaysput.com for more information on scans, tumor markers and alternative testing.)

Biopsy Blunders—Your Need to Know

Contacted by many women, because of my story, who have had much the same experience as I did with "exploding biopsies," I was already convinced that biopsies can cause a diagnosis of breast cancer to go from bad to worse, before ever coming across the previous quoted study.

However, a biopsy gone awry, such as mine, you would think would be the exception. Much to my surprise—in conversations I personally had with women who were also battling breast cancer, I came across it much more than I expected.

In my recovery, and in writing this book, I did not put myself "out there" for people to call me. However, I did speak, or correspond by email, with anyone who made an effort to get in touch with me. But out of the relatively few I did have the opportunity to speak with, I was absolutely astonished at how many women experienced the same unthinkable development. Women who started out by saying, "I've heard about your story, Pam, and after a biopsy my tumor . . . became much larger," "tripled in size," "became much so much bigger." But the one I *could not believe* was when one woman told me, "I had one elongated tumor; the surgeon did *four* biopsies on it and now I have four."

"*Four* biopsies on *one* tumor?" I quizzed.

"The surgeon said she wanted to know if it was *all* cancer. It went from being one elongated tumor to a much larger one—consisting of four distinct tumors that are all attached. Everywhere the surgeon went in with her needle to biopsy, it caused the mass to form another larger tumor. So I now have four in a row."

When I asked her what her diagnosis was, she said, "I don't have one. The surgeon told me she didn't get one—she only wanted to know if it *was* cancer."

What lab would examine breast tissue and not conclude with an actual diagnosis—even if it wasn't ordered by the surgeon? And how could a surgeon not order it?

But the woman I spoke with was specific! It's in my notes: When she asked her doctor for her diagnosis, the surgeon told her, "If you want a diagnosis, we'll have to do another biopsy." (I was thinking, *This even trumps, "Are you sick?"* This was unimaginable!)

When I asked her if I could include this story in my book, she said that she wished I would so others would know ahead of time how imperative it is that a patient asks questions!

I encouraged her to contact the hospital where she had the procedure. There *had* to be a diagnosis—because I didn't think for a pathologist not to do one would even be legal. Malpractice is what I was really thinking! (I don't think someone needs to be practicing medicine with that low of a degree of mentality!)

You have to ask yourself: "Is there such a thing as being 'over-prepared' when it comes to asking the right questions of people in white coats, with degrees on their walls that license them to legally use machines, chemicals, needles and knives to do the only thing they are licensed to do in medicine—which is *practice!*"

Asking a doctor if he or she plans to get an actual diagnosis on a biopsy is like asking a surgeon if he plans to give you anesthesia before he cuts. (Although, anymore, after what I've heard, that would probably be the *first* question I'd ask!)

It just goes to show—you can never ask enough questions! I tell people all the time to ask questions—but who would think you'd need to ask a surgeon *how many* biopsies they planned to do on *one* tumor? And you have to ask yourself if it's a question everyone needs to ask before going under the needle. Travesties like this are just not supposed to happen! And even after speaking with the relatively few women that I have, there have been times when I've said to myself, "I think I've already heard it all!"

But, for me, the one, without question, that was the big eye-opener wake-up call was the one Elonna McKibben asked her oncologist after she had been given only three to six months to live. After hearing this one, I decided when it comes to the medical world, I don't think there's a ceiling on "heard it all/seen it all"—because this takes the cake!

When her oncologist asked her if she would be interested in participating in an experimental chemotherapy being used on the type of cancer she was diagnosed with, Glioblastoma GBM, she said she asked him, "Will it prolong my life—or shorten it?"

I thought, *Wow! What a question!* (Thinking to myself—*Now, that's thinking! I would never have thought to ask a question like that, because what doctor would suggest someone go on a treatment that would actually shorten their life? Right?*)

She said that his answer was, "Shorten it. But don't you want your life to count for something—for research?"

Elonna said, "*No!* Because I plan to *live!*"—(she had four infants at home.)

I was *floored!* All I could think when I heard this was: *How many people would never think to ask a question like that, and, without even knowing it, be signing away their life in an even quicker fashion than the doctor's original prognosis?*

So, I say, a really good question to keep in mind as you contemplate giving the "go-ahead" to any doctor's suggestion of resorting to a procedure that could end up being "life-altering" would be, "What is *the worst* that could happen if I agree to this?"—and then go from there.

With the "exploding biopsies" I kept hearing about (when I thought *my* case was more the exception than the norm) imagine my astonishment in hearing these stories, one at a time, from women in different states who had no contact with each other, all with stories similar to mine. And some of them even *worse!*

And, if I came across so many cases in just the few women who have reached out to contact me, you *know* oncologists have to see it! But why isn't it talked about? Could it be because women who find themselves with explosive growth after a biopsy wind up with a mastectomy as a solution to the problem, regardless of whether they may have only been scheduled for a lumpectomy? You have to wonder how many women who go in for a lumpectomy are asked to sign off on a mastectomy, at "the doctor's discretion," before their surgery (for the patient's own good, of course) and come out having had one. And no one ever knows. Maybe because they are simply told it had to be done, because their cancer was so aggressive and had already spread.

If I could hit "rewind" (and if I weren't writing a book, where the medical world would disregard anything I had to say if I hadn't had conventional diagnostics), I would be inclined to first of all—remind God of how He already had me "covered" in His Word, where He said in it that, by faith, I was already healed! Then I'd get on Protocel® 23, do all of the above, send Willie out to pick up a new cushy goose down comforter and organic popcorn, order Netflix for the long haul and then position myself to expect nothing less than a "full recovery!" Everyone has to make their own choices, but you can bet your bobbles—I would *never* again have another biopsy. I *will* never again even have another mammogram! Too many "user-friendly" ways of staying on top of breast health exist, without my having to go down those dead-end streets in that part of town—ever again! Fool me once, your fault . . . etc., etc.

(But, again, that's just me! You have to do what you feel is right for you—and you *definitely* have to do what you have faith in!)

Mammograms—Detection or Perpetration

And, in the same report, I also found information regarding how radiation causes cancer, and how several years ago the breast cancer rate skyrocketed because of the radiation in mammograms, which is when they started recommending that women wait until after age forty to begin having them yearly. And now, according to who you listen to, the magic number has even been upped to fifty. And haven't we all heard, "You get more radiation from being closer to the sun on one plane flight than you do from an X-ray," from doctors and dentists who insist you have to have those X-rays! I want to say to them, "If they're so harmless and the risk is so minimal, then why don't you stay out here with me when you take it—instead of hiding behind that wall?"

(This of course is not to say that people should *never* get radiation diagnostics or treatments. Doctors, dentists, chiropractors, etc. need that information. They should just use wisdom in determining whether they feel the need for having them is justified, or if it's just an overly interested, or thorough to a fault, practitioner who insists on taking them in amounts that are excessive.)

And this one just *frosts* me! They know "The more mammograms you have at an earlier age, the greater risk you're at for getting breast cancer." BUT in the same breath they're telling us, "However, for those of you who have a family history of breast cancer, or have the gene—well, then, for you—*you* want to begin having mammograms in your 30's!" ... ?

What's that about?

"Early in life mammograms put you at greater risk of having breast cancer"—out of one side of their mouths, and "However, those of you lucky women who have a higher risk factor for being diagnosed with it—well, *you* really need to start having them ASAP!"—out of the other?

Can't you just hear the little man with a squeaky voice in that expert's head going, *"Help me! Help me!"*?

Except when you think about it, you *know* there had to be *two* guys who came up with that moronic train (wreck) of a thought—*because no one person could be that stupid!)*

The following information on mammograms was taken from the same article from www.breastcancerchoices.org:

Is there a danger inherent in the additional radiation exposure?

Answer: Clearly "yes." According to Dr. Gofman, MD, PhD, in Radiation and Human Health: A Comprehensive Investigation of the Evidence Relating Low Level Radiation to Cancer and Other Diseases, ionizing radiation is a known carcinogen, there is no safe exposure level to ionizing radiation, and the effects of radiation exposure are cumulative throughout one's life. Specific to breast cancer, Dr. Gofman presents compelling evidence in his new book, Preventing Breast Cancer: The Story of a Major, Proven, Preventable Cause of This Disease that about 75% of those cancers are caused by exposure to ionizing radiation, principally from medical X-rays. People should not forget the massive and heavily promoted early detection mammogram program in the 1950s and 1960s of women under 50 which was scrapped by the National Cancer Institute because the incidence of cancers caused by repeated radiation exposure was unacceptable. That program "caused between 55,000 and 65,000 future cancer deaths per year!" according to Dr. Gofman, a radiologist with a doctorate in medical physics, who headed a $24,500,000 seven-year study on the effects of radiation on human health.

(See full article, Hibbard W, "Stereotactic Breast Biopsy," 2004 article in MEDICAL ARTICLES BIOPSY section.)

Which is *exactly* why I see "red" over their "pink ribbon" campaigns!

As a side note on the same subject, on May 14, 2007, Brian Williams of NBC News covered a report where he stated, "In the year 2000 a reported 70% of women over the age 40 said they'd had a mammogram within the past two years. That number has now dropped to 66% and they feel it will continue to drop."

Asked if this significant number of women opting out of having their regular mammogram is due to things such as a lack of insurance coverage, a laxness on the part of women in general or whether this was becoming a new "trend," they said they didn't know. So with the considerable decline in numbers of women opting to have their regular mammogram, maybe the "pink promotional campaign" isn't working so well after all.

Or, then again—perhaps it is.

Maybe women have witnessed how this "fund raising" that has raked in billions over the years has purchased no real progress, of any kind, to speak of, and they recognize the system as flawed; they're tired of being told they have to have procedures done whose effectiveness don't justify the risks involved—and they're fed up with frying their breasts on a regular basis.

I'll say this much. Smashing and radiating breasts with a hydraulic press to determine what was going on inside them had to have been the brainchild of a vindictive, evil little man. No woman would have ever come up with the idea—let alone believed it would sell. And I'll tell you something else: If, at the time this machine came to be, men had been subjected to "testigrams" to see what was going on in "places of interest"—they'd have deep-sixed the thing decades ago!—before it ever became this country's diagnostic testing machine of choice—*to detect anything!*

They say "Regular mammograms mean early detection" and "Early detection saves lives." Whatever.

Wouldn't it be interesting, though, if the number of new breast cancer cases *dropped* with the declining number of women having regular mammograms? (Even more interesting would be if they *did*—and they actually *reported* it!)

I Took a Poll

Several months ago I sent out an email to twenty women in my address book who I knew I could include in something like this, to see how they felt and what they thought of when the "pink ribbon campaign" month rolled around; or what they feel or think about when they see one of those "pink ribbons." I wanted to know!

They were all in different states, which I purposely saw to, and all but four out of twenty responded. Out of the sixteen who did, only four had good things to say, of which two were somewhat philosophical, such as how grateful they are they don't have breast cancer and how they feel for the women who do, etc., and two were non-committal. They weren't really against them, but they weren't for them either—which I took to mean that they didn't get regular mammograms. (But I never asked that question—of any of them. I just wanted to know what seeing "pink" did to them or for them.)

But, of the twelve who had negative comments, two basically said they wanted to know where the huge amounts of money were going that were being raised by it, because nothing's changed; three hated it, were sick of seeing it and thought it was a money-making scam with no intention of ever finding a cure, because it certainly hadn't changed or improved much of anything; two thought mammograms didn't detect much of anything and may even cause cancer and would never get them; and one thought they should shoot the guy who invented the machine (or worse!). But two of them are now battling breast cancer, and they had the most to say (as in *way more* to say than the others). And, believe me, they were not at all in favor of the campaign.

And then there was the one who'd already had a mastectomy and chemo. She hates seeing the ribbons. It goes right through her when she walks into a store where there is a huge display, and it makes her want to run, because it reminds her again that she once had it—and it scares her to think . . . it might come back—which is a *perfect* example of what I feel is so wrong with the "pink ribbon" campaign! It plants the seed of: "Breast cancer is out there, and you're going to get it!" Or if someone's already been through it: "It's out there—and it's coming back."

If they really were doing "breast health awareness" I would feel completely different about it. But they aren't! They are deliberately putting fear in the hearts of women about getting breast cancer as a means to an end. Fear and focus—to get the number of women who have regular mammograms *to go up!*

And then there was the time I walked into a store in the small town we live in and saw a box full of "Breast Cancer Awareness Month" paraphernalia. The owner of the store who was sorting through it was very disgruntled. She didn't even know my situation, but out of the blue she started telling me how these "breast cancer people" had called and called her, trying to get her to agree to take a "kit" and display these products for sale in her business. She said, "But now I have to sell it to get my money back, and I hate the thought of making even one dollar profit off this. I wish those people wouldn't call anymore, and the next time they do I'm going to tell them to take me off their list. I think this is a racket." And me? I didn't even know they would set up a marketing system where retailers *would* make a profit off selling things in "pink." (Wonder how much my bank makes off what they peddle.) (And if that was rude, I hope it doesn't count. Because I still have one left I was saving.)

So, setting aside how I feel about it, as the author of this book, just from my little "shoot from the hip" poll and what the shop owner had to say, it doesn't look so good for the "pink ribbon" people. I found it interesting, and I thought you'd want to know. (Or maybe I just didn't ask the right twenty women?)

The Suffering Silent

I didn't take a poll on this; I didn't need to. I received enough calls from women in this position to make me realize there is a whole other category of people out there that no one is talking about. People who have cancer—and are doing nothing! Desperate to find answers, they are searching, because they believe the conventional methods used to fight cancer are worse than the cancer itself. And, in cases of breast cancer, they're convinced it isn't breast cancer that kills—it's when the cancer "metastasizes" to other parts of the body that the body begins to die. So there is actually this whole group of people out there (that may include men, because men can get breast cancer, too) who have been diagnosed with breast cancer, but until they find something like Protocel®, the only thing they are doing is searching. Hoping they have enough time until they find something effective against cancer. They'd rather take their chances in finding a rock solid treatment one day than allow themselves to be victimized by a barbaric system of treatment that doesn't work. They had been doing their best to stay alive, using products and treatments that are known to be effective against cancer, but hadn't been using much in the way of an aggressive approach. I find that chilling.

Then there was Cali. Cali called one day and we became friends. Her situation was the exact opposite of doing nothing, which she says is exactly what she should have done when a physician talked her into a double mastectomy—at the age of thirty—as a form of "prevention" because her mother died of breast cancer. The next twenty years of Cali's life went from one horrid complication to another.

First the implants leaked and Cali was allergic to silicone. Silicone poisoning set in causing a serious infection. They removed the implants but the infection escalated. At one point, Cali became so ill she was rushed in to her doctor, who took one look at her and, right there in his office, tore open the incision that ran the entire length of her torso, in order to release the infection. He told her if he hadn't, she would have died within minutes.

She never was able to detoxify her body from the silicone poisoning, and soon she found herself diagnosed with cancer in her internal organs, which her doctors told her they felt was caused by the silicone. Remember—this girl at the age of thirty was given a double mastectomy and she did NOT have cancer, or any indication that she was at risk, other than the fact her mother died of it.

Cali turned to alternative treatments and had even gone to various clinics. And even Protocel®, like everything else she tried, did not work for her. She felt it was due to the silicone poisoning.

The last I heard from her hospice had been called in. She encouraged me to finish my book and asked if I would tell her story so women would know not to blindly follow a doctor simply because he wants to do a procedure that *he* thinks is a "good idea."

Performing a radical mastectomy on a thirty-year-old woman as a means of breast cancer prevention, when there is no sign of it, would be unconscionable to most doctors. (At least, you'd think, anyway.) But it's chilling to hear the stories of the things women are put through because of a system and doctors who are hell-bent on saving people from themselves—with treatments that kill.

(Breast augmentation today, in the form of saline, versus the silicone that was once used, doesn't seem to involve the same risks if an implant were to be punctured by an accident or a blow, or for some reason happened to leak. Silicone implants, however, are now being

237

revisited, as it's now being said by some in the medical world that they aren't so sure that silicone was then or now would pose that much of a problem—which is another reason why I felt compelled to include Cali's story.)

CHAPTER 19

A Man with a Dream

The "God Given" Answer to Cancer

Considering the perplexing dilemma we find ourselves in, with no real answer to the cancer nightmare based on what we are seeing in our society today, don't you have to wonder how a teenager in the *1930s* could have had the foresight to know he had within himself a gift so extraordinary he knew he couldn't waste it? And wanting so much for his life to count for something he actually prayed and asked God for the cure for cancer? A cure that would work for all types of cancers, that everyone could use and everyone could afford? Where did the "heartbeat" it would take, to get a "bead" on how desperately mankind would be searching in the decades to come for the answer God would give him, even come from—in the 1930s—for Jim Sheridan to be compelled to pursue it his entire life?

A chemical formula that he didn't understand came to him one night in a dream. This chemical formula kept appearing in a recurrent dream, over and over, and he never knew what it meant until he saw it in a book. It was related to cancer, or a carcinogen. It wasn't until a while later that the actual idea for how to make the Protocel® formula also came to him in a dream. But this time it came during a daytime nap, in 1936. And it was the beginning of what became a "personal" dream he would pursue throughout his entire life. (For a more detailed history of how Protocel® was developed, tested and

239

suppressed by the FDA, see *Outsmart Your Cancer,* by Tanya Harter Pierce.)

At one point, he even asked Alden Dow, the owner of Dow Chemical, in Midland, Michigan, to back him financially in the pursuit of developing this cure. The owner told him that, although he would have liked to, he couldn't do it because he knew if he did, he would be funding a project that Jim would spend the rest of his life fighting the bureaucracy over, which would do everything they could to stop it from ever being approved—because there would be no huge profits to be made in an all-natural cure. And he was right.

Test results showing Protocel®'s efficacy came up missing; tests weren't allowed to be run long enough to give Protocel® a chance to kill cancer cells within the timeframe required for Protocel® to work. (Protocel® does not work like a drug.)

There were times when Cancell® (the name for Protocel® at the time) was shut down and the developers of the formula continued to make it and give it away, personally delivering it in brown paper bags to those who had been using it successfully in their cancer battle, so they could continue in their recoveries.

In 1992 it was shut down by the FDA until DSHEA (Dietary Supplements and Health Education Act) was passed by Congress in 1994 that allowed all dietary supplements to come out from under the scrutiny of the FDA and their control, making Protocel® again available to people. And now Protocel® is sold as a dietary supplement, a potent immune system builder and body detoxifier. It is not sold as a cancer treatment. But because of my First Amendment right to free speech, I can tell my story to anyone who cares to listen, including my views and beliefs as I know them to be true, in what occurred throughout the course of my recovery, and my own personal knowledge of just how powerful I know this product is!

Jim Sheridan believed in God, but rather than organized religion, he was looking for a relationship. I, too, had found years ago that God is a relationship God—and He wanted one with me. Jim Sheridan prayed for an answer to cancer—and I needed one. So just thirty miles from the farm I would one day be growing up on in rural Mid-Michigan, Jim Sheridan was setting out to devote his life to perfect a cure for cancer—that would one day, out of all the things I could have researched and chosen, speak to me in such a way that I knew immediately it would be the treatment I would use to win the battle of my life!

How much closer could that man and his formula get to my heart? Of course I will tell my story—to anyone who will listen. And if I can play a role in taking Jim Sheridan and the Sheridan family's dream to the masses, I will feel as though, for my life and opportunity to live, I have given something back. I am alive because of this man's work; because he prayed a prayer; because God answered that prayer in what began as a dream; and because he stayed true to his heart and lived for what he believed in. So how could I not do the same and author this book?

Three Called Him Dad

During the course of writing this book, I asked Marge Sheridan Dubuque some questions about her father. I felt honored to have the opportunity. She has given me permission to share what she wanted me to know about her dad, and this is what she wrote:

> My father handled everything the FDA and others threw at him with his usual grace and good humor. Usually his attitude was, "this is God's project and it is in God's timing" and he could roll with the punches. He once told a newsman who interviewed him that truth is always truth and he knew he had truth on his side and someday it would come out. He was never bitter and rarely angry about anything and I do not think he ever wanted to quit. The only time I ever saw him really discouraged was when the letter came from NCI after the testing telling him they were not going to pursue Entelev®/Cancell®. We had been so sure of the breakthrough because the test results showed that the formula worked on every kind of cancer they tried it on to some degree. My Mom told me he sat with the letter from them in his hand for a very long time.
>
> Once when we were on a family vacation I was sitting and talking to Dad about his work. (By the way, he liked to be called Dad or Daddy and never Father as it was too formal

a term between father and child.) At some point during the conversation he said to me, "I asked God to give me this knowledge, but that I didn't want to become famous or rich." When he said it, I felt a tingle go down my spine and was hit with the absolute assurance that his prayer was going to be answered. However I also knew that it meant that he would not be with us when his work began to gain recognition. I feel he got exactly what he asked God for. Today Jim Sheridan's children and other faithful servants of the project continue to endeavor to hold true to Dad's dream and get his formula to those who need it.

My father's health was failing, especially his memory shortly after the NCI situation. At that time he wrote a letter to his three children and basically said, "I have fought the fight and now due to health issues I am turning God's project over to you, my children." He was still alive and aware when my brothers and I formed the family company, Ella, Inc. He attended many of the early meetings while we were trying to get organized. Dad suffered a stroke and after that until his death in 2001 we cared for him and loved him as always, but he was never the same. Dad was not aware of Protocel® coming on the market, although we did talk to him, and have to believe that, somewhere inside of him, what we spoke was received.

You asked if anything my father said stuck with me or us. He was very patient and full of wisdom and my brothers and I have often laughed at how he taught us to share. Well two of us anyway. There were three pieces of chocolate cake left and my Dad asked who wanted which piece. My older brother Dennis and I picked the same piece and Jim chose another. My Dad then cut a piece off the one Dennis and I had chosen and moved it over to the piece that Jim had picked. At that point we were asked to choose again. Of course Dennis and I chose the biggest piece and Jim chose another. At this point Dad moved the piece he cut off before into Jim's pile and added another piece to it. About this time

Dennis and I got the message that if this kept up we weren't going to get any of that cake and chose the smaller pieces.

In another incident he taught us that things were not what we should value. Jim and I and our dates went to a drive in movie. My parents insisted that my boyfriend and later husband drive as he had the only Ohio driver's license at the time. It was cold and the ground was ice covered. When the movie ended, Gordon tried to drive the car off the mound and fishtailed into the speaker poll leaving a dent in the side of my father's car. My brother Jim and I thought it was funny and ribbed Gordon who was very upset. Knowing our father we knew it was all right, but we did not know Gordon's father who was very different. When we got home, Gordon went to confess to Dad while we stood by. Daddy said to him, "Son, do you know the first thing I do when I get a new car"? Gordon said, "No, sir." Daddy continued, "I go out to the garage and get a hammer and put a dent in the car. That way I know I always put in the first dent and no one else need worry about it." Needless to say we all learned from that and Gordon loved my Dad from that day forward.

You asked about his favorite hymn and I told you "Amazing Grace" which was correct, but my brother reminded me of something else about the hymn. Whenever it was played my Dad stood up and then so did my mother because Dad considered this the ultimate prayer of praise. He did this at his church and so when he stood and then Mother so did others until it became a tradition at their church that whenever this hymn was played everyone stood up. This has gone on and I am sure many do not know why it is still true today.

The move to Detroit came because Dad had gotten his law degree while working at Dow Chemical Company. He moved to Detroit to join a patent law firm. He was always working on "the project" so he later moved on to The Michigan Cancer Society and then Battelle in Columbus, Ohio, to continue his work. (We were the only kids I know who had white mice in residence in our house.) He ran into road blocks in both places and jumped back and forth between the law and "the project" until he retired to work on Entelev® full time.

Dad was a wonderful person who was very smart but at home with everyone. He always made people feel they were his friends and liked everyone. He had a wonderful sense of humor. Along the way he did things like teach his High School math teacher calculus while he was still a student. Once a prize was offered for someone to solve a math problem at his high school and then the teacher offering the reward said if Jim Sheridan is in the audience, he is not eligible for this. I wish everyone could have had a father like him. We were so lucky to grow up in the family we did and we all loved him so much. My Mom was a wonderful supportive woman— not many would have put up with what she did. Once she was particularly discouraged and asked God for a sign as to whether Dad should be pursuing this project. He answered her in a positive way which we all understood and from then on being of great faith she never doubted again.

I hope some of the little I've shared with you gives you a bit of the flavor of the man who I was blessed to call "Dad."

Marge Sheridan Dubuque

For Such a Time as This

The story of how Protocel® was discovered leapt out at me in a way that even *I* didn't understand. At a time when I should have been focusing on my own recovery, which was barely in the infant stage, in a situation where the stakes couldn't be much higher—there was this part of me that already wanted to launch a crusade! I thought it was just the similarities that were getting to me, considering the heat of the moment! But as time went on, I began wondering . . . *Why hadn't Protocel® become a known cure? How could something this good be squelched, and so systematically? Just how much power do "those people," whoever they are, have?*

Jim Sheridan had devoted his whole life to finding a cure for cancer "that would work better than what conventional medicine had to offer, and that everyone could afford," which explained it. There would be no big money in it for Big Pharma. So it was systematically prevented from ever becoming approved.

Well, I was fed up with *"the system."* I've heard for years about natural cures that were bought up by the big drug companies and shelved. Big money could never be made off something that was natural, because something natural could never be patented. When those cancer cures were bought up, they were never intended to be put on the market. Big Pharma didn't even want them known. They couldn't afford to have something that effective out there cutting into their profits.

Finding that hard to believe, are you? Well—think about the "apricot kernel"—Laetrile, practically banned from this country as a means of "saving us" from ourselves. A seed so powerful "they" were concerned it could bring down an entire industry? An apricot kernel for goodness' sake! These people are not only close-minded— they're *paranoid!*

Well—this was one treatment people were going to find out about, and I was just the person to tell them—and somehow I knew I wouldn't be cancer-free before I started.

Ban all these alternative things to protect the public from "quackery"? Well, that's enough right there for me to want to jump on a bandwagon with my own personal soapbox—megaphone in one hand—a copy of *Outsmart* in the other—and let those weenies have what for! God didn't invent "quackery"—if anyone did *it's them!* Like "mutilating and nuking" women's body parts *(if we weren't so conditioned to it)* would ever seem intelligent, necessary and the only responsible, "sensible" thing to do—if they could take off their "conventional treatment cancer-colored glasses" and see that there has to be another more effective, humane and intelligent way to go about "saving" lives.

So, even very early in my recovery, I was already beginning to think at times that maybe this was why I was born. And I told God that if that's what He had in mind, I'd be honored!

I can say for certain that until now I had never seen so many past events in my life tie into present situations. It was so evident I had been equipped by the past to be prepared for the present as I faced this devastating diagnosis. Preparation through situations and circumstances in life to make me who I am today, so when destiny and opportunity presented itself (something others call "luck") I'd be the someone to step up to the plate.

Now there's an oxymoron!—equating cancer with opportunity and destiny! But it's like I've seen my whole life come together over this, rather than, fall apart. Which is why I told God: "If that's what this is about, and You say I'm equipped for this—*I'm Your woman!*"

Was that what all those situations in my life were about? I think it was. *For such a time as this!*

Living Life Inside Out

For as long as I can remember, for me, it's always been about the dream. Daydreams, night dreams, where-I-wanted-to-go-in-my-life and in-my-heart-dreams—it was always about the dream.

I thought Cinderella and Snow White really did end up with their handsome princes. And something told me that if you dream hard enough, often enough, big enough and long enough, you could get *all* your dreams to come true.

However, as a teenager, I had my first hardcore reality check and sadly learned that some dreams don't come true. Some die, some get crushed and some . . . others try to convince you never existed. It's all in your mind, I was told; "Life is a reality—there's no such thing as a dream" I would later hear. But I wasn't buying it. I decided it only *looked* as if dreams didn't come true. And, besides, if they died, got crushed or stolen, you could just get new ones. At least I had to, if I was going to live life at all. Because, to me, life itself was wrapped up in a dream!

In my early twenties some amazing things began happening. I began succeeding at things that even I never dreamed I could, which only fueled my conviction that life was truly about them. And, *thirty-two* years ago, because of it—I wrote a poem. If what I wrote was already that much a part of me back then, how could I not have a heart for a man who lived *his* dream that *too* was fueled by a prayer he prayed to a God he so eloquently served and trusted in—that he knew was listening? Maybe my determination to pick up the cause and carry on Mr. Sheridan's dream was somehow tied to God seeing a throng of people on the horizon who would be searching for answers. And, somewhere in the crowd, He saw me—and knew one day I would use His gift to humanity to save my life—and be willing to find a way to tell others how I did.

A dream that was dreamt in the '30s, written about in the '70s, that is still being pursued in the twenty-first century. A lit torch of burning desire—ignited by a dream!

The Torch of Burning Desire

Dreams are rays of sunshine
that grow within your heart.
Keeping them in focus
is the most important part.

The power of the mind is endless.
Ignited it will seldom tire.
No greater flame was ever lit
than *The Torch of Burning Desire.*

We all have something to offer
and all any man can do is his best,
but delve within yourself and find it—
it's the key to your success.

There'll always be those who discourage you,
show disbelief and bring you despair,
but only you can live your life—
it doesn't matter what they care.

Believe in yourself as a person
and a leader is what you'll become.
Then duplicate yourself in others—
giving is the best kind of fun.

Disillusionment in disguise is a virtue,
without it, inspiration would mean little at all.
The downs in life? Merely stepping stones
to help you climb over the wall.

Surround yourself with people
who think the way you do.
You know there's strength in number,
and they need your support too.

As you grow in your abilities,
strength becomes a way of living.
Your dreams become reality
and you start receiving all you've been giving.

Live for what you believe in!
Non-believers hold no dreams in their heart.
But by the power of example you can show them
that they too can have a fresh start!

Yes, dreams are rays of sunshine.
It's *burning desire* that makes them grow.
With this magic combination,
it's unlimited where you can go!

Let no one sway your thinking—
and let no man *crush your dream!*
God's hand is yours for the asking—
Dreams were made in *The Land of Supreme!*

By
Pamela Hoeppner

CHAPTER 20

A Window to Look Through

Heredity or Logistics?

The fact is, we lost Mom to breast cancer. So even if I don't believe in the heredity factor as being what's behind the insurgency of daughters of mothers who had breast cancer being diagnosed with it *(and I don't—because there is far too much evidence to prove otherwise)*, there is still the fact that Mom was diagnosed with breast cancer—*and so was I.* So how am I so certain that it's more than genetic?

Mom also had been given synthetic estrogen shots, hormone replacement therapy, for twenty years until she got into the world of health and nutrition and no longer needed them. But after twenty years the damage had been done and even Mom was convinced that it was synthetic HRT that caused her diagnosis.

However, Mom having estrogen shots, especially *after* I was born, wouldn't be cause for anything to be "passed down" to me. Right? But—it *did* mean that even Mom might not have been so predisposed to getting breast cancer herself if she'd never had those shots in the first place. And if that were true, what would there be to pass down to her daughters and granddaughters? Doesn't it paint a bit of a different picture than the NCI continues to spotlight, which creates the perfect mindset for acceptance by society that the only defense women have is "early detection"—by having "regular mammograms"!

If synthetic HRT *gave* my mother cancer, then weren't the chances also pretty good that the diagnosis I wound up with came from somewhere, or some *thing*, that had nothing to do with my children's grandmother? And to further press the issue—do you know how many women were given synthetic HRT shots decades ago? Where would those statistics fit into the "heredity" theory? And who do we ever hear address the issue—which is a big one! What about all those statistics? I want all my children and grandchildren, including my sister, Sally, and my niece and nephew, Scott and Shanda, and, one day, their children, to understand that because there was this "thing" in their family history—it doesn't mean they're destined to get it. I want them focusing on feeding deficiencies and eliminating things that can cause it, *rather than allowing themselves to be programmed that the only thing the medical world has to offer as a person's greatest weapon and defense is "detecting it early."* (And it still infuriates me when I think about how they go about it so systematically.)

(Tanya Harter Pierce on pages 17 through 20 of *Outsmart Your Cancer* basically states that as recently as the 1960s, only 1 in 20 American women developed breast cancer. Only 40 years later (which is just *one* generation), that statistic became 1 in 8. Genetics aren't going to change in just 40 years—so there had to be other factors causing an almost triple rise in incidence. And the statistics of every type of cancer incidence have ALL risen over the past 100 years, with the last 40 years or so being the fastest rise for every type of cancer! Again, genetics cannot be a factor over such a short time, which can only mean all the incidence of it has to involve other things.)

And then, Mom had always had a bit of a battle with her weight, as have I all my life. She grew up in Michigan, and, of course, so did I. And we all know that whole scenario from Chapter 18: The one that leaves me wondering if it was her genes I inherited that opened the door for this diagnosis, as much as it was where she and I both lived—Michigan. Iodine-deficient, sun-starved Michigan!—which brings me to Vitamin D-3.

On June 17, 2007, Dr. Manny Alvarez, managing editor of Health News at Fox News.com, reported on the live telecast that due to the mounting compelling evidence pointing to how cancer-protective Vitamin D-3 has proven to be, everyone should be taking it. And that the findings are so overwhelming that even Canada has now issued a blanket recommendation for the entire country that everyone should be taking it as cancer-prevention. He also stated that the Southern states do not have anywhere near the incidence of cancer as do the Northern. And where do I live? Michigan! Ranking as one of the highest in obesity, goiter and breast cancer—where the cloud-cover from the surrounding Great Lakes also makes Michigan one of the most sunshine-starved states in the union!

And, further proof to me for how beneficial it can be to have health care practitioners who treat nutritionally is that, thankfully, one of my health care practitioners had me on 5000 IUs of Vitamin D-3 a year before the overwhelming evidence about the benefits of taking Vitamin D-3 to prevent cancer ever hit the media airwaves and cyberspace. He convinced me to be on it when it wasn't even "cool" to do it.

The push for everyone to be on 1000 to 2000 IUs of Vitamin D-3 is everywhere you look nowadays. Greater amounts, however, of 4000 to 6000 IUs per day are recommended when the concern is that a diagnosis is pending. The reason for cautioning people from taking it all these years was to prevent toxic levels in the blood, which they now know was a mistake. (Fifteen minutes in the sun provides the body with *much more* than 6000 IUs of Vitamin D. But we aren't getting it, because we're either blocking the sun when we're in it, or we live in places where it sun doesn't shine.)

A Cocktail for a Diagnosis

So what else was "brewing" in my life that had handed me this diagnosis—that it turns out even I myself, unknowingly, had contributed to? With what I've uncovered since being diagnosed, there were several more contributing factors I became aware of. (Most of which had little or nothing to do with my mother.)

Iodine deficiency—which was previously discussed in Chapter 17.

The bromine/chlorine factor. I worked at Dow Chemical, as the secretary/clerk for Plant Engineering, in my late teens. Every morning I walked through the plant to the engineering office through a spray-mist of bromine and chlorine (some days worse than others—especially if the wind was blowing and in the right direction) and then back through it again after work. Umbrellas and raincoats didn't protect all the skin from exposure. Engineers who worked out in the plant, and were in it so much of the time, practically on a monthly basis had to replace their denim jackets—the chemical spray would cause the material to rot. The guys also complained of skin rashes and raised or irritated moles. We often talked and joked about the "long-term" effects of it—knowing the possibility of getting cancer from it existed, even though they tried to tell us it didn't. Dow insisted we were safe. And, since anything you put on your skin goes directly into your bloodstream, I was getting a dose of it twice a day, five days a week—probably depleting my already depleted stores of iodine even more (not to mention what I was inhaling). The "daily dose of bromine/chlorine" chapter in my life may have played a bigger role in this diagnosis than I'll ever know.

Burning the midnight oil. I paint and I write. And for years before my kids were born I lived life as a night owl: reading, writing and painting. And even after they were born from time to time, with much of the same in meeting business-related deadlines. The VCR hadn't even been born yet, and so if we were ever going to watch Johnnie Carson, we either watched him late at night or we didn't. Now we know the hours between 10 p.m. and 2 a.m. are when the body floods the system with healing hormones, including melatonin, a youth and longevity hormone. Some say the hours between 9 p.m. and midnight are the most beneficial hours of sleep you can get. And they now say every hour of sleep you get before midnight is worth two hours to the body. Adequate sleep, which some now say is seven hours, but others say requires eight and nine hours, is warfare against weight gain. Less than seven hours' sleep—the waistline grows.

Burning the candle and the midnight oil is what I should have been burning all these years, instead of "artificial light" that robs the body of melatonin. So letting the stars get in your eyes, and welcoming in the moonlight, both contribute to wellness by releasing great "stress-busters" while not robbing you of anything. Unfortunately, Edison had no way of knowing what role the side effect of artificial light in the night would play in breast cancer statistics.

Think outside the bra. And then there was the invention of "the eighteen hour bra." (Which I doubt I ever wore—but I'm sure I wore one well over twelve hours on most days.) An eye-opening book, *Dressed to Kill—The Link Between Breast Cancer and Bras,* by Sydney Ross Singer and Soma Grismaijer, describes what happens in the body, especially lymph drainage in the breast area, when tight-fitting (and especially underwire) bras are worn, and the correlation between the number of hours worn and being diagnosed with breast cancer.

A large percentage of women wear a cup size too small, for a better proportioned look—and too tight of a band around their midriff. And, contrary to what we've all thought, "lifting and supporting" to prevent "sagging" actually encourages it—as the muscles do not get a chance to work to stay toned up—hours and hours during the day. (Maybe burning the bra in the '60s would have done us all a favor if it hadn't been just a fad!)

Well water was what I drank mostly for the first twenty years of my life, being raised on a farm, and well water, like municipal **tap water**, is not at all the best water to drink. Drinking water without "point of use" water treatment is just asking for trouble **because of all the carcinogens.** (Tap water is full of chlorine—a disinfectant that also destroys the "friendly" bacteria in your system that protects you against cancer.) And the only way to bring it back, and bring things back in balance, is to be on a good "pro-biotic."

And because of my **low thyroid—hypothyroidism tendencies,** I almost always battled **adrenal fatigue** and lacked stamina, which also caused my weight to go up and down with the ebb and flow of it all. Because if the adrenals and thyroid ain't workin', ain't nothin' workin'! And, additionally, as we discussed earlier, being on **thyroid medication when a severe iodine deficiency is present can be the perfect set-up for breast cancer,** as Dr. David Brownstein states in his book, *Iodine—Why You Need It—Why You Can't Live Without It.*

Right along with low thyroid and low adrenals comes **Candida.** Everyone has **Candida Albicans** yeast in the body. But it's when Candida takes over and there is more of it than good "friendly" bacteria that it creates the perfect conditions in the body for a diagnosis of cancer. I battled Candida at a time when it was very difficult to control or get rid of, because so few effective formulas existed to successfully treat it, as compared to what is available today.

This "cluster" of issues alone—comprised of hypothyroidism, adrenal fatigue and/or exhaustion; iodine deficiency; and weight gain; creating the perfect setting for Candida overgrowth—can cause the system to spiral downward, finally setting the stage for what, more and more, appears to be—the inevitable.

DDT. On the farm in the 1950s everyone used DDT—a known carcinogen, banned in this country in 1972. Daddy used the atomizer to spray DDT on apple trees often, and, although I was never allowed to be around when he did, I remember playing with it when it was empty and they didn't see. And Mom used it often, too, to spray potato bugs in the garden. An effective insecticide during World War II, DDT was often referred to as the "atomic bomb" of insecticides. It came to be used in this country in the late 1940s. According to an EPA press release in December 1972, its peak year for usage was 1959 when nearly 80 million pounds were applied during the time I was an adolescent.

Further supporting my suspicions of a DDT/breast cancer connection in my case is a study published in *Environmental Health Sciences* entitled, "DDT and Breast Cancer in Young Women: New Data on the Significance of Age at Exposure," states:

> High levels of p,p'- DDT, the primary component of DDT, in women exposed before mid-adolescence, were found to be predict a five-fold increase in breast cancer risk. Many American women heavily exposed to DDT in childhood have not yet reached 50 years of age; therefore the public health significance of DDT exposure in early life may be large.

The above study would suggest that women who fall into the category of "not yet 50" who were exposed to DDT in childhood would do well to be proactive about breast cancer prevention.

(Visit www.thebreaststaysput.com for more information on breast cancer prevention.)

A Glimpse in the Rear View Mirror

As you recall, from the very beginning of this whole breast cancer chapter in my life, I desperately wanted to get safety nets going. I wanted documented information. And I've already covered what I would have done differently. But, in hindsight, I'd feel remiss if I didn't bring up something with regard to my experience with the oncologist, putting another slant on it. Because even though the one and *only* thing the oncologist *did* tell me that was useful information was that the cancer hadn't yet metastasized—the one other significant thing this man did was take a measurement of the mass that had sprung up from the biopsy eleven days earlier. So, if this guy actually did do something of significant *importance* for me, when he really didn't intend to help me at all, how much *more* impact would a compassionate, understanding, skilled oncologist, who is willing to work with you and help you, have on the overall success of your full and complete recovery. *I would never want anyone to think I would suggest approaching any type of battle against a diagnosis of cancer without an oncologist. I went to an oncologist because it was the responsible, wise thing to do.* I still don't regret firing him, though, because after the initial appointment it was like: "Hit one—and drag the doctor." And, to me, it didn't make sense to weigh myself down with someone who was supposed to be *lightening* my load! I found it very unnerving not to have "numbers" and something to measure progress with. So, looking back, this is what I would have done differently.

I would have been more aggressive about dosing. And there were a few things I didn't know at the time, such as being sure to be on adequate enzymes along with Protocel®, to assist the body in processing dead lysed cells, in which I would also have been more vigilant.

My level of exhaustion was not the norm, and I've already covered all the reasons why. (No one needs to push their dosing to try to get to the level of tiredness I experienced, because, again, my tiredness was being caused from more than just the effects of dead cells being lysed away in my body.)

I would have edged up on my doses from 1/4 teaspoonful to 1/3, because, first of all, Protocel® is non-toxic. And I have talked with several people battling cancer who had to go up to 1/3, and even 1/2 teaspoonful to see signs of lysing, such as foam and/or bubbles in their urine, crustiness in their eyes, fatigue, etc. But I would think the need for someone to take more than 1/2 teaspoonful of Protocel®, as a regular dose, would be a rarity.

I would also be certain I never went *more* than six hours between doses (with either formula)—which, to me, means taking that dose in the middle of night. If I'm going to be on Protocel® for cancer of any type, I want to know I'm not leaving anything to chance where dosing is concerned—including being certain I'm taking the *maximum* my body can tolerate, rather than the minimum and hope that, for my particular system, I'm getting enough. (And, again, not what my body can "tolerate" with regard to *high levels* of Protocel®, but how much my body can handle of *the mass exodus of dead, lysed cells* that can sometimes become "backed up" if they can't get out of the body fast enough, which can make for some very interesting "Kodak moments.")

I had *plenty* of warning that something was coming before I ever got into the situation where I experienced such a degree of dizziness and intense vomiting. The tiny picking, shooting *sharp* traveling pains started up, and they intensified with each passing day, as did the exhaustion of feeling like I was walking through "deep" mud. But nothing had prepared me to recognize that this all signaled something was on the horizon—which was yet another reason I felt compelled to tell my story.

Protocel® has been proven, time and time again, to be less toxic than taking one aspirin a day. A person without cancer can take very high doses of Protocel® over an extended period of time and experience no symptoms of any kind. It was the power-dosing I did that caused the cancer to break down faster, that caused my body to struggle to get rid of the extra amount of lysed matter being broken down. So knowing how Protocel® works, and what a number it can do on cancer, I would be "testing the waters" and "pushing the limits" with regard to dosing, to be certain I was taking the amount my body needed to get the job done. (Which could also mean staying right at 1/4 teaspoonful!)

The *Rest* of the Story

So where am I now in all this? Well, I finally got to tell my two friends Valerie and Annette, at the lake, about myself. Valerie was stunned! Actually, she thought I was *nuts!* It was quite humorous! I told her one night while we were all at a wedding reception on the Pointe — under the stars (when the "too much wine" factor may also have been in play).

Well, the next day I was out in our yard and she came home. She had a big smile on her face and walked over, hugged me and said, "I should have expected nothing less out of you. There's no way you'd have gone the route of chemotherapy or anything else they probably tried to tell you that you had to do." She was just so glad I was okay. And we did talk about that notorious "phone call" she and I'd had. And we did have a good laugh!

Then there was Annette. She was hard to pin down because of *all that company.* So one day when it got quiet down there, I walked down to tell her. And as I, so to speak, *spilled my guts*, her face started losing color. Naturally, I went right into my nonstop "no need to come for air" explanation — not realizing that nowhere in what I was saying to her had I stated that I already knew *I was okay!* By the time I did, she was able to start breathing again. (I couldn't believe I did that to her!) She grabbed me and hugged my neck like she was never going to let go — cried and said, "I can't ever lose you! And if I *ever* got that kind of news you would be the first person I'd call, Pam — because I just lost a neighbor to cancer who had been through all that stuff you refused, and it was horrible! I would never, *ever* use that stuff either!"

It was a relief to be able to talk about it. She wanted to know why I hadn't told her. I told her that I just couldn't tell anyone and she understood. I think we were both glad I'd waited until I knew I was okay to tell her — in light of what she'd been going through in losing another friend.

I also had the opportunity to tell Kathy, another dear friend who had lost two of her sisters-in-law to cancer.

We had gone for a boat ride one Sunday afternoon, and Rocky and Kathy were out on their dock, along with several others. They motioned us in and we tied up. And after a bit everyone went for beverages . . . everyone except Kathy and me. Seizing the moment, I told her everything. She was so happy for me and said since she hadn't heard from me, she'd already had me in her "prayer umbrella" where she puts people, to pray for them as God directs. And now she knew why—and she would continue to pray.

Then I told Elizabeth. We were all over at the swimming hole, and I, of course, had stayed in the boat. Elizabeth decided to climb in to sit with me in the sun—and I told her. She was shocked—and then she was so happy! She gave me a great big hug (I got a lot of those from everyone—including the ones later over the phone and through email) and told me she and Mark would tell no one until I was ready one day for everyone to know.

Then I told Joyce when she helped me pull off our huge yard sale—on November 8, in 70-degree weather—(which, in Michigan in November, is a miracle in and of itself!) and we sold everything that weekend! We were sitting in the sun toward the end of the sale when I told her. *No time like the present,* I thought. She looked at me stunned as I told her what I'd been dealing with and said, "Boy, girl—are you *ever* lucky!" (She's actually worked in a hospital mammogram department for years—and I imagine she's seen and heard it all.) I told her that it really wasn't about luck, because Protocel® is a very scientific formula—and she, too, was so glad I was okay! And I knew she'd tell Jake and Mary Jo for me, and Tommy, Johnnie and Iris, and George. Just like Berneda and Noel would tell Jim and Joan and Lisa. Soon everyone would find out.

And then there was Bill and Mitzie, and their daughter Kris. We were standing in line at a community barbeque we all love to go to when I told Mitzie. She was so excited for me, as were Bill and Kris! As it turns out, Pappy, Bill's dad, has been telling people about alternative treatments for years, and Bill and Mitzie purchase books on alternative treatments to give to people they feel might have a need. So with all they knew about alternative treatments, I could have told them about my diagnosis from day one.

Then there were all my other friends, some local and some all over the country. Some of them I got to tell in person, some of them I contacted by phone, and some others told for me: Pat and Jim, Agnes and Bernard, Judi and Jerry, Natalie and Bill, Sally and Jerry, Joan and Verne, Patti, Gerri, Dolly, Del, Asa, Nancy, Connie and Ron, June and John, Sue, Bob and Elaine, Kenny and Char, Marty and Mary, Nancy, Charlene and Bob, Fran and Wayne, Danny and Suzy, Jim and Barb, Guy and Mary, Olive and Harold, Bob and Doris, Gale and Randy, Mary Janet and Dave, and my very close cousins, Mil, Mary, and Caroline, and Teddy and Carol, some of my favorite people in the world—just for starters. It took me awhile, but whether by phone or email or in person, I eventually told them all! And every single one of them was supportive of what I'd chosen to do (especially since they knew it was over—I'm not sure how they'd have reacted if they had found out when it wasn't yet!). And all who didn't hear from me, which was most of them, were very understanding of my having gone into seclusion, including my friends at church.

It was touching and heartwarming to me to know that I have such great friends. Several of them made the comment about what an incredible or very "gutsy" lady I was—which I found surprising. I didn't think of myself as having "guts"—I thought of myself as having "no choice." I did what I needed to do to save my life. And since I know too much about "the other side" of conventional medicine, for me, using something like Protocel® was a no-brainer, no-choice decision.

Some said I was an inspiration. Others said they were glad I didn't tell them, because it would have been hard on them to know what I was dealing with. Some said they knew something was up, when they didn't hear from me like they usually did, and were praying for me because of it. And all said they couldn't *wait* to read my book!

On June 2, Ella's little sister, Penelope Tait Sny was born! Grandbaby #2—weighing 8 lbs. 11 oz. Life is good and it had just gotten better! What a *beautiful* baby! And her little "big sister" Ella adores her. These two little "sugar plums" could not *possibly* be any *sweeter!* Every time I gaze upon these two little "gifts," all I can think of is just how much God was "showin' off" when He put these two little packages together!

So now I will be painting Penelope's nursery—right after I paint more bees, bugs and butterflies in the meadow, next to the life-size tree in "Bugville", that makes up the walls of Ella's room.

To be here for our kids and these grandbabies, and all the other over-the-top events and moments in life, was all I purposed to live for. Like the day they put Ella on the phone to tell me she had just used her potty for the first time and was wearing her new glitter-covered purple flip-flops that she earned for doing it—and I was here to get as excited as she was! And when she told her daddy, at age two-and-a-half, in case he didn't know, "Metamorphosis is when a caterpillar changes outfits into a butterfly . . . I learned it at Grammy's watching *Little Einsteins!*"—I was here to marvel!

And I was here when Josh's band, The Still Out, produced and recorded their first album, *Crystalized*—another *over-the-top* moment in life! And when he entered his first New York City Marathon and finished the 26 miles in 3:50:53—ten minutes under four hours (when everyone told him that in his first marathon it was his job *"to just finish!"*), I was here to answer the phone when he called tearfully exhausted, yet bursting to tell me!

In just four short years, I've watched our children's lives unfold: new homes, promotions, career moves and additions, like "Daisy," Glenn and Kathy's hilariously adorable, very low-to-the-ground miniature dachshund, the cutest little doodlebug on four tiny feet! And the icing on the cake! Just two weeks after Penelope was born, Glenn and Kathy surprised us! They're expecting a baby, too—in January of 2008! *Grandbaby #3!* And it wasn't long before we also learned that *she's going to be a girl!* So soon we'll have three little "dolly-toting stair-steps" to add joy to our family celebrations—and I get to hear and see it all!

It's what I've missed the most about Mom—her not being there all these years to tell things to—to share life and celebrate the moments!

We're getting ready to build on the lake and we've been doing some traveling. And, in addition to painting, I'm thinking of writing another book. A novel. (I'm taking any chances!) I'll spend the rest of my life watching our two favorite little girls grow to become women, as more little "noses" (like the one that's due any day now!), one by one, arrive to become a part of our family. Something I'll never take for granted!

Just as *The Breast Stays Put* goes to print (twelve days after Kathy's due date) Glenn and Kathy's beautiful "little" 9 lb. 7 oz. baby girl, Ava Loren Hoeppner, was born on January 20, 2008—right on PopPop's birthday! He said that is was the BEST birthday present ever! (PopPop and "Uncle Lloyd" were *both* in hopes that we'd get the call today. Two brothers born on the same day, also—six years apart.) And what a precious, content little sweetheart Ava is! This grandbaby thing is the absolute BEST!

Triumph Over Devastation

My cancer-free moment seemed a long time in coming, although my *expected* full recovery was there all along. Hidden enough was my progress that I was able to experience the payoff for all that drama in serendipity-wrapped moments of met expectations that created dividends of answers, solutions and keys—that I might not have continued to pursue—had I known earlier how well I was truly doing! It was the unexpected twist that I never saw coming!

Maybe one day I'll look back and go, "You idiot! *What are you? Nuts?* I can't believe you did that! Did you actually beat breast cancer by taking a bottle of Protocel® and a trip upstairs to bed?" I often wondered, in light of how simple and yet staggeringly miraculous my recovery turned out to be—would people ever believe it? Which is why instinctively, in the beginning, I knew I needed proof if was cancer that I had to beat! And I have it!

The mammogram had already captured images of the "feeler-like" blood vessel system created to set up a food supply. Then added to the mammogram were the scans and reports. The proof of what I was dealing with that was captured on those images would quiet even the most outspoken "Doubting Thomas" who might try to insist that what I had was never actually cancer! The disgusting "roadmap" that was radioactively burned onto those mammogram films clearly shows it was sending "something" out. And if it wasn't in search of a food supply, you can't look at that mess and not recognize, if nothing else, it was setting up "branch offices!"

And then, when you factor in the surgeon's report, where he stated it was "tangerine" size in circumference—and then take into account the explosive 3-D growth in the measurement taken eleven days later by the oncologist, in addition to the ultrasound that revealed all the additional tumors that also materialized within days—had I been dealing with a benign lump or just some crazed lymph node, there would have been nothing to "explode" or "spread."

And the radiologist and MD didn't simultaneously "deep-six" on me over nothing. You can't tell me that was your normal scan-reading reaction!—from either of them!

And then there's the biopsy. The undisputable proof of what God, Protocel® and I beat! I *knew* I'd be glad one day that I'd had it! But would I ever have one again? Not on your life—*or mine!*

So the status of things for me now is that the mass created by the biopsy is all but gone, the fibroids are finally gone, also. All tumor markers are in the safe zone, my liver enzymes are excellent, my DHEA level is perfect, my thyroid is perfect and the test that detects metastasis by Dr. Schandl shows to be in the safe range, and my HCG tumor marker tests that Dr. Schandl has perfected to detect breast cancer also came back low, indicating no breast cancer was detected. The QXCI machine continues to not want to discuss breast cancer where I'm concerned. Which is just fine with me. I don't want to talk about it anymore either.

My plan is to continue to be monitored and use one or two bottles per year of Protocel® for the next several years as maintenance, or more if I feel it's necessary.

Now, as I focus on the future, the more evident it becomes that it was what I had to figure out along the way on my *"road to recovery"* that God wanted in print—to give others that "window to look through." I overcame one of the worst diagnoses known to mankind with a treatment that the FDA, the NCI and the medical establishment officially and emphatically state "Won't work!" And I did it in style—and I lived to tell about it.

Had I a clue of exactly what all was coming I may have been so overwhelmed I'd have felt defeated before I ever started. But I lived it, and even from the very beginning of my recovery when it seemed like nothing was moving, everything was in flux—I was so far into the vision of a full recovery, I only rarely thought about the conse-quences, if what I'd chosen wouldn't work. Because in my spirit, mind and life, it already had (except I could have done with a little less theatrics and *"traumatics"!).*

And the formula that in my case dealt cancer a crushing blow? *My unwavering application of God's Word, as I stood on His healing promises—and blessing my body with non-toxic tools that invited and allowed it to right itself—creating an environment of "life" where death could no longer exist.* That is where I'm convinced my healing came from! The truth of the matter is: I believe I was cancer-free before I ever left the hospital the day of the mammogram. Because of what I knew about Protocel® and *Who* I knew in God.

I am not a breast cancer survivor. I didn't survive anything— because, to me, in order to survive something, you first have to fall victim to it. And I never allowed myself to succumb to taking on the role.

May you go through your entire life never being faced with the overwhelming situation of overcoming something like cancer. But may you also be reminded of all that is available to you—if you one day find you are.

Three Little Kittens Who Lost Their Ribbons

One day there was a knock at my door: I opened it to find standing in front of me a little boy with a basket, and in it were three tiny kittens. All were sporting *"little pink ribbons."*

"Hello, ma'am," he said. "I'm here today in support of Breast Cancer Awareness Month: I'm doing my part in offering my three little *'free* pink ribbon kittens' who, as you can see, are calling attention to die-hard *Conventional Treatments for Breast Cancer.* Would you be interested in one of them?"

I said, "No, I'm sorry, little boy; although this is a very creative way for you to find homes for your three little kittens, and they're really very cute wearing those little pink ribbons, I just wouldn't at all be interested in taking one of them." He thanked me and left.

A week later there was another knock at my door. I opened it to once again find the same little boy with the *same three little kittens,* except this time—*no pink ribbons.*

He said, "Hello, ma'am; due to all the focus being centered around Breast Cancer Awareness Month, I'm doing my part by now offering my little '*free* kittens' who are calling attention to the *good news* that's available to people through living-well *Alternative Treatments for Breast Cancer.* Would you be interested in taking one?"

"Wait just a minute, little boy," I said. "*Last* week you said these were 'little pink ribbon kittens' promoting '*Conventional Cancer Treatments*,' and now you're here *this* week telling me that the very same kittens—*minus the little pink ribbons*—are promoting '*Alternative Cancer Treatments*'? Can you explain to me why the drastic change?"

"Yes, ma'am," he said. "This week their eyes are open."

(*That* was three.)

> *And she proceeded to get on about*
> *the business of living her*
> *"happily ever after."*

The Expected End

Recommended Websites:

www.thebreaststaysput.com
www.outsmartyourcancer.com
www.webnd.com
www.protocelforum.com
www.elonnamckibben.com
www.protocelglobal.com
www.breastcancerchoices.org
www.drbrownstein.com
www.cancerfightingstrategies.com
www.caprofile.net
www.salivatest.com
www.willardswater.com
www.hummingbirdhealth.com

Recommended Reading and Listening:

Outsmart Your Cancer, by Tanya Harter Pierce
Questioning Chemotherapy, By Ralph Moss
What Your Doctor May Not Tell You About Breast Cancer,
    by John Lee, MD, David Zava, PhD, and Virginia Hopkins
Iodine—Why You Need It—Why You Can't Live Without It,
    by David Brownstein, MD
Cancer—Step Outside the Box, by Ty Bollinger
Dressed to Kill: The Link Between Breast Cancer and Bras,
    by Sydney Ross Singer and Soma Grismaijer
What Your Doctor May Not Tell You About Menopause,
    by John Lee, MD and Virginia Hopkins
Adrenal Fatigue, by James L. Wilson and Johnathan V. Wright
Healed of Cancer, by Dodie Osteen
Healing School Series, by Gloria Copeland
Your Best Life Now, by Joel Osteen
Ageless, by Suzanne Somers
The Battlefield of the Mind, by Joyce Meyer

Scripture Reference

Chapter 1

1. See Isaiah 43:26
2. See Isaiah 55:10:11
3. See 1 Peter 2:24
4. See Exodus 15:26
5. See Romans 8:37
6. See Isaiah 54:17
7. See 1 Peter 5:7
8. See 1 Corinthians 2:8

Chapter 3

9. See Psalm 37:23
10. See Proverbs 3:6
11. See Proverbs 16:3

Chapter 11

12. See Ephesians 6:13-14

Chapter 12

13. See Matthew 11:12
14. See Isaiah 45:3
15. See John 15:12
16. See Hebrews 4:11
17. See Ephesians 5:1-2
18. See Isaiah 26:3
19. See Philippians 4:8

Chapter 13

20. See Isaiah 55:8-9
21. See 1 Corinthians 15:55

The Breast Stays Put

To order additional copies
to share visit:

www.thebreaststaysput.com
www.amazon.com
www.barnesandnoble.com
www.xulonpress.com/bookstore.php

To order by phone 24/7:
1-866-909-BOOK (2665)

Retail Outlets
For discount wholesale pricing

Health Food Stores
Healthcare Practitioner Offices
Compounding Pharmacies
Spas
Specialty Shops
(Any retail outlet with regular stores hours)

1-866-381-BOOK (2665)
No minimum order requirements

To Order Protocel®:

www.webnd.com or phone: **1-888-581-4442**